Effective Bullying Prevention

The Guilford Practical Intervention in the Schools Series

Kenneth W. Merrell, Founding Editor
Sandra M. Chafouleas, Series Editor

www.guilford.com/practical

This series presents the most reader-friendly resources available in key areas of evidence-based practice in school settings. Practitioners will find trustworthy guides on effective behavioral, mental health, and academic interventions, and assessment and measurement approaches. Covering all aspects of planning, implementing, and evaluating high-quality services for students, books in the series are carefully crafted for everyday utility. Features include ready-to-use reproducibles, appealing visual elements, and an oversized format. Recent titles have Web pages where purchasers can download and print the reproducible materials.

Recent Volumes

Effective Bullying Prevention

A Comprehensive Schoolwide Approach

ADAM COLLINS
JASON HARLACHER

Foreword by Susan M. Swearer

THE GUILFORD PRESS
New York   London

Copyright © 2023 The Guilford Press
A Division of Guilford Publications, Inc.
370 Seventh Avenue, Suite 1200, New York, NY 10001
www.guilford.com

Printed in the United States of America

Last digit is print number: 9 8 7 6 5 4 3 2 1

The authors have checked with sources believed to be reliable in their efforts to provide information that is complete and generally in accord with the standards of practice that are accepted at the time of publication. However, in view of the possibility of human error or changes in behavioral, mental health, or medical sciences, neither the authors, nor the editor and publisher, nor any other party who has been involved in the preparation or publication of this work warrants that the information contained herein is in every respect accurate or complete, and they are not responsible for any errors or omissions or the results obtained from the use of such information. Readers are encouraged to confirm the information contained in this book with other sources.

Library of Congress Cataloging-in-Publication Data

Names: Collins, Adam (Psychologist) author. | Harlacher, Jason E., 1977– author.
Title: Effective bullying prevention : a comprehensive schoolwide approach / Adam Collins, Jason Harlacher ; foreword by Susan M. Swearer.
Description: New York, NY : The Guilford Press, [2023] | Series: The guilford practical intervention in the schools series | Includes bibliographical references and index.
Identifiers: LCCN 2022033730 | ISBN 9781462550708 (paperback) | ISBN 9781462550739 (hardcover)
Subjects: LCSH: Bullying. | Bullying in schools —Prevention. | Social interaction in children. | BISAC: PSYCHOLOGY / Psychotherapy / Child & Adolescent | EDUCATION / Educational Psychology
Classification: LCC BF637.B85 C645 2023 | DDC 302.34/3—dc23/eng/20220825
LC record available at *https://lccn.loc.gov/2022033730*

About the Authors

Adam Collins, PhD, is the Statewide Bullying Prevention Manager and Multi-Tiered Systems of Support (MTSS) Specialist at the Colorado Department of Education. Dr. Collins has extensive experience researching and implementing bullying prevention best practices at the school, district, university, and state levels. He is coauthor of multiple book chapters and regularly presents at state and national conferences on bullying prevention and MTSS.

Jason Harlacher, PhD, is a Senior Researcher with American Institutes for Research (AIR). He implements school-based MTSS that help all students, including those who are targets of bullying and those who need social and emotional learning support. Prior to joining AIR, Dr. Harlacher worked as a school psychologist, district-level coach, adjunct professor, and state-level consultant. He presents nationally on topics related to classroom management, intensive interventions, and MTSS, and has published peer-reviewed journal articles and several books.

Foreword

Effective Bullying Prevention: A Comprehensive Schoolwide Approach, by Adam Collins and Jason Harlacher, is *the* definitive book on bullying prevention and intervention. Every school, state department of education, and graduate training program in education and psychology should make this book required reading. This is the only book, written by experts with "boots on the ground," that comprehensively links research on school climate, evidence-based curricula, family and community partnerships, data-based decision making, policy, implementation science, multi-tiered systems of support, multiple levels of instruction, and comprehensive assessment systems to practically guide school personnel to create kind schools, free from bullying, harassment, and intimidation.

It is fitting that this book will be published during the first years after the passing of Dan Olweus, the pioneer of bullying research. Dr. Olweus was recognized with a Lifetime Achievement award at the November 2021 World Anti-Bullying Forum in Stockholm, Sweden. His research inspired my own research and the formation of the Bullying Research Network, an international network of over 250 bullying and peer victimization researchers (*https://cehs.unl.edu/BRNET*). The international attention given to bullying research, prevention, and intervention is robust. Since 1999, the research, writing, and public attention given to bullying behaviors has increased exponentially. Bullying reflects a breakdown in healthy relationships, and the tools needed to ameliorate these behaviors are found in this book. It is a comprehensive road map for creating systems that promote healthy relationships and providing systemic change to stop bullying in schools.

Too often, books on bullying rehash what we already know about these behaviors. Too few books provide research-based, *practical,* hands-on suggestions for *what to do.* I'm reminded of a conversation I had with a school principal years ago when he said to me, "To be honest, we know the research finds that bullying is detrimental to kids' learning, development, and success. What we need to know is how to stop it." Drs. Collins and Harlacher examine what they call "look fors and watch outs" when selecting bullying prevention and intervention programs. They are just what school administrators need to know: what should I look *for* and what are *red flags*? As with any industry, bullying programming is fueled by sales, and school leaders are inundated with program options, many of which do not have an evidence base. Programs touting "quick fixes" are likely nothing more than snake oil promises. This book provides coaching for adults working with students and coaches the reader through practical suggestions to create a school environment that is positive and supportive of everyone. It will help state and local school leaders make informed decisions about bullying prevention and intervention strategies that will work in their individual school context.

Drs. Collins and Harlacher provide practical strategies for creating an inclusive culture in schools. In Table 2.1, they outline *how* to build an inclusive culture. I welcome everyone reading this book to think about what you will do to create an inclusive culture that is welcoming and kind. When we set the conditions and expectations for positive behavior, our schools and communities will be places where bullying, harassment, and intimidation do not exist. Together, we can create that world.

SUSAN M. SWEARER, PhD, LP
Chair, Department of Educational Psychology
Willa Cather Professor of School Psychology
University of Nebraska–Lincoln
Co-Director, Bullying Research Network

Acknowledgments

Adam Collins

This book would not be possible without the support of my wife, Kelly, and our two children. Kelly's countless diaper changes and bedtime routines while I wrote made this dream a reality. I remember writing the prospectus for this book at 3 in the morning while trying to teach our infant son how to sleep through the night. By the time this book is published, he will be 5 years old. Our daughter will be 2. The two of them have shown me what it means to truly feel the importance of preventing bullying.

I would also like to acknowledge my doctoral supervisor, Dr. Susan Swearer. Her unwavering support for me from first-year graduate student to author helped me understand how to be a better writer, professional, and parent. My mother and father have also been great supporters in having this book come together, whether it be babysitting or just showing interest in its progress. Finally, I would like to thank my coauthor, Jason Harlacher, for taking me under his wing in the writing of this book. His wisdom and guidance have created something that I believe will help children live happier, healthier lives.

Jason Harlacher

My interest in bullying prevention began when I was a student at Utah State, as my master's thesis was about the emotion regulation of targets of bullying. I was driven to understand why youth would mistreat each other and what schools can do. Since then, I've spent the last 18 years creating positive learning environments in schools; I'm proud that this experience has culminated in a practical and comprehensive book on bullying prevention. I'm thankful for my advisors, colleagues, and professors who shaped my career in this direction: To Tamara Ferguson, my thesis advisor at Utah State, who taught me how to write. To Kenneth Merrell, my doctoral advisor, who supported my growth as a professional and showed me that schools can be supportive of all students. Students have the right to attend school and feel safe and supported, and I hope the practical approach in this book helps to promote this right. I hope this book adds to the resources that schools can use to build schools that reduce bullying and increase the prosocial development of students.

Finally, let me say . . . can you believe it, Adam?! We did it! Who would've thought our little idea a few years ago would become a book in someone's hands? After negotiations, a pandemic, and working full time (from home, to boot), we pulled it off! I'm thankful for our collaboration, your diligence in writing, and your patience as I confusingly insisted on more tables and fewer words, simultaneously. I'm proud of our achievement, so now, let's toast!

Contents

Introduction

For one freshman at Reidsville High School in North Carolina, lunchtime was a lonely time. After being picked on by classmates, this student ate lunch by himself at a table large enough for several people. It's hard enough to navigate high school as a new freshman, let alone being teased or bullied by peers. Demontez Canada and Tyvon Smoot, seniors at Reidsville, heard about the student after his sister texted others his story. They didn't ignore the situation; instead, they reached out to the student and had lunch with him the next day. The freshman was ecstatic, calling these two seniors his "heroes." One small act of kindness inspired others and set a tone in the school, resulting in others reaching out to be "lunch buddies" (Farmer, 2019). "I feel like we inspired other people to do what we're doing," said Canada. Smoot agreed, "What we did, we sent a message out on how being friendly can help somebody's life."

This viral story isn't unique. A fourth grader in Florida wanted to show his fandom for the University of Tennessee. After creating his own design and pinning it to an orange T-shirt, the student was mocked by a few classmates. One social media post later by his teacher and UT's VolShop had made his design into a real T-shirt. The result? Over 110,000 shirts were sold and nearly a million dollars was raised for a nonprofit bullying prevention organization (University of Tennessee, Knoxville, 2019). Celebrities and athletes supporting students who experience bullying or social rejection accompany such heartwarming stories. The cast of *Stranger Things* sent support via social media in hearing that none of the classmates of a student with a *Stranger Things*-themed birthday party had attended. Saddened, his sister posted online, and Millie Bobby Brown and Gaten Matarazzo responded by offering to attend his birthday the following year (Rothman, 2018). In response to incidents of bullying and mistreatment, these are just two examples within the last few years that show the power and capacity of schools to help students in need. By flipping the mistreatment and the culture on its head, these stories show how people can change the climate for youth.

Not all stories involving bullying have pleasant endings. Sadly, students who experience bullying versus those that do not are more likely to have suicidal ideations and attempts (Hinduja &

Patchin, 2018; Van Geel, Vedder, & Tanilon, 2014). Ten-year-old Ashawnty Davis, in Colorado, decided to stand up to a bully, resulting in a fight that was recorded and posted online. She hanged herself 2 weeks later. Her death led to Ashawnty's Law in 2018, which allowed for a statewide bullying prevention policy in Colorado (Colorado Department of Education, 2019). Ashawnty is not alone. Gabriel Taye, only 8 years old, took his life after enduring bullying at an Ohio elementary school (Planalp & Scott, 2020). A middle schooler in California, Rosalie Avila, took her life as well, writing in her journal about the instances of bullying she experienced (Chuck, 2017). Toni Rivers, age 11 (Ducharme, 2017); Brandy Vela, 18 (Hassan, 2016); and Gabriella Green, 12 (Dion, 2018): These are just a few youth who have completed suicide in connection with bullying. Although rare, some targets of bullying respond with violence against others. As reported by the Secret Service, for those school shooters where a motive is known, 33 percent involved being the target of bullying (National Threat Assessment Center, 2021). This was the case for the shooters at Columbine in 1999 (among other motives) and the shooter at Robb Elementary in 2022.

Bullying is a mental health issue. Bullying is a school safety issue. Bullying is preventable. As educators, we have the opportunity, and the responsibility, to support the most vulnerable of our youth. Knowing that acts of bullying can contribute to the death of children, but can also lead to acts of compassion and kindness, we offer this book as a way for schools to stop bullying and protect our youth.

PAST ATTEMPTS TO PREVENT BULLYING

Schools have been trying to prevent bullying for decades. Many attempts included well-intentioned, yet flawed approaches. It is becoming more common knowledge in the field of education that zero-tolerance policies have failed students. Zero-tolerance policies were designed to provide extreme consequences for breaking a school rule on the first offense (Stinchcomb, Bazemore, & Riestenberg, 2006). Enforcing this policy often meant that when students were found to have bullied other students they were immediately suspended or expelled. Although the idea of zero-tolerance policies were likely motivated by good intentions and an effort to reduce school violence (see Ortega, Lyubansky, Nettles, & Espelage, 2016), they were ineffective and potentially harmful to students (Davis, Lyubansky, & Schiff, 2015; Evans & Lester, 2012). The purpose of consequences for behavior should be to reduce the likelihood that the behavior occurs again. Suspension and expulsion often do not teach students skills or fill in gaps that exist in their ability to find other ways to resolve their problems. Moreover, research suggests that zero-tolerance policies may facilitate the school-to-prison pipeline (Heitzeg, 2009) and, in general, discipline in schools is marked by inequity (Losen, Hodson, Keith, Morrison, & Belway, 2015; Porowski, O'Connor, & Passa, 2014).

A common Tier 2 or Tier 3 support for students is to have them join a "lunch bunch" or small group with their peers. In these small groups, they can receive additional instruction and skill building around specific needs. Counselors, school psychologists, and social workers have used this approach for years to help support students with social-emotional learning. Unfortunately, this is not a recommended approach for students who have perpetrated bullying (Dodge, Coie, & Lynam, 2006; Hess, Wirtz, Allroggen, & Scheithauer, 2017). If you have ever seen the movie *Anger Management* with Adam Sandler and Jack Nicholson, then you know how poorly these groups can operate. Even when skilled therapists are facilitating an anti-bullying student group, students may reinforce one another's bullying behaviors by sharing "war stories" and laughing about their exploits (see Dodge et al., 2006).

With the rise in popularity of restorative practices in schools, peer mediation, an older approach, has become a more common way to resolve conflicts between students (Casella, 2000). In peer mediation, two students who are in a conflict come together with an impartial third party who is also a student to arrive at a mutually agreed upon solution. Although peer mediation can be successful in some cases of conflict between students, the unique nature of bullying risks re-victimizing the target of bullying. More common than peer mediation has been the influx of countless one-off assemblies, speakers, and events that schools can find online. Although these resources typically don't claim to cure bullying, they can lead to false beliefs of the school staff that a one-time event means they have done their part to prevent bullying.

Effective bullying prevention involves an ongoing comprehensive effort from everyone. It requires a schoolwide approach (Richard, Schneider, & Mallet, 2012) that includes families, the community, and the students themselves as partners. What years of research have shown us is that to effectively prevent bullying, a comprehensive approach that aligns best practices with successful implementation is required.

COMPREHENSIVE BULLYING PREVENTION

To help schools, educators, and communities address bullying, we offer the Comprehensive Bullying Prevention (CBP) model. We have drawn upon our experience and the literature on bullying, school climate, behavior, social-emotional learning, and multi-tiered systems of support (MTSS) to outline the best practices related to bullying prevention. What we offer here is an evidence-based and systemic approach that changes the fabric of the school to support the development of prosocial skills in students, structured methods to respond to bullying, and partnerships among students, staff, and families. In doing so, a cultural norm is created in which students feel safe, feel confident reporting incidents of bullying, and can build positive relationships.

What's important to understand is that CBP is not a quick fix, one-time event. In fact, research suggests one-time events are ineffective (Ttofi & Farrington, 2009). Rather, it's a restructuring of the school to support positive behavior and the respectful treatment of others. Accordingly, we're offering an effective approach that does require significant resources. This approach takes time to implement, but it can pay off in the long run. To support our readers with implementation, we also discuss implementation science and how it can be used to avoid false starts and support sustainability. The last chapters of the book present an extensive case study that illustrates the step-by-step process schools can engage in to effectively reduce bullying.

CBP is composed of five components that create an exhaustive and systemic approach to bullying prevention. We detail each component more thoroughly throughout this book, but we offer a brief summary of each component in Table I.1.

HOW TO USE THIS BOOK

We have structured this book into two parts. The first part (Chapters 1 through 6) provides an up-to-date review of the research on bullying before delving into detail on the five components of CBP. In the second half of the book (Chapters 7 through 12), we describe how schools can implement CBP by utilizing implementation science (Fixsen, Naoom, Blase, Friedman, & Wallace, 2005). We offer research-based and practical advice for implementation and end with descriptions

TABLE I.1. Features of Comprehensive Bullying Prevention

Component	Definition	Features
School climate	The overall character and tone of the school, including perceptions of safety and relationships among people.	• Intentionally building relationships. • Creating a safe, predictable environment that includes schoolwide expectations, an acknowledgment system, and a discipline structure. • Teaching how to respond to bullying.
Evidence-based curricula	The curriculum or program used to teach students dynamics of bullying, as well as social-emotional learning skills.	• Curricula are evidence based. • Use of a selection process to choose curricula. • Curricula are part of a tiered system.
Family and community partnerships	Intentional collaboration and partnerships among families, schools, and communities.	• School culture is inclusive of all families. • Two-way communication with families. • Intentionally build positive relationships with families. • Increase self-efficacy for supporting children with bullying. • Include families in decision making. • Involve community in the school culture. • Ensure student voice.
Data-based decision making	The use of the four-step problem-solving model to make decisions.	• Measure bullying prevalence in school. • Analyze system and individual students' needs. • Measure fidelity related to bullying prevention. • Measure outcomes related to bullying prevention. • Accessible data warehouse.
Policy	Guidance that outlines responding to and documenting instances of bullying.	• Aligned with district policy. • Aligned with state laws. • Key elements of a strong bullying prevention policy are included (e.g., communication processes, record keeping, form to document).

of case examples. Our intention in this book is to provide the "what" and the "how" in one source. Consequently, we suggest reading the chapters in order to learn the foundational information related to bullying prevention before reading how to implement it.

In Chapter 1, we provide updated research and information on bullying. We describe current statistics related to bullying, how bullying occurs, and why it lingers in schools. We introduce the five components of CBP and discuss how they fit within an MTSS framework.

The next few chapters describe each of the five components. Chapter 2 provides an overview of *school climate*, which is a foundational component of effective bullying prevention. Our readers will learn what school climate is, how it relates to bullying, and the critical elements for creating a positive school climate.

Chapter 3 covers *policy*. When a bullying prevention policy is comprehensive, it provides stability and reassurance to all stakeholders. We discuss the critical features that should be included in a bullying prevention policy, explain how to use a school handbook policy to provide families with answers before they even know what questions to ask, and review the pitfalls to avoid when drafting a policy.

In Chapter 4, we describe the use of *evidence-based curricula* in reducing bullying rates. We describe the difference between the terms evidence based and research based, as well as where educators can find reviews of evidence-based curricula for bullying prevention. We provide a framework for making decisions about what curricula to choose before describing a list of commonly used bullying prevention curricula. Finally, we discuss how curricula are used across the tiers within MTSS.

In Chapter 5, our readers learn the importance of *family and community partnerships*. A theme of this book is the importance of context, environment, and family and community in reducing bullying. To that end, this chapter describes how schools can partner with families and the community to fully realize their potential in preventing bullying. We offer practical strategies for engaging families, students, and the community as well as how those strategies fit within the social-ecological model.

In Chapter 6, we discuss the use of *data-based decision making*, arguably the "glue" that holds all the components together. We describe the four-step problem-solving model (PSM) and demonstrate how the model can be used to evaluate the impact of CBP. We also share how to utilize the PSM with individual students who experience bullying and offer tips for effective use of the PSM.

Beginning with Chapter 7, we move into describing how to implement the five components of CBP. Our readers will learn about *implementation science* and its active implementation frameworks. We begin by discussing *usable innovations* and situate CBP as such an innovation to implement. Next, we describe *improvement cycles* and how they align with the PSM.

In Chapter 8, we discuss the *implementation teams* that lead bullying prevention efforts. We describe the form and function of the team, including the roles and responsibilities of members as well as the key features that truly make a team effective.

In Chapter 9, our readers learn about *implementation drivers*, which are the factors that enable or facilitate successful implementation. We discuss how teams can address each driver for their site, leading to sustainable and effective implementation.

Beginning in Chapter 10 and continuing through Chapter 12, we share a case example of CBP being implemented through the *stages of implementation*. In doing so, we offer an actual and practical view of how the model is implemented. Since the case study in these chapters is fictional, we use gendered pronouns to represent the characters.

By outlining the *what* and then the *how*, we are offering a comprehensive and unified approach that can be seamlessly integrated with other behavior and school climate initiatives within a school. As demonstrated within the case study chapters, utilizing the approaches described in this book provides educators with an effective way to blend and braid bullying prevention within the fabric of the school.

A note on language: Unless otherwise indicated, we use the pronouns *they/them/their* when referring to a single individual. We have made this choice to be inclusive of readers who do not identify with masculine or feminine pronouns.

CHAPTER 1

Bullying Prevention, MTSS, and Implementation Science

BULLYING, PREVENTION, AND INTERVENTION

When the late Dan Olweus first published his book *Aggression in the Schools: Bullies and Whipping Boys* in the United States in 1978, the academic study of bullying was nascent. The book itself was based on the research Olweus had completed earlier that decade. There were no peer-reviewed journals dedicated to bullying prevention, no international conferences focused on how to reduce bullying, and certainly no broad understanding of bullying as a concept by school staff across most of the western world. The mere concept of something like cyberbullying wouldn't even be investigated for decades. Today, studies are conducted on bullying across the world, and there is even a journal, *International Journal of Bullying Prevention,* specifically dedicated to preventing bullying and cyberbullying at any stage in the process (O'Higgins & Hinduja, 2019).

Since the birth of bullying prevention science, there have been a multitude of approaches to curb its existence and impact. Olweus himself developed a bullying prevention approach that has been implemented since mid-1980s in the United States. As the research on bullying began to clarify its unique form of aggression and consequences, bullying prevention practices began to take shape. It wasn't until the Columbine High School shooting in 1999 that the field of education began to view bullying in a significantly different light (R. M. Thomas, 2006). In the over 20 years since that tragedy, there have been dozens of approaches to prevent bullying and cyberbullying. What has become clear, however, is that a comprehensive approach addressing the myriad of factors influencing bullying (e.g., school climate, policy, effective implementation) is necessary to see its sustained elimination (Gaffney, Farrington, & Ttofi, 2019; Ttofi & Farrington, 2011).

BASICS OF BULLYING

Definition of Bullying

The definition of bullying has been debated among scholars for decades. In their 1987 article, Dodge and Coie suggest that bullying is "unprovoked" aggression. Olweus (1993, 1994) put forth that not only does bullying involve aggressive behavior, but behavior that is also intentional, repetitive, and characterized by an imbalance of power between the target and the perpetrator. More recently, the Centers for Disease Control and Prevention (CDC) weighed in on the definition of bullying by convening a group of expert bullying prevention researchers. As described by Gladden, Vivolo-Kantor, Hamburger, and Lumpkin (2014), this multiyear endeavor culminated with a "uniform definition" of bullying that attempted to navigate common critiques of the definition of bullying, specifically, the fact that a single act can be considered bullying. The three factors that differentiate bullying from other forms of aggression according to the CDC definition is that the aggression is (1) unwanted, (2) marked by a real or perceived imbalance of power, and (3) repeated or is highly likely to be repeated.

The third factor in the definition of bullying is especially prevalent when considering cyberbullying. Indeed, when bullying occurs through an electronic medium, it is almost instantaneously repeated given the fact that social media posts or texts can be so easily shared. As defined by Hinduja and Patchin (2023), cyberbullying is deliberate, repeated harm through the use of electronic devices. Although not overt, the authors further suggest that cyberbullying is typically also characterized by an imbalance of power. This imbalance of power through an electronic medium can look different from what occurs in face-to-face bullying. For example, if one student has possession of embarrassing photos or videos of another, that student can be considered to have power over the other. With the ever-changing nature of online media, it can be also be difficult for educators to even speak the same language as their younger students when it comes to cyberbullying. If a student tells their teacher that they were "catfished," and the teacher mistakes the conversation as one about angling without realizing that the student is referring to an online interaction, the teacher could easily miss an opportunity to address that student's concerns. On their website, *cyberbullying.org*, Hinduja and Patchin (2023) provide a regularly updated glossary of online terms related to cyberbullying that educators should know. A copy of this glossary can also be found in Appendix A.

One of the most important aspects of preventing bullying in schools is understanding what bullying *is* and what bullying *is not*. For example, bullying and conflict are separate acts that require separate responses on the part of school staff. Whereas bullying is defined by an imbalance of power, conflict often includes students of relatively equal power who are having a disagreement or argument. Moreover, if students who are in a conflict realize that they are causing harm, they will stop the conflict in most cases. Harassment is another term that some use interchangeably with bullying even though they are two different concepts. As outlined by the U.S. Department of Education's Office for Civil Rights in 2010, bullying can be deemed "discriminatory harassment" if the bullying is based on a federally protected class (e.g., race, sex, gender) (Ali, 2010). It should be noted, though, that not all harassment is bullying since harassment does not have to be repeated or marked by an imbalance of power (see Table 1.1).

It is also important to understand the different roles students embody when bullying occurs. The first role is that of the *perpetrator,* or the student who engages in the act of bullying. The *target* is the one on the receiving end of the perpetrator's bullying. A *bystander* is a student who witnesses bullying occurring. Research suggests that there is at least one bystander in over 80%

TABLE 1.1. Bullying, Conflict, and Harassment

Bullying	Conflict	Harassment
Unwanted.	Disagreement or argument.	Unwanted.
Marked by real or perceived imbalance of power.	Those involved have relatively equal power.	Those involved may have equal or unequal power.
Repeated or likely to be repeated.	Although conflict may be ongoing, it generally stops if those involved perceive they are hurting someone.	Conduct is based on a federally protected class.

of bullying incidents (Hawkins, Pepler, & Craig, 2001; Pepler, Craig, & O'Connell, 2010) and that bullying prevention programs can increase the degree to which bystanders act to intervene in these incidents (Polanin, Espelage, & Pigott, 2012).

Although some bystanders attempt to prevent bullying, others do not. Research originating from the work of Salmivalli, Lagerspetz, Björkqvist, Österman, and Kaukiaimen (1996) has found four different types of bystanders. The first two types support the perpetrator of bullying. An *assistant* is a student who actually gets involved in the bullying incident. For example, an assistant may watch out for teachers or block the path of a target so they can't leave. A *reinforcer* is a student who encourages the bullying by laughing or providing other forms of attention that supports the perpetrator. The third type of bystander is a *defender*. Sometimes referred to as an *upstander*, this is a student who comes to the aid of the target. The last type of bystander is known as the *passive bystander*, a student who witnesses bullying occurring, but neither supports nor defends the target. Although this role may seem neutral, by staying silent and doing nothing, passive bystanders implicitly reinforce the idea that bullying is acceptable in the school culture.

Although not typically differentiated within the empirical literature, we suggest that there is a difference between a target of bullying and a victim of bullying. In bullying research, the term *victim* is commonly used to describe a student who is the target of bullying, regardless of whether or not that student actually suffered negative consequences from the bullying. Not every attempt at bullying is successful. When bullying does not cause harm or when we simply do not know if the bullying led to negative consequences, we owe it to students to avoid labeling them as victims. If we refer to students as victims, we encourage them to self-identify as victims. Researchers and practitioners alike can empower the targets of bullying by avoiding the label of victim unless it is truly warranted. See Table 1.2 for a summary of the roles within bullying.

Types of Bullying

Even when educators understand the components of bullying and how it differs from conflict or harassment, it can still be difficult to know if a behavior is bullying when seen in the moment. This is why it can be helpful to also know what the different types of bullying look like. As part of the work by Gladden and colleagues (2014) on a uniform definition of bullying, the different types of bullying were also enumerated and defined. You may notice that cyberbullying is not listed as a type of bullying. This is because it is technically viewed as a location where bullying occurs (Gladden et al., 2014).

TABLE 1.2. Roles within Bullying

Role	Definition
Perpetrator	The aggressor during a bullying incident. This person has more power than the target of the bullying.
Target	The individual for whom bullying is intended. This person has less power than the perpetrator of the bullying.
Bystander	The individual(s) who witnesses a bullying incident.
Perpetrator-target	An individual who is in the role of both a perpetrator and target.
Victim	An individual who is targeted for bullying and experiences negative consequences (e.g., anxiety, dropping grades) as a result.

Physical Bullying

This type of bullying is what many view as the traditional form of bullying. It involves the use of physical force against the bullying target. It can include, but is not limited to, hitting, spitting, pushing, and kicking. These incidents of bullying are usually the easiest to spot. An example of physical bullying from popular culture can be seen in the movie *The Karate Kid*. The main character in the movie, Daniel, moves to a new town and is repeatedly physically attacked by a group of teenagers from a karate dojo. At one point, Daniel is physically bullied to the point of becoming unconscious. Eventually, Daniel is able to remove the imbalance of power the other teenagers hold over him by learning karate.

Verbal Bullying

Verbal bullying includes both oral and written communication that causes harm to the target. Common examples of verbal bullying include calling someone names, written notes that are threatening, inappropriate sexual comments, and threatening someone verbally. A popular culture example of verbal bullying is found in the television show *Ugly Betty*. In the show, Betty Suarez works as an executive assistant at a fashion magazine. The majority of her coworkers have greater power over her due to the fact that they hold higher positions than she does and because they are ostensibly more attractive. Using this power, they continually humiliate and insult Betty because of her appearance.

Relational Bullying

This type of bullying is designed to harm a student's relationships and/or reputation. Relational bullying can be perpetrated either directly to the target or indirectly about the target. For example, direct relational bullying can include excluding a peer from activities. Indirect relational bullying often takes the form of spreading false or harmful rumors. In the movie *Mean Girls*, relational bullying is front and center with the main characters. One scene highlights how relational bullying can be used in an attempt to improve one's social standing. The main character, Cady Heron, is a new student at a high school and attempts to connect with her peers by disparaging another student. A separate character, Regina George, takes the opportunity to spread rumors about the targeted student.

Damage to Property

Although less common than the other forms of bullying, damaging one's property is a type of bullying. As described by Gladden and colleagues (2014), examples include taking a targeted student's property and refusing to return it or destroying the targeted student's property in front of them. An example of this type of bullying comes from the television series *Family Matters*. In one scene, a main character, Laura, is working at her aunt's diner, Rachel's Place. A group of teenagers enter the diner, and the leader of the group sexually harasses Laura before asking her on a date. After being rebuffed, the leader of the group purposefully breaks a glass on the floor. Later in the episode, Laura and her aunt enter the diner to find it has been vandalized. This example also demonstrates the importance of including the community in bullying prevention efforts because many students are connected to community establishments.

Prevalence of Bullying

How bullying is measured can, and often does, vary by study and researcher. As mentioned earlier, the definition of bullying is still debated among scholars. It can easily be seen then how changing the way in which bullying is defined can change prevalence rates. Even the order with which questions are asked can affect prevalence rates (Huang & Cornell, 2015). Some research surveys students, whereas other research uses observation or staff input. Rates of bullying can change depending on the state from which a sample was derived. These fluctuations and variances between empirical studies further suggest the importance of using local data systems to guide decision making. Schools need to have an understanding of the prevalence of bullying within their unique site, because even data at a district level can paint a picture that differs from the reality at one specific school.

Given these caveats, understanding the general prevalence of bullying, including those who are more at risk of being targets, can provide schools with a broad understanding of how to support their students. There are several national studies on the prevalence of bullying that provide longitudinal data on bullying rates, including the School Crime Supplement (SCS) of the National Crime Victimization Survey, the Youth Risk Behavior Surveillance System (YRBSS), and the Health Behavior in School-Aged Children Survey, which is conducted every 4 years across the United States and Europe. The SCS in particular is useful because it is administered to students as young as 12 years old, whereas other surveys are only administered to students in high school across the United States. The most recent data from the SCS come from 2017 (U.S. Department of Education, 2019) and show that 20.2% of students report being the target of bullying. The most common way students reported being bullied was that they were the subject of rumors (13.3%), and females were more likely to report being the target of bullying (23.8%) compared to males (16.7%) in the study. In general, the prevalence of cyberbullying is significant, albeit less prevalent than face-to-face bullying (Eyuboglu et al., 2021; Gaffney, Farrington, Espelage, & Ttofi, 2019). Across several studies, the rates of cyberbullying have been found to be roughly half that of face-to-face bullying (Eyuboglu et al., 2021; Iannotti, 2013; see Rivara & Le Menestrel, 2016).

Results from the SCS also align with empirical research on how likely students are to be the target of bullying based on specific demographic information. Research on the prevalence of bullying by grade level has consistently found that students are more likely to be involved in bullying during middle school, that incidents of bullying decrease as students progress through high school, and that the prevalence of cyberbullying increases as students get older (see Rivara & Le Menestrel, 2016; U.S. Department of Education, 2019). The same results are found in the SCS with students in sixth grade reporting the highest rates of bullying (29.5%) and students in twelfth grade reporting the lowest (12.2%). Household income has been identified in some studies as a potential risk factor for students experiencing bullying (Lemstra, Nielsen, Rogers, Thompson, & Moraros, 2012), though it has been suggested that other social-ecological factors may explain these connections (Barboza, Schiambrg, Oehmke, Korzeniewski, Post, & Heraux, 2009). At the school level, socioeconomic status is commonly assessed by examining the percentage of students who qualify for free and reduced-price lunch. In the SCS, students with reported household incomes between $7,500 and $14,999 were the most likely to also report being bullied (26.6%) and those with household incomes below $7,500 (26.2%) a close second. Those students with household incomes above $35,000 are the only group that reported bullying rates below 20%.

An important question asked on the SCS concerns the location where bullying occurs. The top two locations students report being bullied have stayed fairly consistent over multiple SCS surveys: in a hallway or stairwell (43.4%) and in the classroom (42.1%). The location of hallways or stairwells seems reasonable to anyone who has been in a middle or high school during a passing period. There is less adult supervision given the number of students and, given the design of some schools, more secluded areas can provide cover for bullying to occur. But what about the classroom? It is not because teachers are being vigilant about addressing bullying in their classrooms. It is likely because this is where students spend the majority of their time while at school.

Bullying and Federally Protected Classes

While bullying can and does affect the lives of students from many backgrounds, there are several federally protected groups of students that are more likely to experience bullying in schools. Federally protected classes or groups are defined in anti-discrimination laws in the United States. This includes Title VI of the Civil Rights Act of 1964 (prohibiting discrimination based on race, color, or national origin), Title IX of the Education Amendments of 1972 (prohibiting discrimination based on sex), and Section 504 of the Rehabilitation Act of 1973 and Title II of the Americans with Disabilities Act of 1990 (prohibiting discrimination based on disability status). All of these protected classes are listed in a 2010 Dear Colleague letter from the Office of the Assistant Secretary for the Office of Civil Rights (Ali, 2010) as areas that may constitute discriminatory harassment depending on the circumstances surrounding bullying.

There have been few studies on how race or ethnicity influence the likelihood that students will experience bullying (see Rivara & Le Menestrel, 2016). What limited research has suggested is that it is not one's race in particular that leads to an increased chance of being the target of bullying, but if a student's race or ethnicity is in the numerical minority in their school they are more likely to experience bullying (Graham & Bellmore, 2007). However, more recent data have suggested that students identifying as Black and Latinx were significantly more likely to report being the target of bullying (Gage, Katsiyannis, Rose, & Adams, 2021). In related data from the most-recent SCS, student reports of the reasons why they were bullied found race (9.5%) to be the second most-cited reason after appearance (29.7%; U.S. Department of Education, 2019). Separate research has suggested that greater ethnic diversity is correlated with lower rates of bullying and harassment as self-reported by students (Felix & You, 2011; Juvonen, Nishina, & Graham, 2006). This finding seems reasonable when one considers the necessity of an imbalance of power for bullying to occur: the numerical majority ostensibly has power over a numerical minority. Again, research in this area is still limited, and more studies are needed to fully understand the role that race and ethnicity play in students' experiences of bullying.

An area of significant research in the field of bullying in recent years has been the experiences of students who identify as lesbian, gay, bisexual, transgender, queer, or other (LGBTQ+). Research has consistently demonstrated that LGBTQ+ students are more likely to be the targets of bullying (Espelage, Aragon, Birkett, & Koenig, 2008; Garofalo, Wolf, Kessel, Palfrey, & DuRant, 1998; Russell, Everett, Rosario, & Birkett, 2014). On the most recent YRBSS survey of high school students from 2019, students identifying as gay or lesbian were most likely to report being the target of bullying (37.3%), with gay male students in particular reporting targeting rates of 43.7%. In comparison, straight students reported being the targets of bullying at a rate of 17.1%, with only 14.0% of straight male students reporting being the target of bullying. In short, gay male students are three times more likely to experience bullying than straight male students.

Fortunately, empirical research has also examined what is effective at preventing bullying of LGBTQ+ students. Kull, Greytak, Kosciw, and Villenas (2016) examined the impact that district bullying prevention policies have on improving the school climate for LGBTQ+ students. Their findings revealed that students in districts with bullying prevention policies that enumerate LGBTQ+ students specifically as protected against bullying report greater school safety, less victimization based on their sexual orientation, and less social aggression than students in districts with unenumerated policies or no policies. These findings are in line with other research suggesting that enumerated policies may be most effective at reducing bullying for LGBTQ+ students (Hatzenbuehler & Keyes, 2013; Saewyc, Konishi, Rose, & Homma, 2014). Moreover, when schools have Gender and Sexuality Alliances (GSA) or similar student clubs, LGBTQ+ students are more likely to report that their school has a positive climate (Kosciw, Clark, Truong, & Zongrone, 2020).

Similarly to students who identify as LGBTQ+, students with disabilities have consistently been shown to be at greater risk for involvement in bullying regardless of role (Bell Carter & Spencer, 2006; Blake, Zhou, Kwok, & Benz, 2016; Farmer et al., 2012; Gage et al., 2021; Rose & Gage, 2017). Moreover, this disparity can be found in children as early as preschool (Son et al., 2014). Although some research has been conducted on how different types of disabilities (e.g., learning disability, autism spectrum disorder) are more or less likely to be involved in bullying, additional studies are needed to provide reliable data.

Impact

As discussed earlier, bullying is marked by an imbalance of power and repetition. These factors are integral not only to understanding the difference between bullying and other forms of aggression, but also in determining the degree to which students are impacted by the bullying they experience (Cougnard et al., 2007). Ybarra, Espelage, and Mitchell (2014) found that, from a nationally represented sample of adolescents, students who reported bullying without endorsing an imbalance of power or repetition had the lowest rates of negative consequences interfering in their daily lives.

In contrast, students reporting the highest rates of interference were those who reported a power imbalance and a repetition of bullying. Research on cyberbullying has found similar results, with increased severity of cyberbullying being correlated with increased severity of depression (Didden et al., 2009).

Targets

Involvement in bullying, regardless of role, has been shown to be correlated with negative academic, behavioral, and health consequences. For students who are the targets of bullying, the most immediate consequences can be that of injury if the bullying is physical. Health effects can also be long lasting. In a longitudinal study by Bogart and colleagues (2014), researchers found that students with the worst mental and physical health as indicated on a self-report were those who had bullying experiences in both the present and the past. In the same study, the least likely students to have poor physical health outcomes were those that had never been the target of bullying.

Similarly, students who have been the target of bullying are more likely than their non-bullied peers to report symptoms of depression, anxiety, and self-harming behavior (Juvonen & Graham, 2014; Kidger et al., 2015; Klomek, Sourander, & Elonheimo, 2015). This disparity in internalizing symptoms is present in both face-to-face and cyberbullying contexts (Patchin & Hinduja, 2006). Unfortunately, the internalizing impacts of bullying can be long lasting. A study by Bowes, Joinson, Wolke, and Lewis (2015) examined the depressive symptoms of students at both age 13 and then later at age 18. Those students who had reported being bullied at age 13 had higher rates of depression 5 years later at age 18 compared to students who had not been bullied. The authors concluded that roughly one-third of the explanation for depressive symptoms at age 18 could be attributed to the bullying the participants experienced as students at age 13.

In addition to the negative internalizing symptoms students who have experienced bullying endure, externalizing symptomatology has also been demonstrated through multiple research studies. Specifically, targets of bullying are more likely than uninvolved adolescents to use alcohol, cigarettes, and inhalants within the next 12 months (Tharp-Taylor, Haviland, & D'Amico, 2009). Alcohol and drug abuse and dependence have also been shown to be connected to experiencing bullying (Radliff, Wheaton, Robinson, & Morris, 2012), but more research is needed in this area to fully understand the impact bullying has on later substance use (McDougall & Vaillancourt, 2015). Other studies have shown connections between experiences as the target of bullying and increased violence and crime (Gibb, Horwood, & Fergusson, 2011).

Academically, students who are bullied have been shown to score lower on standardized tests and to receive lower course grades (Espelage, Hong, Rao, & Low, 2013). Targets of bullying have also been found to be at greater risk for overall lower academic achievement (Nakamoto & Schwartz, 2010; Neary & Joseph, 1994). Perhaps related to these outcomes, the same students are at increased risk for absenteeism compared to their non-bullied peers (Vaillancourt, Brittain, McDougall, & Duku, 2013). These negative academic connections to being bullied can be seen as early as kindergarten (Ladd, Ettekal, & Kochenderfer-Ladd, 2017).

Perpetrators

Studies examining the impact that being the perpetrator of bullying, and not simply aggression, has on students is extremely limited. Moreover, in the research that does exist, the consequences of perpetrating bullying are not as clear as those for students who are the targets of bullying. This result may be due to the fact that some students who bully are actually perceived by their classmates as popular and as having strong social skills (Peeters, Cillessen, & Scholte, 2010; Thunfors & Cornell, 2008).

A meta-analysis by Gini and Pozzoli (2009) examined 11 studies on the role students play in bullying situations and their later reports of psychosomatic problems (e.g., headache, stomachache). Results from the meta-analysis showed that perpetrators of bullying had elevated reports of psychosomatic problems compared to students who were not involved in bullying. Interestingly, there were also significantly higher reports of psychosomatic problems with youth who reported being the target of bullying or a perpetrator-target. A longitudinal examination of how bullying experiences in childhood may later predict psychotic symptoms (e.g., hallucinations, delusions) was conducted in 2014 by Wolke, Lereya, Fisher, Lewis, and Zammit. The study assessed over 4,500 students between the ages of 8 and 11, then followed up with the same individuals when they were 18 years old. Results from the study found that being involved as a perpetrator or target of bullying as a child may increase the risk of developing psychotic symptoms as an adolescent.

Perpetrator-Targets

In general, the outcomes for students involved in bullying as perpetrator-targets are worse than any other role (see Rivara & Le Menestrel, 2016). Students who are perpetrator-targets of bullying have been shown to have worse physical health (Wolke, Woods, Bloomfield, & Karstadt, 2001) and greater sleep problems (Hunter, Durkin, Boyle, Booth, & Rasmussen, 2014) compared to those who are not involved in bullying. Students who are perpetrator-targets have also been found to be more likely than other students in other roles to have report suicidal ideation (Holt et al., 2015). To be clear, existing research does not confirm a causal link between bullying and suicide; however, it does show that students who experience bullying are at increased risk of suicidal ideation and attempts (see Rivara & Le Menestrel, 2016).

Social-Ecological Theory

When we have a better idea of all the influences impacting our students, it gives us a more complete understanding of how to tackle issues of bullying. This can be done more formally as a Tier 3 support or informally when trying to figure out what may be leading to the bullying in your school. One of the most prominent theories that can help frame the many factors involved in bullying is social-ecological theory. This theory was first introduced by Urie Bronfenbrenner in 1979. The idea behind the theory is that there are unseen influences from our students' environments that affect their behaviors, beliefs, and emotional development. Through Bronfenbrenner and others who subsequently elaborated upon his theory, these influences are organized into five different systems, the microsystem, the mesosystem, the exosystem, the macrosystem, and the chronosystem, which we define in the next section. Table 1.3 features a complete list of the systems, questions to ask yourself to better understand your students, and considerations for how to address concerns that arise.

Before diving into the five different systems it's important to note the characteristics of the individual student as well. This is another reason why building positive relationships with your students is so vital. Even just starting with basic demographics like your students' age, socioeconomic status, and gender can be helpful. Knowing that a student is female, for example, lets you

TABLE 1.3. Questions and Considerations across the Social-Ecological Theory

System	Questions	School supports
Individual	• How old is the student? • Does the student have a disability? • Does the student identify as LGBTQ+? • Is the student a numerical or historically marginalized minority?	• Active GSA is a student group in the school. • Students in special education receive push-in supports to reinforce that they are part of the general education classroom. • The school makes intentional efforts to celebrate all cultures and traditions.
Microsystem	• What is the primary language spoken in a student's family? • How safe is the student's neighborhood? • Does the student's family have a documented history of child maltreatment? • What do students value at the school (e.g., athletic performance, academic achievement)?	• Bullying prevention materials are available in multiple languages for families. • The school partners with local youth organizations in the community to reinforce prosocial behaviors. • All students are provided trauma-informed educational practices. • Staff intentionally highlight the achievements of all students, regardless of their popularity.
Mesosystem	• What are the relationships like between families and the school? • Are there common locations in the community where families visit? • What community organizations exist that partner with the school? • Does the student attend a before-or-after school care facility?	• The school embodies a culture where all families are welcome. • The school partners with neighborhood before-and-after-school care centers to align behavioral expectations. • The school utilizes a community resource map to structure organizations and businesses as potential partners.
Exosystem	• What is the school board policy on bullying? • What laws exist in the state related to bullying? • Does the student's family receive social services or other government services? • What media does the student consume regularly? • Does the student qualify for free or reduced-price lunch?	• The school handbook anti-bullying policy is aligned with the district school board anti-bullying policy. • Leaders at the school actively push for effective district school board policy on bullying prevention. • The school provides and/or connects families to low- or no-cost resources (e.g., food, clothing). • Educators are generally aware of the youth culture.
Macrosystem	• Is bullying considered a rite of passage in the culture of the school or district? • Do families believe it is the school's role to support social-emotional development in their children?	• The school clearly explains the connection between behavior and academic performance to families. • The school makes intentional efforts to include families in decision making on behavior expectations in the school.
Chronosystem	• How have beliefs about bullying changed over time? • How does current technology impact the school and students? • What recent events have begun to shift the macrosystem?	• The school clearly demonstrates the impact bullying can have on students. • The school culture leans into current health and societal changes that affect students socially, emotionally, and behaviorally.

know that statistically she is more likely to be involved in cyberbullying compared to her male peers. Do you know how a targeted student responds when facing more common adversities, such as having difficulty understanding an academic concept or not getting selected for the lead role in a school play? This information can give you insight into how resilient the targeted student may be when facing bullying. We know that students with disabilities are more likely to be involved in bullying (Gage et al., 2021), and knowing what disabilities the targeted student has can help you decide what interventions to consider. Finally, think about the strengths that you know the targeted student possesses. How can those strengths be used to support the student in overcoming the impact of bullying?

Microsystem

The microsystem includes factors directly connected to students themselves. It includes the students' home, school, and neighborhood. The activities, roles, and interpersonal relationships that influence students' development are represented in the microsystem. Some of the most common factors within the microsystem are students' socioeconomic status, relationships with teachers, relationships with family members, relationships with peers, recent loss, family views on the value of education, and extracurricular activities. Any of these factors can provide a buffer against or be a risk factor for bullying.

Research has shown that the microsystem of the family can have a profound impact on the likelihood that students are bullied. In 2008, Holt and colleagues conducted a study looking at how family characteristics impacted the rate at which children were bullied. One interesting finding from the study was that parents reported that their children were involved in bullying at a lower rate than the children themselves reported being involved in bullying. As shown later in the chapter, this observation holds true for teachers as well as parents. The researchers also found that home environments marked by greater rates of criticism, fewer rules, and more child maltreatment were risk factors for being the target of bullying. Risk factors associated with being the perpetrator of bullying included homes environments with a lack of supervision, child maltreatment, and exposure to domestic violence. These results were also reinforced by a later meta-analysis of familial risk factors conducted by a separate set of researchers (Lereya, Samara, & Wolke, 2013). Although as educators we are limited in our ability to shield students from many of these factors, having knowledge of them allows us to consider which students may need Tier 2 supports related to bullying prevention.

Mesosystem

The mesosystem represents the interactions between two or more different settings in which the student resides. If you have watched the movie *The Karate Kid*, then you have seen an example of a mesosystem. In one scene, the main character, Daniel, gets chased by several students from his school and tries to get home before they catch him. The students eventually catch up with Daniel and physically attack him. Just before he is knocked unconscious, Daniel sees the handyman from his apartment complex, Mr. Miyagi, fending off the student attackers. Daniel's microsystems of school and home interact, and the interaction creates a mesosystem.

A real-world example of a mesosystem involving bullying would be the interaction between a student's familial value of education and the way peers value education. If a student's family places a high value on doing well in school, but the student's peers think being smart means being a "nerd," then they may be at an increased risk of being the target of bullying. Conversely, if there is congruence between family and peers about the value of education, the student may be less likely to be targeted for bullying. Thinking of what is valued at your school, where might these interactions lead to an increased likelihood of bullying? Maybe there is a high value placed on athletic achievement. Perhaps your school is geared toward performing arts, and those students who excel in this area are more protected from bullying they would otherwise experience. Understanding how these different microsystems interact can give you a head start on preventing bullying.

Exosystem

The final three systems indirectly impact students but can still have profound consequences. Outside of the mesosystem is the exosystem. Students are not directly interacting with the exosystem, but the events that occur within this system affect students. For example, decisions made by students' school board will change their experience at school, but students are not typically directly interacting with the school board to make decisions. In the past several decades, many school boards have developed or updated their bullying prevention policies. When they are able to use the most up-to-date research, such as disavowing zero-tolerance policies, the impact on bullying can be great even if it is a decision made at the policy level. Laws in students' cities, states, and country are another example of how the exosystem can influence their experiences of bullying. Each year, states propose new laws around bullying. In Wisconsin in 2019, a law was proposed that would fine the parents of students who bully other students $313. Moreover, several states have made cyberbullying a misdemeanor offense with the potential for a fine.

Macrosystem

Outside of the exosystem lies the macrosystem. This system reflects the culture and belief systems that may indirectly influence a student. Although bullying occurs in countries throughout the world, it can look very different depending on the culture. For example, bullying in Japan, known as *ijime*, is largely characterized by groups of students bullying weaker peers in a psychological way (Naito & Gielen, 2006). This type of bullying is compared to the traditional view of bullying in American culture that focuses on physical aggression. Changes in the macrosystem occur less frequently but can have a sweeping impact. In America, cultural changes can often be seen through the lens of television and movies. If you have ever gone back and watched shows from even just a few decades ago, the shift in culture can be readily apparent. The first season of the show *Friends* aired in 1994 and is rife with jokes that show the culture's fear of being perceived as a homosexual or not masculine. In one episode, a father is mortified that his young son prefers to play with a Barbie doll and tries to convince him to play with soldiers instead. In another episode, a character, Joey Tribbiani, starts wearing a unisex bag that looks like a large purse in an effort to land an acting job. The first time one of his friends sees him wearing the bag, he states, "Wow. You look just like your son, Mrs. Tribbiani." Just 4 years later in 1998, the first television show staring an openly gay character, *Will and Grace,* premiered. American culture continued to shift, and in 2015 the United States legalized marriage between same sex couples. To be sure, students who identify as LGBTQ+ are still at an increased risk for experiencing bullying; however, the culture has evolved to be more accepting.

Chronosystem

The final system that affects the development of students is the chronosystem. This system refers to the time in which students live. As recently as the 1980s, cyberbullying was not a concept that bullying prevention researchers would have been able to predict. In current times, it is such a concern that legislatures around the country pass laws that criminalize it. More recently, the impact of the COVID-19 pandemic has changed how bullying occurs. Before in-person learning was discontinued for schools across the country in the spring of 2020, Asian American students began reporting bullying related to the virus and their ethnicity. In one example posted online by a parent in Georgia, her Asian American daughter was touched by other students, who pretended that she was the most contagious child, in a game they called coronavirus.

Placing bullying experiences in the context of the social-ecological model, as described earlier, can help you when problem solving for individual students' bullying concerns or at the schoolwide level. Moreover, by understanding the different effects of each system, you can begin to predict how bullying may change in your school. Are school boundaries being redrawn this year? How might the change in feeder neighborhoods influence the types of bullying that occur? Is your school adding new clubs? How might this decision affect the culture, and thus bullying, in your school? When we are able to consider our students' individual characteristics within the context of their environments, we are better able to prevent bullying.

COMPREHENSIVE BULLYING PREVENTION

Having outlined how bullying is defined, its prevalence, and the context that reinforces it, we now offer a way to address it. Comprehensive Bullying Prevention (CBP) is a schoolwide approach that reinforces a positive school climate, engages the community, and outlines structures to actively preventing bullying and to address specific instances of bullying (National School Climate Center [NSCC], n.d.; cf. McIntosh & Goodman, 2016; Sugai & Horner, 2006). CBP is composed of five components: (1) school climate, (2) policy, (3) evidence-based curricula, (4) family and community partnership, and (5) data-based decision making. We describe each component briefly here before discussing how best to organize the components in a systemic manner.

School Climate

School climate refers to the overall quality and character of the school (NSCC, n.d.; Thapa, Cohen, Guffey, & Higgins-D'Alessandro, 2013). Specifically, it includes the perceptions of safety and security of the students and staff, the quality of relationships among students and staff in the school, the extent to which the staff emphasizes teaching and learning, and the actual physical environment (NSCC, n.d.). To create a positive school climate, schools develop a safe and predictable environment that has an intentional focus on positive student–staff relationships. Additionally, the staff and students are given methods and tools to respond to bullying, whether they experience it directly or witness it as a bystander (see Ross, Horner, & Stiller, 2012). By creating a positive climate, schools establish a culture that reinforces prosocial skills, discourages unwanted interactions and bullying, and establishes the positive treatment of everyone in the school community.

Policy

The next component is policy, which provides guidance and organization on the expectations for the treatment of students and how staff can respond to and investigate incidents of bullying. Within the policy, schools outline the exact steps and procedures that families, students, and staff members should take when bullying occurs. It includes how staff members should immediately intervene when they see bullying, investigate incidents, and document incidents for record keeping. Overall, schools use the policy to establish the positive treatment of all students and reinforce that bullying is not tolerated at the school.

Evidence-Based Curricula

A critical piece of CBP is the use of curricula to intentionally teach students prosocial skills to navigate the school setting. In particular, the chosen curriculum is used to teach students about bullying dynamics, social-emotional learning (SEL) competencies, and how to manage instances of bullying they may experience. Schools use a universal curriculum with all students, and then use additional lessons or other curricula for students who need additional support.

Family and Community Partnerships

In creating a context that reduces bullying, schools must include families and the community. Schools use intentional strategies to build relationships between families, students, the community, and the school, which help to reinforce expected behaviors across multiple settings. When families are included as true partners in bullying prevention efforts, schools are better equipped to use practices that are both evidence based and parent approved. Moreover, when bullying incidents do occur, schools that have already developed relationships with families are in position to be supportive instead of defensive.

Data-Based Decision Making

Data-based decision making is the use of data to make decisions regarding fidelity of implementation and the effectiveness of the practices used within CBP. Schools gather a variety of data to make decisions about implementation and the impact their efforts have for students, the staff, and families. To organize decision making and use data well, schools can use the four-step problem-solving model as an organizing heuristic (Deno, 2016; Good, Gruba, & Kaminski, 2002; Shinn, 2008). With the problem-solving model, schools can identify and resolve problems that arise, and they can engage in continuous improvement cycles to ensure that their efforts are beneficial.

CBP AND MTSS

Having described the five components of CBP, the idea of implementing all the components cohesively may feel overwhelming. We are well aware of initiative fatigue in schools, as schools often are asked to take on too much and end up with scattered approaches (Elmore, 2000; Newmann, Smith, Allensworth, & Bryk, 2001; Schmoker, 2006). The last thing we want is for schools to implement bullying prevention in a disconnected manner. To create a context that supports implementation and a coherent system, schools can adopt a comprehensive systems approach to bullying prevention, which is reflective of a multi-tiered system of supports (MTSS) (cf. Bradshaw, 2013 and Sugai & Horner, 2006).

At its core, MTSS is a service delivery model. It's a way to organize a school's systems so that supports and services can be provided to students in an effective and efficient manner (Jimerson, Burns, & VanDerHeyden, 2016; McIntosh & Goodman, 2016). In practice, this means that schools provide instruction or support to students based on data, not labels, and they put processes in place to ensure that these supports are effective in meeting the needs of students, staff members, and families (Sugai & Horner, 2006). Because MTSS is a schoolwide framework for coordinating, providing, and monitoring supports provided to students (Jimerson et al., 2016; McIntosh & Goodman, 2016), implementing bullying prevention within MTSS is a sensible and natural fit. Schools can capitalize on the organizing systems of MTSS to ensure that bullying prevention is systemic and sustainable.

MTSS provides the shell within which bullying prevention is organized (McIntosh & Goodman, 2016; Sugai & Horner, 2006). Specifically, schools can orient the practices and efforts related to bullying prevention within instructional tiers (Stoiber & Gettinger, 2016). At Tier 1, schools provide students a safe and positive school climate in which they all are taught schoolwide expectations that encourage safety, empathy, and responsibility (George, Kincaid, & Pollard-Sage, 2009). The adults work to build relationships with one another, with students, and with families. The staff make intentional efforts to connect with families and communities, educate them on bullying prevention, and enlist them as partners in building a safe and supportive school (Cohen & Freiberg, 2013). The staff also use evidence-based curricula to teach all students about bullying prevention, SEL, and ways to respond to conflict. At Tiers 2 and 3, the staff can use additional interventions and curricula to further support students involved in bullying, connect with families and the community, and provide additional guidance and education around bullying prevention (cf. McIntosh & Goodman, 2016). All of these practices represent the CBP components of *school climate, evidence-based curricula,* and *family and community partnerships.*

The *policy* component is a core feature of MTSS, as the staff and administrators outline the efforts of the school to prevent bullying across all three tiers of support. Within this component, the school outlines an effective bullying prevention policy that provides structure and guidance for how to respond to incidents of bullying, the use of data, and how problems around bullying are solved.

Finally, the school will use the *data-based decision-making* component of CBP throughout all of MTSS. Schools engage in data-based decision making as they evaluate the benefit of their bullying prevention practices (Deno, 2016; Hosp, 2008). In particular, the staff will regularly screen all students multiple times a year to identify the rate of bullying within the school, thus allowing the school to gauge the overall prevalence of bullying and to identify those students who need support (cf. Clemens, Keller-Margulis, Scholten, & Yoon, 2016; PBIS Apps, 2020). Staff members will also evaluate how well the various components are being implemented and benefiting students. For example, they will evaluate the extent to which the school climate is positive and the extent to which they are engaging families in a positive and beneficial manner.

Schools can use the MTSS framework as a foundation and structure within which their efforts to prevent bullying can be organized, so we hope our readers understand that MTSS is a framework that can bring the components of CBP to light. Certainly a school could use the components outside of an MTSS framework, but it would likely result in a disconnected and unsustainable system (Sugai & Horner, 2006). As such, we have framed bullying prevention within an MTSS framework so that schools and staff can create the necessary systems for sustainable change (cf. Jimerson et al., 2016).

Implementation Science

In addition to framing bullying prevention within MTSS, schools will also want to consider implementation science as a means to ensure sustainability. Despite the fact that empirical studies on bullying have been providing educators with research-based prevention approaches for decades, difficulties still persist in translating research into real-world practice. This has been an issue that bullying researchers have worked on addressing for years (Swearer, Espelage, & Napolitano, 2009). One of the most effective ways to bridge this gap is through implementation science. As defined by Rogers (1995), implementation science is the study of methods and strategies that facilitate the use of evidence-based practice and research into real-world application by practitioners and policy-makers. In other words, implementation science tells you how to take research and put it into practice. At the end of each CBP core component chapter, you will find a Practice Profile that aligns with the principles of implementation science. These Practice Profiles define each component and provide readers with an understanding of what the component looks like when implemented as expected. The second half of this book covers implementation science in depth to support your understanding of its concepts and how they are applied to bullying prevention efforts in schools.

CHAPTER 2

School Climate

Walk into the entryway of any school and you'll immediately notice its tone and feel through the design and layout of the physical space, the posters on the walls, the interactions among students, and so forth. Such elements encompass a school's climate, which refers to the quality and character of a school (NSCC, n.d.). It includes not only how safe students feel (socially, emotionally, intellectually, and physically), but also the relationships within the school and the value placed on academic learning (Bosworth & Judkins, 2014; NSCC, n.d.; Thapa et al., 2013; Wang & Degol, 2016). The NSCC (2007) summarizes a positive school climate well:

> A . . . positive school climate . . . includes norms, values, and expectations that support people feeling socially, emotionally, and physically safe. People are engaged and respected. Students, families, and educators work together to develop, live, and contribute to a shared school vision. Educators model and nurture an attitude that emphasizes the benefits of, and satisfaction from, learning. Each person contributes to the operations of the school as well as the care of the physical environments. (p. 5)

From reading this summary, you can probably surmise that there are four domains that comprise school climate: (1) the feeling of safety within the school; (2) the relationships among the people in the building; (3) the teaching and learning practices used, including the value placed on academic achievement; and (4) the institutional environment (NSCC, n.d.; Thapa et al., 2013). We share a summary of these four domains in Table 2.1.

HOW IS SCHOOL CLIMATE RELATED TO BULLYING?

Imagine how you feel walking into a new setting, such as the Department of Motor Vehicles: there are people, lights blinking, long lines, a packed waiting room, and everyone is anxious to get in and get out! Usually there isn't much structure or direction other than a sign that says "take a number

TABLE 2.1. Four Domains of School Climate

Domain	Description	Example of positive school climate
Safety	The extent to which students feel safe to express their social needs, emotions, and intellectual pursuits without fear of adverse experiences or disregard for their perspective. It also includes how physically safe from violence students and staff are.	There are clear expectations that value each student's experience, and students perceive the rules within the school as fair. Adults are seen as caring and supportive. Adults reinforce expectations that align with bullying prevention.
Community and relationships	How connected people feel to one another within the school. It includes the qualitative nature of the interactions between students and between students and the staff, as well as how connected students feel to the school itself.	The student–student and student–staff relationships are positive, supportive, and focus on inclusion. Students feel connected to the school and value its community. There are strong relationships with the staff.
Teaching and learning practices	Refers to the emphasis and focus on learning, as well as the instructional practices used within the school.	There is a clear focus on learning and achieving academic goals within the school. Effective instructional practices are used throughout the building.
Institutional environment	Encompasses the physical layout of the school, its structural organization, and the adequacy of resources.	The building layout facilitates positive interactions and behavior (e.g., schedules minimize disruption, areas are supervised by staff), resources support learning and climate, and class size is manageable. The staff uses active supervision as a method for bullying prevention.

and please have a seat." When you're finally called up for your turn, it turns out the paperwork you brought with you isn't what's needed (what the website said and what the clerk is saying are two different things). What a stressful and agonizing experience. Now contrast that to a department store with health protocols in place to manage a pandemic. As you enter the store, you see signs stating that masks are to be worn, along with arrows on the floor indicating the direction of traffic. There are people to remind everyone of where to walk and of how to proceed through the store, and stations set up for hand sanitizer and waste bins. All this together creates a predictable environment so that customers and store employees know what to expect and how to engage with the environment. This is the notion behind building a positive school climate. There's structure, predictability, and reliability in the environment. Because of that structure, the likelihood of bullying occurring is reduced and both students and teachers are better equipped to respond to incidents of bullying.

A school climate establishes the foundations and norms that can either encourage or discourage bullying (Bradshaw, 2013; Good, McIntosh, & Gietz, 2011; Wang, Berry, & Swearer, 2013). In an environment with a positive school climate, students feel valued and cared for by the staff, and they report confidence that the staff will handle issues that arise (Thapa et al., 2013). Students frequently have positive interactions with staff members, and the staff members in turn have positive relationships with each other (Bosworth & Judkins, 2014; Thapa et al., 2013). This atmosphere creates a setting in which students feel safe, are encouraged to pursue their interests, and feel supported with their needs (Thapa et al., 2013). Increased graduation rates, lower rates of violence and delinquent behavior, and fewer incidents of bullying are just some of the benefits associated with a positive school climate (Klein, Cornell, & Konold, 2012; Thapa et al., 2013).

The environment created by a positive school climate arguably makes responding to bullying easier for the staff and students (Bradshaw, 2013; Cohen & Freiberg, 2013). In fact, when rules are broken or unexpected behaviors like bullying occur, there are clear procedures to respond to it in a fair and equitable manner (Good et al., 2011; Horner, Sugai, Todd, & Lewis-Palmer, 2005; Thapa et al., 2013). Students are provided specific language and methods to use in order to appropriately respond to a bullying incident they experience or witness (Good et al., 2011). For example, students may be taught to assertively tell the perpetrator of bullying that the behavior is not okay and to then alert an adult (Ross et al., 2012). The burden on students to manage instances of bullying or unwanted behavior is lessened, as they are simply reinforcing a social norm instead of trying to establish one (Ross et al., 2012; Wang et al., 2013). Adults also have a clear structure and response for managing such incidents (Cohen & Freiberg, 2013; Good et al., 2011). Further, there is consistent adult awareness and supervision throughout the school (Wang et al., 2013). When students do experience or witness a bullying incident, not only do they feel safe in reporting it, they also feel confident that it will be heard and appropriately managed (Aldridge, McChesney, & Afari, 2018; Eliot, Cornell, Gregory, & Fan, 2010). By creating a positive school climate, schools establish a foundation in which empathy and kindness are the normative ways to treat others, as opposed to aggression, harassment, or bullying (Bosworth & Judkins, 2014; Wang et al., 2013).

IMPROVING SCHOOL CLIMATE

To create a positive school climate and lay the foundation for bullying prevention, we offer three broad strategies: (1) intentionally building relationships among (a) students and (b) students and teachers (Cohen & Freiberg, 2013; Jennings & Greenberg, 2009); (2) creating a safe, predictable environment (Cohen & Freiberg, 2013; Horner et al., 2005); and (3) explicitly teaching students how to respond to incidents of bullying (Cohen & Freiberg, 2013; Good et al., 2011; Ross et al., 2012). These best practices address three of the four domains of school climate outlined by the NSCC. The one best practice not addressed in this chapter is teaching and learning practices. Discussing teaching practices and academic instruction is outside the purview of this book, but we offer a few resources for our readers to consider, including *Leaders of Learning* (DuFour & Marzano, 2011), *Professional Learning Communities at Work: Best Practices for Enhancing Student Achievement* (DuFour & Eaker, 1998), *Integrated Multi-Tiered Systems of Support: Blending RTI and PBIS* (McIntosh & Goodman, 2016), and *Explicit Instruction: Effective and Efficient Teaching* (Archer & Hughes, 2011). Here we focus our attention on three best practices related to bullying prevention and school climate.

Intentionally Building Relationships

Imagine a student named Jill who witnesses another student, Judy, being verbally bullied in the hallway. Jill doesn't know Judy very well. They run in different crowds and only have one class together, so she isn't sure if the perpetrator is joking with Jill. Instead of asking, Jill closes her locker and continues to class ("Not my concern," she thinks to herself). Jill misses an opportunity to support a classmate because she has never met Judy. Now imagine if Judy and Jill had met last week because the school held a "get to know your classmates" event. They spent 15 minutes interviewing each other with questions given to them by their classroom teacher. In this alternative scenario, when Jill notices Judy being bullied, she asks Judy if everything is okay. By creating personal connections among students, schools can reduce isolation among them, create positive social norms regarding the treatment of others, and help students feel more connected and valued (Gest, Madill, Zadzora, Miller, & Rodkin, 2014; Jones & Kahn, 2017; Van Ryzin & Roseth, 2018; Yoder & Gurke, 2017). Given this outcome, it's not a surprise that a key component of a positive climate that reduces bullying is intentional efforts to build relationships among students and among students and the staff (Good et al., 2011).

As one strategy for building relationships among students, the school can hold events or activities for all students to attend that promote positive prosocial behavior and friendly relationships among people in the building. For example, the school can structure grade-level or schoolwide events to celebrate the school community, such as a field day, a community breakfast, or festival. The school can provide activities for students to learn about peers with whom they don't always spend time, such as developing an interview protocol of questions to ask and have a social mixer or ice cream social for students. The school can also highlight a few students each week and provide a venue for the school to learn about that student, such as a public display about the "student of the week."

The staff can organize service learning projects to build community and relationships among students and the staff. For example, students could construct a local garden within the community, spend time working with a local charity or nonprofit, or restore a designated location in the community (Harlacher & Rodriguez, 2018). Such projects can be connected directly to bullying prevention. For example, the local garden can include plaques that describe acts of kindness done by students in the school. Specific projects can also be developed around spreading kindness and support, including cleaning up parts of the community or partnering with other grades to teach students about respect and responding to bullying incidents. By having such events, school staff can create opportunities for students to interact with peers with whom they normally wouldn't spend time. Building personal connections among students can increase the likelihood that students report incidents of bullying they may see.

Classroom Circles

Schools can also ask teachers to provide a platform to discuss classroom issues and to provide a space for students to share insights about themselves or to raise issues (Kriete & Davis, 2014). This morning advisory time or "classroom circle" allows students to greet each other by name, share news or personal information about themselves, and complete a group activity to foster connection among the students. Teachers can use this time to encourage relationships, practice prosocial skills, or foster community in the classroom by having students learn more about one another. Targets of bullying can have a voice, and all students can have a platform to share concerns regarding how others are treated. To be sure the classroom circle is positive and beneficial to students, teachers can establish behavioral expectations (we discuss what they are later in the chapter) and create a process and structure for the circle.

Daily Positive Greetings

Staff can also conduct daily greetings with students to further develop relationships and create a positive climate. Cook et al. (2018) developed a strategy that facilitates positive interactions between the staff and students and also gives the staff an opportunity to set students up for success when they enter a classroom. The strategy consists of three steps: (1) teachers greet students at the door with a verbal or nonverbal gesture (e.g., elbow bump, high-five, fist-bump), (2) provide general or personal feedback to set students up for success (e.g., "Let's make sure you complete your work today" or "Remember to be respectful and use kind words today"), and (3) provide behavior-specific praise to students ("You're here on time, so I can see you're being responsible"). This method affords teachers a brief moment to connect personally with each student, precorrect any issues, and provide prompting or encouragement for using certain behaviors or prosocial skills (Sugai, 2020). For targets of bullying, teachers can use this time to connect with them and remind them that they can come forward if they are being targeted. For perpetrators, teachers can focus on ensuring they treat others well. Schools that use this approach schoolwide can guarantee that all students have a positive interaction with an adult each day, thus facilitating connections and relationships with students.

School Communities

It's perhaps not surprising that the smaller the school, the higher the feelings of school safety and school connectedness among students (McNeely, Nonnemaker, & Blum, 2002; Thapa et al., 2013). Although schools can't simply reduce the number of students in their building, they can create school communities or smaller networks of student communities to create a "smaller" feel (Lee & Freidrich, 2007). For example, a *respect team* can be formed that helps to teach weekly lessons on respect or empathy as a means of reducing bullying. Other student teams can be formed that offer supervision throughout the school or that create connections among students by befriending students or offering greetings and cards on holidays, birthdays, and on other important days (see Good & Lindsay, 2013; Martinez et al., 2019). Larger schools may be perceived as having higher rates of bullying, but in reality there isn't a clear connection between a larger school and higher rates of bullying (Klein & Cornell, 2010). Consequently, creating connectedness and building relationships among students can be a potential way to gain some of the benefits associated with a smaller school by default.

Given all these strategies, schools can ensure a positive climate by building relationships within the building. In turn, students will feel less isolated and safer coming forward to report bullying (Bosworth & Judkins, 2014; Thapa et al., 2013; Van Ryzin & Roseth, 2018; Wang et al., 2013).

Creating a Safe, Predictable Environment

In addition to building relationships, schools can create a positive school climate that reduces bullying by ensuring a safe and predictable environment (Harlacher & Rodriguez, 2018; Horner et al., 2005). To create such an environment, school staff can begin by teaching and reinforcing a set of schoolwide expectations to all students. The staff can also establish a discipline system for how to respond to incidents of unwanted behavior, including acts of bullying.

Schoolwide Expectations

By outlining schoolwide expectations, schools provide all students with a common understanding of expected behavior, how to get their needs met, and how to navigate the environment successfully (George et al., 2009; Lynass, Tsai, Richman, & Cheney, 2012). Readers will see the connection to the Positive Behavioral Interventions and Supports (PBIS) approach here, but this common understanding forms a foundation of predictability, safety, and structure. From this foundation, a climate can be created that reduces the likelihood of bullying occurring and, if it does occur, students and teachers know who to turn to for support or assistance (Bradshaw, 2013; Cohen & Frieberg, 2013).

Each school creates a set of three-to-five schoolwide expectations. These expectations describe general behavior that is expected across all school settings and clarify what is acceptable. They also communicate to students what to do in each setting and how to treat others, thus making clear that bullying is not allowed within the school (George et al., 2009; McKevitt & Braaksma, 2008). The expectations are created and agreed upon by the staff and students in the school, and they represent the norms and cultural values of the school community (Harlacher & Rodriguez, 2018; Lynass et al., 2012). All expectations are positively worded, action oriented, culturally and developmentally inclusive, and are limited in number (as more than five is difficult for students to remember; George et al., 2009).

The most commonly used expectations in schools are "Be Safe, Be Respectful, Be Responsible." They are often used because they cover a vast range of behavior within a school (Lynass et al., 2012). Schools can use acronyms for their expectations, such as PAWS—Productive, Act Safe, Work Responsibly, Show Respect—or TEAM—Take responsibility, Eager to learn, All are welcome, Manage yourself. They may also use mnemonics, such as "the four B's—Be Safe, Be Responsible, Be Respectful, Be Caring" —or visuals, such as a picture of a paw to match with a PAWS acronym, to help students remember and recall the expectations.

The expectations span common settings in a school, thus creating a schoolwide matrix (see Figure 2.1). The matrix lists the most common settings within the school across the columns and the schoolwide expectations within the rows. The cells of the matrix are then populated with positively stated rules. Whereas the schoolwide expectations are general descriptions of behavior across all settings, the rules are concrete and clear descriptions of behavior relative to a given setting (Harlacher & Rodriguez, 2018; McKevitt & Braaksma, 2008). Teachers use the matrix to indicate what each rule "looks like and sounds like" across common settings, thus providing clarity and structure (George et al., 2009). Although we provide an example with written text, it's key to consider the developmental needs of your students. For example, some schools may include visuals or icons to communicate the rules and expectations to ensure that their younger students, who are still learning to read, can understand the matrix (Harlacher & Rodriguez, 2018; see Beckner, 2013). Overall, teachers can use the matrix as a visual prompt for the rules and expectations for students, as well as a teaching tool for when students need correction on using the expectations (Harlacher & Rodriguez, 2018; Simonsen & Myers, 2015).

Schools can intentionally embed rules regarding bullying and the treatment of others in the matrix. For example, rules such as "allow others to sit with you" or "stand up for someone if they are being cyberbullied" are two examples of embedding such rules into the matrix. With the rise of cyberbullying over the past several decades, the staff will want to include explicit rules for digital spaces and online behavior. Moreover, one of the best practices for preventing cyberbullying is to

	Classroom	Hallway	Cafeteria	Bathroom	Online
Be safe	• Use materials appropriately. • Keep hands, feet, and objects to self.	• Walk on the right side of the hall. • Use handrail on the stairs.	• Keep food on your tray. • Follow the line procedures.	• Keep water in the sink. • Use soap when washing hands.	• Keep your passwords secret. • Keep personal information personal.
Be respectful	• Be mindful of others' learning. • Follow the dress code. • Take care of materials and property.	• Hold the door for others. • Use a quiet voice. • Be mindful of others' learning in classrooms.	• Use good manners. • Allow others to sit with you.	• Respect others' privacy. • Go quickly so others don't wait long.	• Comment on and write only things you would say to someone in person. • Stand up for someone if they are being cyberbullied.
Be responsible	• Be prepared with your materials. • Work diligently and ask for help when needed.	• Keep hands, feet, and objects to self. • Go to where you're going.	• Clean up your area when you're done eating. • Throw away all trash and recycle your recyclables.	• Wash hands, flush, throw trash away. • Return to class promptly.	• Log out of websites when you finish using them. • Tell an adult if you see someone is in danger.

FIGURE 2.1. Example of a behavior matrix.

teach digital citizenship. This means explicitly explaining to students how to be safe, respectful, and responsible online, and teachers can show students how to report cyberbullying to the school or to the social media company on which the cyberbullying occurs. For students who are in high school, a helpful activity can be to have them Google themselves. Their social media profiles are often one of the first links that appear. From there, students can see firsthand what information anyone in the world can get about them if they don't restrict access to their profiles. Further, teachers can ask their students if they would want a prospective boss or college to see what is easily accessible about them online.

Additionally, the rules illustrated in the matrix can include routines, which are structured steps students take to accomplish a task or to have a need met, that can be taught to students (Harlacher, 2015; Simonsen & Myers, 2015). For example, the "follow the line procedures" in the "Cafeteria" and "Be Safe" cells in Figure 2.1 is a routine that was taught to students (i.e., 1. Stand behind the person at the end of the line. 2. Have your card out to pay. 3 Speak clearly when asking for your food item. 4. Say please and thank you.). By outlining clear expectations, rules, and routines, schools can develop predictability and structure that contribute to a positive climate.

Teaching and Reinforcement of Expectations

In addition to outlining expectations, the staff will want to explicitly teach students how to use them (Harlacher & Rodriguez, 2018). Just as academic skills are explicitly taught to students, the staff can explicitly teach behavior. Although we could point out many ways to teach students expectations, the creation of a lesson plan is a key starting point. The lesson plan includes examples and nonexamples of the expectation, activities to practice the expectation, methods for the staff to prompt the expectation, and data to monitor use of the expectations (Langland, Lewis-Palmer, & Sugai, 1998). The lesson plans are then used throughout the year to teach students the expectations, beginning with an introductory event, such as an assembly or an overview shared during their homeroom. Following the introductory event, there is active teaching of the expectations in the setting. Groups of students are taken to a given location (e.g., the hallway) and are explicitly taught the expectations for that setting (cf. Taylor-Greene et al., 1997). Booster sessions of the expectations are then used during the year to both correct for increases in rates of problematic behavior and to also proactively mitigate predictable times when behavior is worse (e.g., after a holiday break; George et al., 2009; Harlacher & Rodriguez, 2018). Teaching and feedback are critical pieces for creating a safe and predictable environment (Freeman, 2019). Following the initial teaching, the staff will want to provide ongoing practice and feedback to students on their use of the expectations. We offer a variety of examples in Table 2.2 on ways for students to practice expectations and embed them throughout the school.

The staff can also acknowledge students' use of expectations by frequently using behavior-specific praise (BSP). BSP is precise verbal feedback provided to students contingent on performing a given behavior or using a certain skill (Lewis, Hudson, Richter, & Johnson, 2004; Simonsen, Fairbanks, Briesch, Myers, & Sugai, 2008; Sutherland, Wehby, & Copeland, 2000). For example, "Thank you, Henry. You came into class quietly and started on your bell work right away" or "Jeremiah, I saw you invited Benny to sit with you during lunch. That's very kind." Specific praise is different from general praise, which offers up positive, yet vague, statements of what a student is doing (e.g., Way to go! Awesome! That's the best!).

Teachers can use BSP to intentionally promote and strengthen the schoolwide expectations as well as acts of empathy and kindness as a means of preventing acts of bullying. Teachers can praise students for acts that are counter to bullying, such as listening to others, inviting others to be a part of an activity, or acknowledging other's perspectives and thus create a welcoming environment.

You may have heard the concern that reinforcement can harm a student's intrinsic motivation or that students "should just know already." However, when used effectively, reinforcement actually does not show a detrimental impact on a student's motivation (Akin-Little, Eckert, Lovett, & Little, 2004; Cameron & Pierce, 1994). External reinforcement is a temporary teaching tool used to strengthen a specific or targeted skill; it's not something given all the time for every skill or behavior. Once the skill is learned and the student is fluent, the external reinforcement can be applied to a different skill. This is why it's important to initially pair verbal praise (i.e., behavior-specific praise) with a tangible reinforcer; over time, the tangible reinforcer will be removed, leaving the natural and verbal praise behind as a maintaining reinforcer (not to mention a more cost-effective one!). In this manner, reinforcement serves as a bridge between initially learning a skill (in this case, a schoolwide expectation) and the inclusion of that skill into the student's repertoire (Daly et al., 1996; Haring, Lovitt, Eaton, & Hansen, 1978). The reinforcement provided within the acknowledgment system is also used as a tool to encourage future use of the skill and to communicate close approximations of the skill (Alberto & Troutman, 2013; Simonsen et al., 2008).

TABLE 2.2. Examples of Embedding and Practicing the Expectations

Method	Description
Skits	Students or the staff create skits acting out use of the expectations.
Songs	Students write a song about the expectations. A contest can be held and the winning song can be sung each week or month to start the school day.
Videos	Students and the staff develop videos in which they illustrate examples and nonexamples of the expectations.
Weekly or monthly focus	An expectation is chosen and students are reinforced for that particular expectation heavily for a week or month. For example, respect can be chosen, and students earn two tickets (instead of one) for being respectful. This can be helpful during the first few weeks when expectations are first introduced.
Monthly teaching	An expectation is chosen and related skills are taught each week. For example, the focus is "be responsible" for September, and each week, a related skill is taught during a class attended by all students. The skills can be (1) using your planner, (2) setting personal goals, (3) expressing anger safely, and (4) admitting mistakes.
Character perspective	Students are asked to reflect on a story read or a historical figure about how the character or person used or did not use the schoolwide expectations (George, 2009).
Tracking tickets	During a math class, students examine data on the number of tokens provided to students to determine which grade level or classroom earns the most, the probability of getting a ticket, or which expectation is reinforced the most (George, 2009).
Short essays	As part of an English language arts lesson, students write essays about how they demonstrate the expectations.

Initially, students need a high rate of BSP and even tangible reinforcement to get them to "buy in" to using the expectations (George, 2009; Harlacher, 2015). During initial learning, external reinforcement (e.g., a tangible reward) may provide motivation to use the skill (Alberto & Troutman, 2013; Daly, Lentz, & Boyer, 1996; George et al., 2009). Over time, as the skill is developed (and internal motivations are naturally developed by the student), the external reinforcement can be gradually faded. The tangible reinforcement is no longer needed and instead our language (i.e., BSP) can serve as the natural reinforcement (Alberto & Troutman, 2013).

In addition to BSP for use of the expectations, the staff can provide longer-term reinforcements. For example, teachers can pair the BSP with a tangible token, such as a paper ticket, sticker, or adult signature (George et al., 2009; Harlacher & Rodriguez, 2018). These tokens are given out on a regular basis (e.g., typically daily, but at least a few times a week) and can provide that initial motivation to learn and use the skill. Students can then use the tangible tokens as "money" and purchase items from a school store (Harlacher & Rodriguez, 2018). Such items can include school supplies, electronic devices or accessories, or free social rewards (e.g., first in line to lunch, homework help pass, time with a staff member or peer).

Other ideas for long-term reinforcement include announcements of the names of students who have earned a certain number of tickets, a special identification card to acknowledge students who have displayed positive behavior over an extended period of time, phone calls home to families about their students' positive behavior, raffles or drawings for larger items, or admission into school events or dances (George, 2009; Harlacher & Rodriguez, 2018). In particular, the staff can provide a method for students to submit acts of kindness, which can be shared via social media or daily announcements. For example, a student can report that a fellow student was kind or supported another student who was a target of bullying, and they can be publicly acknowledged. In doing so, the school can further reinforce a climate that prevents bullying.

Discipline Structure

As part of a predictable, safe environment, schools also create clear procedures for discipline and responding to unwanted behavior, including bullying. This structure not only provides a "road map" for staff to follow when managing issues, but it also provides predictability for students (Harlacher & Rodriguez, 2018). One factor that contributes to ongoing bullying can be ambiguity about what is or is not bullying, as well as uncertainty among staff members on how to adequately respond to prevent further acts of bullying (Bradshaw, 2013; Harlacher & Rodriguez, 2018). By creating a discipline structure, both students and teachers will have clarity about how to respond to behavior, including not just acts of bullying, but also harassment, unwanted teasing, and other forms of mistreatment.

An example of a discipline structure is illustrated in Figure 2.2. As you can see, the structure provides clarity on teacher-managed versus administrator-managed behaviors and consistent,

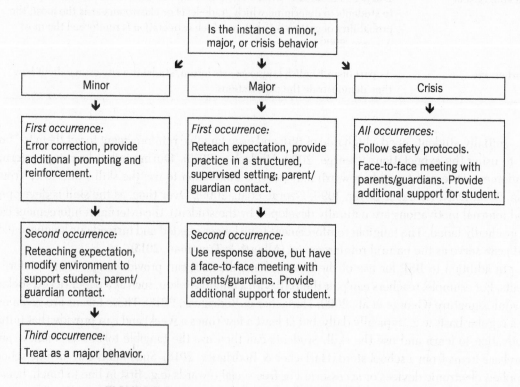

FIGURE 2.2. Example of a schoolwide discipline process.

predictable staff responses to behavior. By providing this structure, all staff and students have a sense of how behavior is managed. This removes the guesswork and clears up any inconsistencies that may occur for the staff. It also eases any anxiety or uncertainty that students may have when it comes to discipline.

TEACHER-MANAGED VERSUS ADMINISTRATOR-MANAGED BEHAVIOR

Schools can organize behaviors into three broad categories: *minor, major,* and *crisis.* Minor behaviors are those managed by the classroom staff, such as disruption, defiance, or not having materials for class. Major behaviors are those managed by the administration and include behaviors that significantly disrupt the learning environment, including bullying, fighting, harassment, vandalism, or stealing. Crisis behaviors are ones that pose an immediate threat to safety or student–staff well-being, such as the possession of weapons, the use of drugs or alcohol, or threats toward the self or others.

In delineating different categories of behavior, the school creates a structure that allows the school to match the appropriate amount of resources to a given response to a behavior (George et al., 2009; Harlacher & Rodriguez, 2018). For example, imagine that a teacher sends a student to the office for verbally saying to a classmate, "You're dumb." Although the remark is inappropriate, administrators and office-level staff likely don't need to intervene in this situation given its lack of severity. However, if a student was verbally abusive toward a classmate numerous times or engaged in a physical confrontation with a classmate, a teacher would refer this sort of behavior to the office to be managed. By outlining which behaviors classroom staff versus office staff manage, the school is able to avoid an overexpenditure of resources on behaviors that don't warrant it.

By clarifying major, minor, and crisis behaviors, schools can ensure that all staff in the building are clear on what constitutes certain responses and what does not. In doing so, schools can indicate where and which types of bullying fit within the structure. As an example, we have outlined different types of behaviors in Table 2.3, along with different levels of bullying (readers can also visit the national center on PBIS for additional resources on defining behaviors at *www.*

TABLE 2.3. Examples of Definitions for Minor, Major, and Crisis Behaviors

Minor behaviors	Major behaviors	Crisis
Defiance: *Student does not comply with directions or talks back.*	Fighting: *Student is involved in a mutual incident that entails physical violence.*	Weapon possession: *Student has a weapon in their possession.*
Disrespect: *Student is socially rude or dismissive to adults or other students.*	Possession of drugs: *Student has illegal drugs, substances, or paraphernalia in their possession.*	Threat: *Student makes a statement or message that threatens the safety of themselves or others.*
Minor bullying: *Student teases or calls students names but it occurs infrequently.*	Major bullying: *Student is intentionally harming another person repeatedly.*	Threat (bullying): *Student makes a statement or message of retaliation that threatens imminent harm or the safety of themselves or others.*

pbisapps.org). Because staff members may have different views and tolerances for certain behaviors over others, and they may be fuzzy on what exactly constitutes bullying, defining behaviors for each category can be an iterative process. Moreover, to create buy-in from all stakeholders, school leadership can include staff in the decision-making process. The school staff should frequently revisit definitions and the resulting staff response to ensure consistency over time (George et al., 2009; McKevitt & Braaksma, 2008).

PROCEDURES FOR RESPONDING TO BEHAVIOR

Given the three categories of behavior, schools should outline specific ways to respond to each type (George et al., 2009; Harlacher & Rodriguez, 2018). This comes in the form of a flowchart or table that provides step-by-step responses and procedures. At each step, the school staff has certain strategies that can be used. Creating such a process provides clarity and predictability for staff and students responding to bullying as well as to other behaviors. There are no surprises or unknowns about how the staff or students will experience the response to an unwanted behavior; instead, there are clear procedures, and predictability is established. In outlining these responses and structures, staff members can align their intervention approach with their handbook and the district's policy for students who engage in bullying.

As illustrated in Figure 2.2, when an incident occurs, staff members follow the prescribed steps using an agreed-upon method for responding. For initial offenses, the general approach is to provide error correction to the student and then reinforce the desired skill or schoolwide expectation (Harlacher & Rodriguez, 2018). Error correction is a quick and simple process in which the staff member points out the student's error, asks the student to perform the correct skill or behavior (modeling, if needed), praises the student's use of the behavior, and then moves on (Watkins & Slocum, 2004). Following repeated incidents of a behavior, additional reteaching and corrective consequences are used to ensure the desired skill is learned (see *Second occurrence* and *Third occurrence* in Figure 2.2). Generally speaking, the student is retaught a schoolwide expectation, and adjustments to the environment are made to support the student's use of the new behavior or skill (Alberto & Troutman, 2013; Harlacher, 2015). As such, teachers use the discipline structure to reteach missing skills or strengthen infrequently used skills. By providing a structure for managing behavior, the staff has a transparent, predictable, and clear process for responding to behaviors that the staff should manage and behaviors that the administration should manage. They have steps for how each type of behavior (i.e., minor, major, and crisis behavior) will be handled and by whom.

For minor acts related to bullying, the staff can follow procedures outlined in Figure 2.2, which generally includes error correction and increased supervision or teaching of schoolwide expectations to ensure the perpetrator doesn't repeat the minor bullying. For major acts of bullying, we recommend that schools investigate the incidents according to the school district policy and handbook. They can enlist the support of office staff and develop a plan that addresses the issue. We discuss these approaches in greater depth in Chapter 3.

Classroom Management

Given that over 40% of bullying occurs within the classroom (U.S. Department of Education, 2019), teachers will want to use effective classroom management as a means for lowering the rates of bullying. In fact, teachers who use effective classroom management generally have lower rates of bullying (Koth, Bradshaw, & Leaf, 2008). Effective classroom management includes five key principles: (1) identifying and teaching expectations, (2) creating routines and structure, (3) reinforcement of the expectations and routines, (4) actively engaging students in a variety of ways, and (5) a process for responding to unwanted behavior (Greenberg, Putman, & Walsh, 2014; Oliver, Wehby, & Reschly, 2011; Simonsen et al., 2008). By using the five practices, teachers can create consistency and predictability in their classrooms to support bullying prevention and a positive school climate.

The expectations, behavior matrix, procedures to acknowledge students for use of the expectations, and procedures to respond to incidents of unwanted behavior that are used schoolwide can also be used in the classroom as well (Harlacher 2015; Simonsen & Myers, 2015). Each teacher uses the schoolwide expectations as their classroom expectations, including a behavior matrix specific to their classroom and their classroom routines (George et al., 2009; Harlacher, 2015). Within the matrix, teachers can provide more nuanced rules or skills related to bullying prevention for their particular students. For example, a preschool teacher may include "use kind words" or "ask others to play with you" as a means of creating connection in the classroom and reducing forms of bullying. However, at the high school level, a teacher may include "respect other's points of views" or "speak up if you see cyberbullying" within their matrix. With the matrix, a teacher can generally outline behaviors and skills that create a positive climate and incorporate routines or rules that actively prevent bullying. To create consistency between the schoolwide system and each classroom, we recommend that teachers use the same expectations in their classroom and that their teaching and acknowledgment methods align with those of the school.

Strong classroom management also includes a focus on learning and on a variety of ways to engage students during academic instruction. Generally speaking, high rates of engagement and active responding in a classroom can lead to lower problematic behavior and improved academic outcomes (Brophy & Good, 1986; Haydon et al., 2010; Haydon, Marsicano, & Scott, 2013; Sutherland et al., 2000; Sutherland & Wehby, 2001). Teachers can vary the types of responses students use during instruction. They include individual oral responses, such as calling out answers, or peer-to-peer responding, such as cooperative learning and peer tutoring. Teachers can also use written responses (e.g., white boards, guided notes) and physical responding (e.g., gestures, electronic polling, premade cards with answers) (Harlacher, 2015; Haydon et al., 2010).

With respect to bullying, teachers can incorporate cooperative learning groups as helpful ways to not only engage students, but also to break down barriers or cliques between classmates. The jigsaw method is a cooperative learning strategy in which students work in groups to learn academic content together. Each student in the group is assigned a number that corresponds to certain academic content. For example, imagine that students are learning about the life of Malcolm X. The students are placed into groups of four and assigned a number. Malcolm X's life is segmented into four sections (i.e., (1) early life and childhood, (2) prominence with the nation of Islam, (3) departure from nation of Islam, (4) assassination and influence), and each student's number corresponds to a section they are learning about. Students then get into "expert groups" with other students who have the same number, within which they discuss and become experts on their given section. After mastering the material, students return to their original groups and take turns teaching the members of their group about their section. Students are given a piece of the content to learn about, after which they all share what they have learned and put together entire "puzzle" of the content.

The jigsaw method is an effective strategy for not only for academic learning, but also as a way to break down cliques among students and build empathy and perspective taking for each other (Aronson, 1978, 2002; Aronson & Patnoe, 2011). In this manner, it can be used to improve student relationships, reduce isolation among students, and improve the collegiality among students. For students involved in bullying, the use of cooperative learning can lead to decreases in bullying and victimization marginalized (Van Ryzin & Roseth, 2018). Further, students can be taught a prosocial skill and then asked to use it during a cooperative learning activity. For example, teachers could teach students how to demonstrate empathy and perspective taking, and then students can engage in the jigsaw method to practice the skill (Aronson, 1978).

Explicit Teaching of Responding to Bullying

A key component of a positive climate that reduces bullying is actively teaching students how to respond to incidents of bullying and disrespectful behavior (Cohen & Freiberg, 2013). Teachers and staff teach every student specific words and actions to use when they witness or experience a bullying incident (see Ross et al., 2012 and Stiller, Nese, Tomlanovich, Horner, & Ross, 2013). For example, students can be taught a three-step process in which they tell their peer(s) to stop the bullying, walk away from the behavior, and then tell an adult (Ross et al., 2012). These steps are successive and used in sequence, moving to the next step when the previous one does not work (e.g., after telling their peer to stop and walking away, an adult is told if the behavior persisted). These steps create a cultural norm in which bullying incidents are not reinforced or encouraged. This language or method of responding to bullying can then be placed on the matrix in Figure 2.1 as a rule (i.e., "Use Stop-Walk-Talk"; Ross et al., 2012).

Additionally, schools can align the ongoing teaching of the schoolwide expectations with lessons on skills or character-education traits or SEL competencies (Barrett, Eber, McIntosh, Perales, & Romer, 2018; Bradshaw, 2013). In doing so, the staff can teach all students prosocial skills related to conflict resolution, healthy communication, and bullying prevention. For example, in Figure 2.1, the behavior matrix under a "be responsible" expectation can list "own your emotions" or "express your feelings safely," and students can be taught what the skill looks like (Barrett et al., 2018; Good et al., 2011). By teaching students SEL skills, encouraging them to listen to others, and to have empathy, schools can contribute to building relationships among people within the building and create an environment where bullying is not tolerated.

Physical Environment

The physical environment is a consideration when thinking about school climate and bullying prevention, as it incorporates the overall structure, layout, and state of the school campus, as well as the resources available to staff and students (NSCC, n.d.). Imagine walking into a school that is clean and freshly painted. The hallways are orderly and not overly crowded, class sizes are manageable, and students seem able to move about the building with ease. Contrast this environment to one that has graffiti on the walls or papers strewn about. The hallways are loud and crowded, and even the lightning is dim. They are all factors that can impact the overall school climate, the former example communicating pride in the school, the latter suggesting that the staff and students are less concerned with their building. In elementary schools, the layout of the playground can contribute to the frequency of bullying as well. Is there a clear line of sight for the staff to view students or are there corners around which students can hide? We offer two methods of how schools can address the physical environment.

Active Supervision

Students report feeling less safe in unsupervised areas of a school (Astor, Guerra, & Van Acker, 2010), so schools can create a safer climate by simply increasing supervision. The use of *active supervision* can be a cost-effective and easy strategy to not only increase the protection of students, but it can also be used to build connections and relationships among teachers and students. Active supervision is the ongoing monitoring of students by staff members, in which students are provided feedback and experience a positive interaction with them (DePry & Sugai, 2002). With active supervision, staff members are asked to have frequent and positive interactions with students, during which the focus is primarily on recognizing students for who they are and their prosocial behavior. It consists of three parts: movement, scanning, and interaction. Staff members *move* about a location (e.g., cafeteria, playground) and *scan* for instances of prosocial behavior by students (such as students using the schoolwide expectations). They then *interact* with students, providing BSP to reinforce students' use of the prosocial behavior. They can use the interaction as an opportunity to learn about the student, provide a positive interaction for the student with an adult, and/or to simply to offer praise. Active supervision is also a means of monitoring behavior and correcting any instances of bullying that may occur. Teachers can identify and address specific instances of bullying they witness.

Schedule

A second consideration for the environment includes adjusting the schedule to accommodate student interactions and traffic patterns. For example, if the hallways are overcrowded because all students return to classes after lunch at the same time, there is an opportunity for reduced supervision and thus, for students to bully others away from the staff. We recommend considering how the schedule can be examined to support a manageable number of students in the hallways during passing periods, at lunch, or on the playground. Schools can also consider altering the schedule to allow the staff to use active supervision with a manageable number of students. Further, the school can coordinate the schedule in relation to some of their methods for creating connections among students. For example, teachers can be given time on a rotating basis to conduct classroom circles or to hold certain school community meetings. Alternatively, staff can be given time each week to connect with parents and students around bullying prevention.

In Figure 2.3 (on page 38), we provide a school climate practice profile to operationally define this component of CBP.

Core Component: School Climate		
Definition: The overall character and tone of the school, including feelings of safety and positive relationships among the people in the building (e.g., students to students, students to staff).		
Expected Use	**Developmental Use**	**Unacceptable Use**
All staff use distinct strategies or methods to build relationships with and among students.	The staff lets relationships form "organically" with and among students.	The staff do not actively support the building of relationships with and between students.
The school has three-to-five schoolwide expectations that are explicitly taught multiple times throughout the year.	The school is developing its three-to-five schoolwide expectations; however, the expectations may not be explicitly taught or taught only once each year.	The school does not have three-to-five schoolwide expectations, or the expectations cannot be translated into rules for various settings.
The school consistently uses an acknowledgment system to reinforce expected behaviors.	The school has an acknowledgment system, but students are not consistently acknowledged or long-term reinforcement is intermittent.	The school does not provide recognition or feedback to students or recognition is not behavior specific.
The school implements an equitable and consistent discipline system that includes how staff can respond to bullying.	The school inconsistently uses a discipline structure or uses one that lacks responding to bullying.	The school incorporates a heavy use of punishment when responding to behavior incidents.
Students are adequately trained and respond appropriately to bullying.	Only some students are adequately trained and respond appropriately to bullying.	Students are not adequately trained or respond inappropriately to bullying.

FIGURE 2.3. School climate practice profile.

CHAPTER 3

Policy

Most school staff members and families have looked at some form of a school policy. It is often what we turn to when there is a question that needs to be answered about how the school operates. "How early can I drop my kid off at school?" "What days are early release, again?" "How do I enroll my student for honors classes?" Unfortunately, when families read about anti-bullying policies, it is often only after an incident has occurred. An even greater concern is having a school handbook that doesn't include any information on bullying or just states that bullying is not tolerated. When schools are able to communicate a strong anti-bullying policy in their school handbook, it can go a long way to alleviating concerns and preventing small issues from becoming scandals.

The goal of an anti-bullying policy should be to provide structure and guidelines for families and students so that they know the steps the school takes to prevent bullying. A secondary goal is that, if bullying does occur, the policy should provide stability for everyone involved such that they know how the school will respond to keep everyone safe. To use a sports analogy, if the school is your team and the staff are the players, then the policy is your playbook. The same way that all players on a team should know their playbook in and out, so too should the staff know the school's bullying prevention policy. If a staff member sees bullying occurring, they should know immediately how to respond to effectively protect all students. When a staff member receives a bullying report, they should know where to bring the report and understand how the investigative process will play out.

SCHOOL HANDBOOKS AND DISTRICT POLICY

When working with schools to prevent bullying and the topic of policy comes up, we often get the sense that policy is not something that can be easily changed. It makes sense that if you are an individual teacher who bought this book because you are passionate about preventing bullying, when you read that it is best practice to revise the district anti-bullying policy, it can feel like an insurmountable task. Although it is true that it's more difficult to influence district-level policy, it can be a much more manageable endeavor to review and revise your current school handbook. In fact, it is likely that your school handbook's section on bullying prevention hasn't been updated in quite some time and your administration would appreciate someone taking the lead to bring it up to speed.

The main difference between a school handbook and a district policy is that the school often has greater agency in developing the content of its handbook. Changing district policies almost always requires a vote by the district school board. Since school board members are elected officials, it means that the process is at least somewhat political. Before you close this book and put it on a shelf in your classroom or office, remember that you can have a powerful impact on how bullying is prevented by addressing it in your school handbook. A school handbook can provide much greater detail on how bullying is prevented and addressed than a district-level policy. Often, district-level policies are written in "legalese" and do their best to avoid any legal liabilities for the district.

To be clear, the vast majority of school boards pass anti-bullying policies because they genuinely want to prevent bullying in their districts. The challenge for districtwide policies, however, is that they must be all encompassing for every school in the district, including grades kindergarten through 12, alternative education campuses, online schools, charter schools, and every other unique setting in the district. We go into more detail later in the chapter on the key elements to include in an anti-bullying policy, but remember that if the policy is in your school handbook, you can tailor it to the uniqueness of your school.

It should also be noted that even though you have more control over your school handbook's anti-bullying policy, it doesn't mean you can go rogue against your district's policy. If the district policy states that families of the student accused of bullying will be informed of the allegation prior to the start of any investigation, your school policy should align with this approach. You certainly do not want to be in a situation where you have trained your staff on how to respond to reports of bullying just to have the district come back and be unable to defend the staff's actions in the case of litigation.

HOW TO FIND YOUR DISTRICT POLICY

You likely have a copy of your school handbook tucked away in a desk or on a bookshelf somewhere. But how can you find the bullying prevention policies for your district? The easiest way is to simply give a call to the district office's main contact line. Almost every district has its board policies online for families and the community to access, but they can be difficult to find. You can also try doing a Google search with your school district's name followed by "bullying policy." If you're lucky, the webpage or even a PDF of the actual policy will be in the first few search results. More than likely, you will simply be given a link to the main school district's webpage. From there, you will need to find the district school board's webpage where you can search for its collection of policies. Developing policies is one of the main functions of a board of education so the board typically makes its policies readily available.

When you do find the collection of policies from your school district, you will then need to find the bullying prevention policy among the myriad of policies that the board has adopted. A resource that districts use more and more often is an online system called "BoardDocs." This program allows school boards to document their meetings digitally and also serves as a way to share meeting minutes and policies with the public. If your district uses BoardDocs, then all you have to do is use their search function and type in *bullying*. The district's bullying prevention policy will be listed as a policy item that you can then view and download. If your district documents its meetings using BoardDocs, you will also see a list of agenda items in which bullying has been discussed by the board.

STATE MODEL POLICIES

Just as it would be prudent to align your school handbook with the district's policy on bullying prevention, it is prudent for the district policy to align with state law. There is no federal anti-bullying law, so as you can imagine the laws against bullying vary widely across the states. Some states have extensive laws regulating everything from family notification to consequences. Others are more limited in their approach and connect bullying closely with harassment laws. Moreover, new laws are being introduced and passed on a yearly basis. Several states have taken a more punitive approach by making bullying a misdemeanor offense. Other states and municipalities have been more creative. In 2019, a city in Wisconsin introduced an ordinance that would charge fines up to $313 to the parents of students who bully. In North Tonawanda, New York, a law was passed that could result in the jailing of parents if their children bully others.

The good news is that despite the myriad of state laws and unique approaches that address bullying, many states also have model policies. These policies are typically developed by the state's department of education in accordance with that state's laws on bullying. Another positive development is that many state model policies include more than just the one- or two-page legalese of a dry policy. State model policies are typically available on a department of education website that also includes a wealth of other bullying prevention resources. Some states even go as far as providing sample reporting or investigative forms that schools and districts may use to support their bullying prevention efforts. An example of a state model policy from Colorado can be found in Figure 3.1.

If you are interested in knowing your state's model bullying prevention policy, the federal Department of Health and Human Service's website *stopbullying.gov* has a list of all model policies by state with links. Not every state has a model policy, but the vast majority do. *Stopbullying. gov* also has a collection of the laws within each state that address bullying. In addition to the collection of laws and model policies, the website is also a great general resource for how to support schools, families, and students with bullying prevention.

BUILDING A STRONG BULLYING PREVENTION POLICY

Bullying among children has been studied for decades, but the research on bullying prevention policies in schools has been less robust. Despite this fact, there are several key pieces that, when included in a district- or school-level policy, have been shown to improve the lives of students.

A study by Kull and colleagues (2016) examined how specific language in a district's bullying prevention policy impacts the safety of students within that district's schools. In their study, over 7,000 LGBTQ+ students from nearly 3,000 unique school districts were surveyed about their feel-

Colorado Bullying Prevention and Education Best Practices and Model Policy

NOTE: Colorado school districts are required by law to adopt a specific policy concerning bullying prevention and education (C.R.S. 22-32-109.1(2)(a)(I)(K)). Each school district must ensure that its policy, at a minimum, incorporates approaches, policies, and practices outlined in the Colorado Bullying Prevention and Education Model Policy. Districts should consult with their own legal counsel to determine appropriate language that meets local circumstances and needs. Districts have discretion to determine the specifics of their bullying prevention policies and supports.

Statement of Purpose

The Board of Education supports a secure and positive school climate, conducive to teaching and learning that is free from threat, harassment, and any type of bullying behavior. The purpose of this policy is to promote consistency of approach and to help create a climate in which all types of bullying are regarded as unacceptable.

Bullying and other behaviors as defined below are prohibited on district property, at district or school-sanctioned activities and events, when students are being transported in any vehicle dispatched by the district or one of its schools, or off school property when such conduct has a nexus to school or any district curricular or noncurricular activity or event.

Prohibited Behavior

- Bullying
- Retaliation against those reporting bullying and/or other behaviors prohibited by this policy
- Making knowingly false accusations of bullying behavior

Definitions

Bullying is the use of coercion or intimidation to obtain control over another person or to cause physical, mental, or emotional harm to another person. Bullying can occur through written, verbal, or electronically transmitted expressions (i.e., cyberbullying) or by means of a physical act or gesture. Bullying is prohibited against any student for any reason, including but not limited to any such behavior that is directed toward a student on the basis of his or her academic performance or any basis protected by federal and state law, including, but not limited to disability, race, creed, color, sex, sexual orientation, gender identity, gender expression, marital status, national origin, religion, ancestry, or the need for special education services, whether such characteristic(s) is actual or perceived.

Retaliation is an act or communication intended as retribution against an individual who reports an act of bullying. Retaliation can also include knowingly making false accusations of bullying or acting to influence the investigation of, or the response to, a report of bullying.

False accusations of bullying are those made knowingly by an individual or group of individuals with the purpose of causing harm to another individual and which are false.

Prevention and Intervention

The Superintendent will develop a comprehensive program to address bullying at all school levels and that the program is consistently applied across all students and staff. This program will be designed to accomplish the following goals:

1. To send a clear message to students, staff families, and community members that bullying and retaliation against a student who reports bullying will not be tolerated.
2. To train school staff on an annual basis in taking proactive steps to prevent bullying from occurring, which includes but is not limited to, training on the bullying prevention and education policy, how to recognize and intervene in bullying situations, and positive school climate practices.
3. To implement procedures for immediate intervention, investigation, and confrontation of students engaged in bullying behavior.

(continued)

FIGURE 3.1. Example of a model bullying prevention state policy.

4. To initiate efforts to change the behavior of students engaged in bullying behaviors through reteaching on acceptable behavior, discussions, counseling, and appropriate negative consequences.
5. To foster a productive partnership with parents and community members in order to help maintain a bullying-free environment across settings.
6. To support targets of bullying through a layered continuum of supports that includes, but is not limited to, individual and peer counseling.
7. To help develop peer support networks, social skills, and confidence for all students.
8. To support positive school climate efforts that clearly define, teach, and reinforce prosocial behavior. This includes intentional efforts to promote positive relationships between staff and students as well as students with other students.
9. To designate a team of persons at each school who advise the school administration on the severity and frequency of bullying. The team of persons at the school may include, but need not be limited to, school resource officers, social workers, school psychologists, health professionals, mental health professionals, members of bullying prevention or youth resiliency community organizations, counselors, teachers, administrators, parents, and students.
10. To survey students' impressions of the severity and frequency of bullying behaviors in their school.
11. To include students in the development, creation, and delivery of bullying prevention efforts as developmentally appropriate.
12. To provide character building for students that includes, but is not limited to, age-appropriate, evidence-based social and emotional learning as well as information on the recognition and prevention of bullying behaviors.

Reporting

Any student who believes they have been a victim of bullying and/or other behaviors prohibited by this policy, or who has witnessed such bullying and/or other prohibited behaviors, is strongly encouraged to immediately report it to a school administrator, counselor, or teacher.

Investigating and Responding

As part of the Superintendent's comprehensive program to address bullying, procedures will be developed with the goal of immediate intervention and investigation in response to reports of students engaged in bullying and/or other behaviors prohibited by this policy. Procedures will include, to the extent appropriate as determined by the investigator and designated administrator, and in accordance with applicable law and local school board policy and procedures, notification to parents/guardians of the results of bullying investigations and their right to appeal investigatory findings to the district.

Supports and Referrals

As part of the Superintendent's comprehensive program to address bullying, procedures should be developed with the aim toward accomplishing the following goals:

- Initiate efforts to change the behavior of students engaged in bullying behaviors.
- Support targets of bullying in ways that avoid increasing their likelihood of discipline.
- Support witnesses of bullying.

A student who engages in any act of bullying, retaliation and/or other behaviors prohibited by this policy is subject to appropriate disciplinary action including but not limited to suspension, expulsion, and/or referral to law enforcement authorities. The severity and pattern, if any, of the bullying behavior will be taken into consideration when disciplinary decisions are made. Bullying behavior that constitutes unlawful discrimination or harassment will be subject to investigation and discipline under related Board policies and procedures. Students targeted by bullying when such bullying behavior may constitute unlawful discrimination or harassment also have additional rights and protections under Board policies and procedures regarding unlawful discrimination and harassment.

FIGURE 3.1. *(continued)*

ings of safety and victimization at school. Next, the district anti-bullying policies in those students' districts were examined to determine if they specifically prohibit bullying based on a student's sexual orientation, gender identity, and/or gender expression (SOGIE). Results from the study showed that, compared to students in districts with generic anti-bullying policies or no policies at all, students in districts explicitly prohibiting bullying based on SOGIE status reported less targeting based on their sexual orientation and gender expression while also reporting greater school safety. Moreover, on most measures of being targeted for bullying and safety, there was no difference for LGBTQ+ students in districts with generic policies versus no policy at all against bullying. An important takeaway from the results of this study is that just referencing protected classes (for example, stating that bullying is prohibited, including against "federally protected classes"), without specifically naming those protected classes does not provide the same benefit to student safety. This is important because, as we mentioned before, district-level policies can easily become political. Since compromise and debate are common in politics, watering down enumeration in this way could eliminate its potential benefit.

In addition to the language that is contained in the policy, there are also key elements of a bullying prevention policy that make it effective. The website *stopbullying.gov* outlines important components of an effective policy, and many state model policies include the same components. You can find a list of the elements in Table 3.1. Over the next several pages, we will delve in depth into each of these elements so that you come away with a strong understanding of how they could be incorporated into your school's own policy.

Definition

As we discussed in Chapter 1, the definition of bullying can be complicated and is not even agreed upon among scholars. Our job is to make sure that there is a common understanding of how bullying is different from other forms of aggression (namely conflict) so that students, families, and staff members are all on the same page. In the definition section, you can let stakeholders know that for a school to consider a behavior to be bullying, the investigation of the behavior needs to show that (1) there was an intent to harm, (2) the behavior was repeated or is likely to be repeated, and (3) there was a power imbalance. You should also let families know that even if a behavior doesn't rise to the definition of bullying, the school will still address the issue to make sure that all students in the school feel safe. The behavior will simply be addressed under a different policy on student conduct.

Prohibition against Bullying

Typically following the definition of bullying, the school's policy will have a statement declaring that bullying is not allowed in any form at the school. Given that bullying is such a common term in America and across the world, many state model policies include other prohibited behaviors in addition to bullying itself. The two most common behaviors that are listed as not being allowed in school are (1) knowingly making false reports of bullying and (2) retaliating against students who report bullying. Students are very aware that when adults hear the word *bullying* that it carries a different weight than saying a student was "mean," "called me names," or "didn't let me play with them." Unfortunately, this awareness also means that students have learned that if they really want

TABLE 3.1. Key Elements to Include in a Bullying Prevention Policy

Element	Description
Definition	• Clearly define bullying and how it differs from other forms of aggression.
Prohibition against bullying	• State that bullying is prohibited and specifically name federally protected classes for whom bullying is prohibited. • State that knowingly making false statements is prohibited and is subject to the bullying prevention policy. • State that retaliation against those making reports of bullying is prohibited and is subject to the bullying prevention policy.
Scope	• Consult with the district and legal counsel as necessary. • State the circumstances in which the bullying prevention policy will be used.
Prevention and intervention	• Describe the prevention efforts used by the school and district, including any evidence-based programs. • State that any adult witnessing bullying should intervene immediately. • Describe the training and coaching that staff receive on bullying prevention and intervention. • Describe how families and the community can be involved in bullying-prevention efforts.
Reporting	• List the ways that students and adults can report bullying. • Provide a description or flowchart of the process for investigating bullying in the school.
Investigation	• Describe the investigative process. • State the protections that students are afforded if they are accused of bullying. • Describe the factors that go into determining whether or not bullying is substantiated.
Consequences	• Provide a graduated list of consequences, both supports and punishments, that students may receive. • Describe the factors that are considered when selecting consequences.
Communication	• Consult with the district and legal counsel as necessary to know if there are laws dictating how soon families must be notified. • State the time frame in which families are notified that their children have been named in a bullying report.
Record keeping	• Describe the record-keeping process used by the school to support data-based decision making. • Describe the protections that are provided by the school to ensure the confidentiality of records.

to get another student in trouble, they can falsely claim that they were bullied by that student. Although not as common, the student reporting a bullying incident may receive consequences if it comes to light during an investigation that the report was fake and intended to harm another student. It's also important for the staff to consider the intent of a false report of bullying. If a student reported bullying to a teacher but did so without knowing how bullying is different from conflict, we wouldn't then punish the student, we would reteach. It boils down to the student's intent in reporting a bullying incident.

Retaliation is another area somewhat unique to bullying. Research suggests that the majority of students who experience bullying do not report the incident to adults (Petrosino, Guckenburg, DeVoe, & Hanson, 2010). One of several reasons for a reluctance to report may be because students are fearful that doing so will just make the problem worse. As members of the school staff, we can help to alleviate that worry by making it clear in our policy that retaliating against students because they made a report of bullying will result in consequences in accordance with the anti-bullying policy.

Scope

The scope of the school and district's anti-bullying policy is a vital yet legally fraught area. By scope, we are referring to situations in which the school has the right to address bullying behavior. This issue most often comes up when students are bullied off school grounds, outside of school hours, and/or not during school-sanctioned events (dances, sporting events). With the proliferation of smartphones, the question of scope has become even more common due to cyberbullying. Does the school have the right to administer consequences to a student for something done at their home on the weekend?

The short, and admittedly unsatisfying, answer is: it depends. Whether or not a school can respond to a bullying situation outside of school-sanctioned events and hours depends on whether or not the student's speech or actions disrupted the educational process. This interpretation emerged from the case of *Tinker v. Des Moines* in 1969. In this Supreme Court of the United States case, a 13-year-old student and several of her friends were suspended from school for wearing black armbands to protest the Vietnam War. The American Civil Liberties Union (ACLU) represented the students in court, arguing that their right to free speech had been violated by the school district. The Supreme Court agreed in a 7-2 ruling, stating that students do not "shed their constitutional rights to freedom of speech or expression at the schoolhouse gate" (*Tinker v. Des Moines Independent Community School District*, 393). The exception to this rule is speech that interferes with the educational process.

For example, let's say a student is cyberbullied on a Sunday evening, and when they come to school on Monday dozens of students are making passing comments to them about what happened online. It gets to the point that the student begins crying in class and can't focus on learning. Even though the precipitating event occurred on Sunday off school grounds, it is having an effect on the student's ability to access a free and appropriate education and thus may be within the scope of the school to address. In these cases, it can also be helpful to check with your district's legal counsel on when you are allowed to address these types of bullying incidents.

A final note on the issue of scope is that in June of 2021, the Supreme Court of the United States issued a ruling in the case of *Mahanoy Area School District v. B.L.* The central issue in the case is whether or not public students can be punished for their speech off campus. A high school student, later self-identifying as Brandi Levy, in 2017 posted a Snapchat photo of herself with her middle finger up and an expletive-filled caption reading, "F*** school F*** softball F*** cheer F*** everything." Despite the fact that the photo was only visible for 24 hours to just her 250 friends, a screenshot was shown to her coaches and she was suspended. As you remember, the *Tinker* case involved students who were expressing their speech on school premises. The *Mahanoy* case now sheds light specifically on the right a school has to punish students for their speech off school grounds. In an 8-1 vote, the Supreme Court sided with the student, and for the first time referenced bullying in its decision. Specifically, the Court wrote that a school *can* regulate student speech that occurs off campus in certain circumstances including "serious or severe bullying" (Totenberg, 2021).

Bullying Prevention and Intervention

A component that is worth including in your policy is the bullying prevention and intervention efforts at your school. Doing so is a way for you to tout all the work your school puts in to support the safety of students. You can discuss the evidence-based curriculum that is being implemented and describe how students are taught expected behaviors in all areas of the school every year. If you have annual events that support bullying prevention by including families and the community, include them in your policy. You can help alleviate concerns around bullying by letting families know everything you are doing to stop it.

This is also where you can create a shared understanding of how adults should intervene in bullying situations. When adults see bullying, they should intervene immediately to ensure everyone's safety. After intervening, adults should *not* attempt to mediate the situation between the students. If it is a true bullying situation, the power imbalance between the students can still play out, even if there is an adult present. A great, yet hard to watch, example of this is demonstrated in the documentary *Bully* that was released in 2011. In one scene, the principal of a middle school does the right thing by intervening when she sees bullying between two boys. After she intervenes, though, she forces the two boys to come together, apologize, and shake hands. The student who was bullying holds out his hand and stares down the student he was targeting. Having just been bullied, the student who was targeted doesn't want to shake hands. The principal then reprimands the targeted student until he provides a limp handshake without making eye contact. Obviously, the principal had good intentions and wanted to resolve the problem between the students; however, without proper knowledge and training, the best of intentions can actually make bullying worse.

In the prevention and intervention section of policy, it can also be helpful to describe the training and coaching that the school provides on bullying. Studies have shown that when teachers receive training on bullying prevention, they are more confident in their ability to intervene (Alsaker, 2004) and that when teachers are not provided training, they are unlikely to intervene (Bauman, Rigby, & Hoppa, 2008). If you are following the CBP approach, then your staff will be receiving training at least once each year. State this fact in your policy. Some schools offer parent education nights when families can visit the school and learn about the warning signs of bullying and how to respond if they think that their child is being targeted. Other schools may have communitywide events in October during bullying prevention month. Put these annual family, school, and community partnership events in your policy so that it is clear how much value your school places on preventing bullying.

Reporting Bullying

Let's assume that despite our best efforts, bullying is still occurring in the school. How should someone formally let the school know about an incident? We need to make it as easy as possible for students, families, and the community to report bullying. If the school does not know about the bullying, it can't do anything to stop it from happening again. Perhaps the most common response a family member may give a child who is being bullied is to "tell your teacher." Although this is certainly an option, as a school we should have multiple methods for allowing someone to report bullying so we give ourselves the best chance to address it.

Some students may have a strong relationship with their teachers and feel comfortable reporting bullying; however, by providing several different options for reporting, a school can improve its chances of receiving reports. An approach that is becoming more and more common is having an anonymous reporting box in the school. Students are able to take a blank reporting form, fill in the information (including their name if they want), and put it in a locked collection box. The collection box should be checked by a staff member every day. Another option is the development of an online reporting system. For example, in Colorado, a system is available from the state called Safe2Tell. This online system was developed in the wake of the Columbine High School tragedy as a way for anyone with knowledge of an issue about school safety to anonymously report the incident. Students, families, or community members can go to the Safe2Tell website, submit a form, and the report will be sent directly to the school administration. Since its creation, bullying has consistently been one of the top three most reported incidents to Safe2Tell. Regardless of the method of reporting, one of the first steps a school should take is to check in with the alleged target of bullying to ensure the student's safety.

The ultimate goal of having a reporting process is that the school will be able to act on any report it receives to provide for the safety of all students. To this end, the data that are collected on the reporting form need to allow the staff the chance to gather more information during an investigation. You can find a collection of basic questions to include on a reporting form in Table 3.2. Remember that the form should be developmentally appropriate given the age of the students in your school. You wouldn't want to have a 20-question form for an elementary school. Rather than asking the question, "Where did you see the bullying?" which calls for an open-ended response,

---

TABLE 3.2. Items to Include on a Bullying Report Form

- Name of the person making the report (optional)
- Are you willing to have a school staff member contact you for more information? (Yes / No)
- Contact information of person making the report (optional): (Phone / Email)
- Full name of the person(s) who was targeted
- Grade level of the person(s) who was targeted
- Teacher of the person(s) who was targeted
- Date of the incident(s)
- Location of the incident(s)
- Were there any witnesses? (Yes / No)
- What were the names and grades of witnesses
- Describe the event in detail

---

provide prewritten response options that students can simply circle or check. Having prewritten response options also makes it easier for you to use the data for problem solving because it removes subjectivity. For example, instead of trying to figure out if "drama" should be categorized as verbal or relational bullying, you will know exactly how to code each type of bullying. As an added plus, it makes the report faster to complete.

It's also important for those submitting a report to understand that the school can only adequately follow up on a report to the extent of the information provided. The form should make it clear that the person submitting the report can remain anonymous, but doing so may affect how much information can be gathered about the bullying incident. Encouraging reporters to provide a list of people who also witnessed the bullying incident can go a long way to helping investigate the incident. Moreover, research suggests that, more often than not, bullying occurs with other students around (see Rivara & Le Menestrel, 2016), so there are likely to be other students who witnessed the incident. An example of a reporting form that could be used at the elementary or secondary school level can be found in Figure 3.2.

In addition to developing a reporting form, a school needs to create the infrastructure to sustain reporting efforts. This includes designating who will be the lead for collecting and organizing the reports that come in. Typically, this point person would be a member of the bullying prevention implementation team. The role of this individual is to regularly collect the bullying report forms submitted via a multitude of methods, document the reports for problem-solving purposes, and provide them to the person in charge of investigations. Having a point person for all bullying reports is helpful because it limits the possibility of a report going missing or not being investigated. Every staff member in the school should receive training on how to respond if a student reports an incident of bullying, and every staff member should know the person in the school to contact so that a formal report can be made. Having the point of contact for all bullying reports be part of the prevention committee also increases the sustainability of the school's intervention system. If there is turnover at that position, the implementation team is able to quickly adjust to assign a new staff member in the role. Also be sure to have a backup for this staff member for days when they are out of the building.

Another way that schools can improve their bullying prevention infrastructure is by providing a flowchart of the process that occurs once a report of bullying is made. Beginning with a report being received by the school staff, the flowchart can depict the steps that ultimately lead to students either receiving consequences for being involved in an incident or the determination that bullying cannot be substantiated. Having a flowchart of the standardized process is helpful for both staff and families. An example of what a flowchart may look like is shown in Figure 3.3. As you can see, even if the report does not result in substantiated bullying, the school staff should also try to determine if other codes of conduct have been violated. For example, if there was a physical fight in the hallway between two students and it is determined that the event is not likely to be repeated, it may not be substantiated as an incident of bullying; however, it likely violates another student code of conduct related to safety.

Investigating Bullying Reports

Having a standardized process for investigating reports of bullying is vital to maintaining trust with families and students. This is true for both students who have been targeted as well as for students who have allegedly perpetrated bullying. Remember that we want to avoid a situation where students are able to falsely submit a report of bullying to get another student in trouble. Our inves-

Bullying Report Form

All reports may be made anonymously.
False reports of bullying are punishable as outlined in school policy.

Today's date: _____

Name of person making the report (optional): _____

Are you willing to have a school staff member contact you for more information? (Optional)   **Yes**   **No**

Contact information of person making this report (optional):

Phone: _____   Email: _____

Details

Full name of student(s) who was targeted: _____

Grade level of the student(s) who was targeted: _____

Teacher of the student(s) who was targeted: _____

Full name of student(s) who bullied: _____

Date of the bullying: _____

When the bullying happened: _____

Where the bullying happened: _____

Did anyone else see the bullying?   **Yes**   **No**

If so, please provide the names and contact information. If students, specify grade: _____

_____

_____

_____

Please provide a description of the bullying and any supporting documentation: _____

_____

_____

_____

_____

(Use additional pages, if needed)

- -

FOR OFFICE USE ONLY

Received by: _____   Date: _____

Position/Title: _____

Date submitted for Investigation: _____

FIGURE 3.2. Example of a Bullying Report Form.

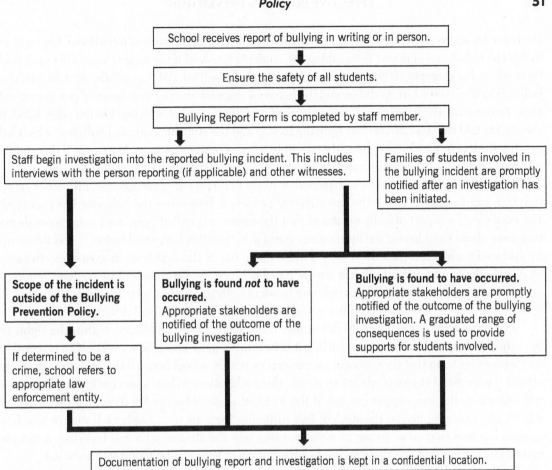

FIGURE 3.3. Flowchart of a school report of bullying.

tigative process should ensure that no student is unduly punished for something they did not do. Think about it. If a police officer told you that someone had accused you of committing a crime and you knew that you didn't do it, wouldn't you want to know the process for proving your innocence?

The first place an investigation starts is with the report that was submitted. In addition to having a reporting form, schools should have a standardized investigation form. This form guides the investigator toward determining if the report of bullying can be substantiated. A copy of the bullying report should also be provided as a reference for the school investigator so that they have the details of the alleged incident. When investigating reports of bullying, it can be easier to start with getting facts about the students involved. For example, if the report states that the bullying happened in the cafeteria during lunch, you could speak with the adults who typically work lunch duty. Do the students listed in the report actually have lunch at the same time? Do they usually sit together? Do they typically have to be reminded to follow rules? If the adults on duty find out that the students listed as witnessing the event are not even in the cafeteria during that time, then it may alter the types of questions they ask those students when speaking with them.

The goal of the investigation is to find out the truth about the incident. Since the investigation is about bullying, schools should keep in mind several unique considerations compared to a typical incident report. Specifically, it will need to be determined if there was an imbalance of power, if the behavior was repeated or likely to be repeated, and if the behavior was intentional. One way to assess the imbalance of power is by asking the students involved if the targets were able to defend themselves. For example, if the targets were being verbally bullied, did they tell the student who was bullying to stop? If the targets did so, and the behavior stopped, then an imbalance of power may not exist. In this case, the incident may be considered conflict instead of bullying. On the other hand, if the targets told the student who was bullying to stop and the student continued bullying, which led to other student bystanders laughing, then an imbalance of power may exist. Moreover, if the student who was bullying was told to stop and didn't, then it suggests that there was an intent to harm.

Determining if the behavior is repeated or likely to be repeated can also be difficult. A question that can be asked during the investigative process is how often the behavior has occurred. For example, if a report of bullying stated that the target was called "gay" for having gym shorts that were above their knees, the investigator could ask, "has this happened before?" and follow up by asking the student if they think they will be made fun of the next time in gym class. In cases of cyberbullying, repetition is almost always possible given the nature of online content. Students are able to repost or retweet a cyberbullying incident with the click of a button. Even if content is removed or a student is blocked online, screenshots can still be taken and distributed.

The investigation can also help determine if the scope of the incident is within the rights of the school to respond. As discussed earlier, it is becoming more common for schools to respond to incidents of bullying that do not occur on campus or within school hours if the bullying adversely affects the targeted students' ability to access their education. When interviewing students who were targeted, the investigator can ask if the incident made it harder for them to learn while in school. For example, maybe the student had difficulty focusing on a teacher's lesson or was late to class because they were trying to avoid running into the student who was bullying. A sample investigation form that considers all the factors described here can be found in Figure 3.4.

At the completion of the investigation, the school staff should come to a formal conclusion on whether or not the incident of bullying was substantiated. Unfortunately, at times this can be a subjective conclusion. Short of the student accused of perpetrating bullying admitting to the incident, the staff will need to use the results of the investigation to determine if it is believed that bullying occurred. Considerations should include the accounts of witnesses, whether the bullying incident fits a pattern of behavior of the student accused of bullying, and the relationship between the students involved. If it is determined that bullying did occur, consequences for all the students involved should then be considered.

Consequences for Bullying

When we talk about consequences, we don't mean punishments. Yes, punitive consequences have their place in response to bullying, but our initial focus should be on support. If we truly want to prevent bullying from occurring again, then we must consider the reason bullying occurred in the first place. In fact, an individualized support plan can be created following the 4-step problem-solving model we outline in Chapter 6. From a behavioral perspective, bullying serves the purpose of either gaining attention (whether it be positive or negative) or obtaining something tangible (think of the stereotype of stealing a student's lunch money). Taking it one step further, we can use social-ecological theory to better understand the context of bullying. Maybe a student was bullying another student for attention, but why did the student feel the need for attention in the first place? Understanding the contextual factors surrounding the student's desire for attention (for example,

Bullying Investigation Form

*Attach any reports, documents, evidence, and written accounts
of the alleged bullying incident(s) to this form.*

Date of Bullying Report: _____

Date Investigation Started: _____

Person Completing Investigation: _____

Date Bullying Report Received: _____

Date Investigation Completed: _____

I. Initial Review

Is the bullying incident within the scope of the bullying prevention policy?   **Yes**   **No**
- *If No, the report should be promptly investigated pursuant to the applicable school board policy.*
- *If Yes, promptly investigate the report pursuant to the bullying prevention policy.*

If possible criminal conduct is described in the report, was law enforcement notified?

Yes   **No**   **N/A**

    Date: _____   Contact Person: _____

    Status, if known: _____

_____

II. Bullying Report

Does the person making the report want to remain anonymous?   **Yes**   **No**

  Name of person making report: _____

Is the person making the report also the target of the bullying?   **Yes**   **No**

III. Investigation Interviews (if applicable):

Person Making Report of Bullying

Name of interviewee: _____

Description of the event in general: _____

_____

_____

_____

_____

(continued)

FIGURE 3.4. Example of a Bullying Investigation Form.

Bullying Investigation Form *(continued)*

Date the event occurred: _____

Time the event occurred: _____

Location where the event occurred: _____

Type of bullying that occurred: _____

How the targeted student responded: _____

Was the targeted student able to defend themselves?   **Yes   No**

Was this the first time that something like the behavior described happened?   **Yes   No**

Does it seem likely that the behavior will happen again?   **Yes   No**

Did the behavior seem like it was done on purpose to hurt the targeted student?   **Yes   No**

Notes: _____

Bullying Witness

Name of interviewee: _____

Description of the event in general: _____

_____

_____

_____

_____

Date the event occurred: _____

Time the event occurred: _____

Location where the event occurred: _____

Type of bullying that occurred: _____

How the targeted student responded: _____

Was the targeted student able to defend themselves? **Yes No**

Was this the first time that something like the behavior described happened? **Yes No**

Does it seem likely that the behavior will happen again? **Yes No**

Did the behavior seem like it was done on purpose to hurt the targeted student? **Yes No**

IV. Findings

Based on the information from the report and interviews, is the above incident bullying?   **Yes   No**

- *If No, file the report form and this investigation form in a secure location and notify all parties of the findings of the investigation.*
- *If Yes, determine appropriate consequences for students involved, notify stakeholders of the findings of the investigation, and place all forms in a secure location for recordkeeping.*

FIGURE 3.4. *(continued)*

the culture of the school, gang involvement in the neighborhood) can lead the staff to consider more supportive consequences.

Consequences should also be considered for students who have been targeted. Depending on the impact of the bullying, supports can be provided that help students who have been targeted to process the event with a school counselor or psychologist. If the student who was targeted does not currently feel safe, a staff member can work with the student and their family to develop a safety plan. Safety plans can be tailored to each student's unique situation, but typically include jointly agreed upon procedures that help the student feel safe enough to learn. This could mean the student is allowed to have early passing periods to reduce the opportunity for bullying to occur in the hallways. Maybe the student is allowed to have priority seating in the cafeteria during lunchtime. Having the students themselves provide guidance on what would make them feel safe is a great place to start. They often have ideas that we as adults would not think of as options. Once the safety plan is agreed upon by all parties, the plan can be signed and distributed to the staff who need to support its implementation.

Understanding that the purpose of consequences should be to prevent future incidents of bullying, the next step is to determine how consequences are laid out in the school policy. One clear, structured way to organize consequences is by starting with those that are least severe and time intensive. From there, the list of consequences can gradually increase in severity and intensity. Ensuring that potential consequences are listed in a graduated fashion aligns with the use of multitiered supports (Leff & Waasdorp, 2013) and is common in state model policies. Figure 3.5 is an example of a graduated range of consequences that starts with quick, easy responses to the behavior. From there, the consequences become more severe up to the point of suspension or expulsion and the involvement of law enforcement.

Once a graduated range of consequences have been created, it is helpful to provide guidance to the school staff on how to select consequences. Moreover, the factors that go into determining which consequences are selected can be laid out in the policy. Table 3.3 provides a list of potential factors that can serve to influence the consequence that is selected for both the perpetrator and the target of bullying. Providing this graduated range of consequences and the factors that go into determining which to select in your bullying prevention policy can help the staff when the inevitable question, "What happened to the kid who bullied my child?" arises. It's easy to understand why families want to know that some sort of punishment was doled out to the perpetrator of bullying. It's also easy to understand why families can be frustrated when schools have to tell them that, due to federal privacy laws, they can't say what consequences the student received. Instead of responding to families by telling them that you are not able to give them any information, you would now be able to point them to your bullying prevention policy and tell them that the school followed their policy related to bullying, including consequences for the perpetrator.

Communication of Bullying

Communicating with families is one of the most vital aspects of an investigation. The last thing you want is for a family to say that bullying was reported and "the school did nothing." Unfortunately, there are multiple stories in the news every year in which parents make this claim about their school. Even when schools do inform families that their child was named in a bullying incident report, there are still concerns about how long it took the school to inform the family. One place you can look to for guidance on how soon families should be informed about a bullying report is in

Targets of Bullying:

- School personnel and parent communication
- SEL skills instruction
- Increased check-in and feedback opportunities with adults
- Additional adult supervision
- Implementation of a safety plan
- Reassignment of seat in class, lunch, or on the bus
- Referral to school counselor, social worker, school psychologist, or other support staff

Perpetrators of Bullying:

- School personnel and parent communication
- SEL skills instruction
- Increased check-in and feedback opportunities with adults
- Supports focused on increasing empathy, communication skills, and the impact of bullying
- Additional adult supervision
- Behavioral contracts: a written statement listing expected behavior of the student and how school staff and/or families will provide support
- Reassignment of seat in class, lunch, or on the bus
- Daily behavior report cards: adherence to expected behaviors is scored for each school period
- Referral to school counselor, social worker, school psychologist, or other support staff
- School/community service
- Removal of desired activities
- Detention: detainment of a student for disciplinary reasons before, during, or after school
- Saturday/evening school: detention programs on Saturday or during other nonschool hours
- In-school suspension for one-half day or more, with a family member contacted
- Prohibition from entering certain areas of school
- Reassignment of classes
- Out-of-school suspension, including a conference with the family and reentry plan
- Referral to law enforcement
- Reassignment to another school or mode of transportation
- Other alternatives to suspension and expulsion, in which the school, student, and family agree to a set of requirements that, while in good standing, prevent removal

Bystanders of Bullying:

- School personnel and parent communication
- SEL skills instruction
- Increased check-in and feedback opportunities with adults
- Implementation of a safety plan
- Referral to school counselor, social worker, school psychologist, or other support staff

FIGURE 3.5. Example of a graduated range of consequences.

TABLE 3.3. List of Potential Factors That Influence Consequences

- Developmental appropriateness
- History of being the perpetrator or target of bullying
- Severity of the bullying incident
- Availability of supports at the school, family, and community level
- If the bullying behavior also broke the law
- The type of bullying that occurred (e.g., destruction of property)
- If the bullying was traditional or cyber in nature

your state's model policy. Some state model policies have specific time frames, such as 24 hours, while others use broader guidance such as "in a timely manner."

Regardless of the time frame your school selects, in most cases, families of all the students involved need to be contacted so that they are aware of the incident and have the opportunity to speak with their child. Schools should make at least three contacts with families when there is an investigation of bullying. The first one is to inform the family that their child has been named in a report on bullying. The second is to let families know the outcome of the investigation. The last one is a follow-up call after several days to see if there are any concerns that have arisen since the end of the investigation. Depending on the role the student played in bullying, there are certain topics that the school should cover in these phone calls.

One area of family communication that merits extra consideration from schools is speaking with families about the reason why their child was targeted. Specifically, if a student is bullied because of their SOGIE status, the school will want to avoid unintentionally outing students to their families. This issue becomes more complex because it is also not recommended that schools simply forgo notifying families of bullying. In fact, several states have laws specifically requiring schools to notify families if a student is involved in bullying. The LGBTQ+ advocacy group GLSEN (Gay, Lesbian, and Straight Education Network) suggests in their model anti-bullying policy that families of students involved in bullying should be notified, "provided that such notification does not endanger the health, safety or well-being of any student" (GLSEN, 2019, p. 5). Moreover, civil rights groups suggest that it is a violation of students' privacy rights to out them to their families. With states considering different laws each year related to bullying prevention and notification, it unfortunately leaves those at the school and district level on unsteady ground in terms of notifying families. The best approach may be to simply follow district guidance based on state laws and to use your best judgment regarding the safety of the student.

Record Keeping of Bullying Incidents

As you will read in Chapter 5, using data to help improve your bullying prevention efforts is extremely valuable. In addition to collecting student survey data and office report data on student behavior, keeping records of substantiated and unsubstantiated reports of bullying can support staff decision making. Due to the sensitive nature of bullying reports, records should be kept in a secure location to ensure confidentiality. Typically, schools keep bullying reports in the same location as student individualized education plans and 504 plans. This allows the bullying prevention implementation team to be able to quickly access reports when needed.

Digitally recording bullying report data in a database management system can also be an option for schools to support their ability to analyze data. For example, if a report of bullying is substantiated and the school is in the process of determining what consequences will be administered, they can quickly filter a digital database by the perpetrating student's name. If there are several previously unsubstantiated reports of bullying, the school can examine the context of each one to help gain a better understanding of any patterns. These patterns could then inform the types of supports the student may need to reduce future incidents of bullying. Alternatively, filtering the report data by the names students who are targeted can inform which students could benefit from additional supports or reteaching on how to respond to being the target of bullying.

In Figure 3.6 (on page 58), we provide a policy practice profile to operationally define this component of CBP.

Core Component: Policy		
Definition: Guidance that details how to respond to and document instances of bullying, including communication with families and procedures with the staff.		
Expected Use	**Developmental Use**	**Unacceptable Use**
The school handbook policy is fully aligned with the district school board policy.	The school handbook policy is aligned with some district policies on bullying prevention.	The school handbook policy is in conflict with the district policy.
The school handbook policy is fully aligned with state law.	N/A	The school handbook policy is in conflict with state law.
The school bullying prevention policy includes the key features shown to be effective in preventing bullying.	The school bullying prevention policy includes key features shown to be effective in preventing bullying; however, federally protected classes are not enumerated or consequences for involvement in bullying do not include supports for students.	There is no school bullying policy or the policy includes zero-tolerance or forced-mediation procedures.
School staff are trained on the bullying prevention policy at least once each year.	The bullying prevention policy is mentioned during other school trainings but staff are not directly trained on their responsibilities.	No training is provided for staff on the bullying prevention policy.

FIGURE 3.6. Policy practice profile.

CHAPTER 4

Evidence-Based Curricula

As we touched on in the previous chapter, the curriculum within CBP is used to educate students about bullying and to give all stakeholders the ability to prevent it. As such, it can be used to provide students more explicit instruction on how to respond to bullying incidents, on how to use and apply given SEL skills, and on how to understand the bullying dynamics that serve to reinforce or minimize it. The curriculum can also supplement the schoolwide expectations and teach students how to build and cultivate relationships. Using a curriculum is important, as it has been shown to be associated with a 19–23% reduction in the perpetration of bullying and a 15–20% reduction in being targeted (Gaffney, Ttofi, & Farrington, 2019; Ttofi & Farrington, 2011). It's also critical that schools select and use an *evidence-based* curriculum, so we begin this chapter by discussing this term.

WHAT IS EVIDENCE BASED?

If you have ever attempted to purchase an educational curriculum you will have heard a myriad of terms meant to suggest that the program is effective: *research-based, theory-based, evidence-informed, evidence-based* (see Table 4.1). So what *does* "evidence based" actually mean? The term was originally used in relation to the medical sciences. It represented an approach to solving a problem that joined a physician's expertise with clinical evidence from external research (see Woodbury & Kuhnke, 2014). In other words, it was originally used to describe not only the fact that a program had independent research showing its effectiveness, but also that it relied upon the experience of a trained implementer. In the field of education today, the latter part of this equation is often overlooked, as most curricula are designed to be implemented by even the most novice teacher with some basic training.

TABLE 4.1. Definitions of Different Descriptors of Evidence for Bullying Prevention Curricula

Term	Definition
Research-based	Findings from research and research methodology are used to create the curriculum.
Theory-based	The curriculum is guided by a theory for how it impacts bullying and is developed in line with that theory.
Evidence-informed	Existing results from research are used to develop the program.
Evidence-based	The curriculum has studies that demonstrate its effectiveness.

Now that we know what the term means, why is it important to select a program that is evidence based? It's the same reason you likely look at reviews when you are shopping online. Purchasing an evidence-based program is like getting a curriculum with an overall 5-star rating (and all the reviewers are actually real). The product has been tested and approved by researchers in the field of bullying prevention, and they claim that it is effective. Choosing such a program gives you the best chance to successfully prevent bullying.

Even when schools do use evidence-based programs, research suggests that it may be difficult to obtain successful results. A study by Yeager, Fong, Yeon Lere, and Espelage (2015) found that bullying prevention curricula are effective through grade 7 but decline in effectiveness starting in grade 8. By grade 10, anti-bullying programs were actually shown, on average, to *increase* bullying, though not to a statistically significant level. The study's authors make clear that this finding does not mean that high schools should not try to prevent bullying; rather, they suggest trying to understand the reasons why what is successful in younger grades is not successful in high school. There are several different possibilities, including the fact that bullying in the upper grades takes on a less directly aggressive form, that social skills deficits may impact bullying rates in the lower grades but not in the upper grades, and that students in high school desire greater autonomy, which may influence how they perceive being taught lessons on social skills.

There are also a plethora of programs and curricula that claim to prevent bullying but are not evidence based. This does not mean that they are "bad" programs by any means, but it does indicate that there may be more risk associated with the program not being effective. There are several reasons why a program may not have data or research showing its effectiveness. The program may be new, and there has not yet been an opportunity to conduct any research. Another valid reason is that research is expensive. If the developers of a curriculum want to conduct a rigorous study on the effectiveness of their program, they likely need people on staff who know how to conduct the research or have to provide funding to outside organizations that could do the research. Given this information, it doesn't mean that efforts to prevent bullying are pointless. Rather, it shows that the effectiveness of the program is just one factor to consider when selecting a program for your site. We discuss a selection process later in this chapter.

HOW TO FIND EVIDENCE-BASED PROGRAMS

Now that you know the terms associated with evidence-based programs and research, where does one find these programs? If you take the approach of simply using Google to search "evidence-based bullying prevention programs," the first several results that pop up will be ads for programs that likely don't have a strong evidence base. Thankfully, there are several organizations that use a rigorous process to review and provide guidance on the evidence base of bullying prevention programs. We discuss three sources here (see Table 4.2).

The National Institute of Justice (NIJ) is the research, development, and evaluation arm of the United States Department of Justice. Their website, *crimesolutions.gov*, is an online clearinghouse of all the programs that NIJ has reviewed. The website assesses the strength of the research conducted on programs and practices related to a host of criminal justice services, including bullying prevention. Reviewers at the NIJ have combed through scientific studies of different bullying prevention programs (so you don't have to!) and have organized their findings with a rating of each program's effectiveness. Whereas the NIJ reviews programs and practices related to criminal justice, Blueprints for Healthy Youth Development (more commonly known as Blueprints) reviews those that are focused on reducing antisocial behavior and promoting healthy development among youth. Similar to NIJ, there is a standardized review process that culminates in programs receiving a certification denoting the program's effectiveness. The last organization we highlight is the Collaborative for Academic, Social, and Emotional Learning (CASEL). CASEL has many areas of focus, including research and policy around SEL. In particular, CASEL has reviewed programs related to SEL and has compiled resources for both elementary and secondary grade levels (see *https://casel.org/guide*). A unique aspect of CASEL's reviews is that they also describe the program design and implementation support of different programs. Several evidence-based bullying prevention curricula include the core components of SEL in their programs. This is a great finding because research suggests that SEL can improve student behavior (Durlak, Weissberg, Dymnicki, Taylor, & Schellinger, 2011).

TABLE 4.2. Finding Evidence-Based Programs for Bullying Prevention

Source	Information
National Institute of Justice (NIJ)	*crimesolutions.gov* Rates programs related to criminal justice, including bullying prevention, on a 1–4 scale (No Effects, Inconclusive Evidence, Promising, Effective) of the program's effectiveness.
Blueprints for Healthy Youth Development	*www.blueprintsprograms.org* Rates programs on healthy development on a 1–4 scale (Non-Certified, Promising, Model, Model Plus) of the program's effectiveness. Recommend using only programs with Model or Model Plus to address bullying.
Collaborative for Academic, Social, and Emotional Learning (CASEL)	*https://casel.org/guide* Summarizes evidence-based and well-designed programs that teach SEL competencies.

LOOK FORS AND WATCH OUTS

On your journey to find a curricula for bullying prevention, you now know what evidence based means (versus research based) and where to search for a program. Before we discuss a detailed selection process, we offer some immediate "look fors" and red flags. When researching programs to reduce bullying in your school, it can be helpful to have an idea of some key things to look for that suggest the program has a good chance of success when implemented. There are also some red flags that you should watch out for that may mean that the program will be less effective.

First, look for a strong presence of research on the website of the curriculum. When programs have research showing their effectiveness, the information will often be easy to find on their websites. For example, the Second Step curriculum, which has several peer-reviewed studies demonstrating its effectiveness at reducing bullying and aggression (Espelage, Low, Polanin, & Brown, 2013; Espelage, Low, Polanin, & Brown, 2015; Espelage, Rose, & Polanin, 2015), has a section on its website called "research." If you go to this page, you will find details on not only how their program was developed using research, but also the studies conducted to evaluate the effectiveness of their program.

Obviously, any program is trying to sell you on how great its product is when you visit its website. This being the case, watch out for programs using the words "research" and "evidence" but there are no actual studies evaluating the effectiveness of the specific program. An anti-bullying curriculum could be based on dozens of studies, but if no study has been conducted to examine the effectiveness of the program itself, you don't really know if it can reduce bullying. Watch out for programs that only discuss research on bullying in general terms but little about the specific program being offered. For example, a program could say, "our program was developed using the principles of psychology and research on bullying prevention." While this may be true, it says nothing about the effectiveness of the program.

The second "look for" is the *type* of research the program is using to suggest the effectiveness of their program. As just mentioned, the Second Step curriculum has several studies that have been peer reviewed. Peer-reviewed studies are typically viewed as more rigorous because other researchers review the research and have to give their thumbs up that it is a strong study before it can be published. Additionally, experimental studies provide more conclusive evidence of a curriculum's impact compared to quasi-experimental designs or correlational research. In particular, group designs with random assignment to conditions provide stronger evidence (Fraenkel, Wallen, & Hyun, 2018). Additionally, watch out for programs that may provide data, but the data provided are just from surveys of people who have attended their trainings. Although having this information may be better than not doing any research, relying solely on trainees' opinions of how bullying has improved can be misleading. Research has shown that adults, including teachers, often underestimate the amount of bullying that is occurring in a school (Rupp, Elliott, & Gresham, 2018). These data should not be discounted entirely, but it is important to understand their limitations. An even bigger red flag to watch out for is a program that focuses largely on client testimonials. These testimonials are typically hand selected by the program's designers to make the program sound as good as possible and do not reflect an independent review of the program itself.

Third, look for programs that understand the complexity of bullying and avoid ones that claim to have a "simple" or "easy" solution for bullying. There are no magic solutions for eliminating bullying in schools. Research on bullying prevention curricula suggest that the most effective programs have multiple components and are implemented schoolwide (Farrington & Ttofi, 2009). You can often find information on how the creators of a program view bullying in the section of the website that describes the program. For example, the RULER program, developed by the Yale Center on Emotional Intelligence, has a webpage on how the program works (*www.ycei.org/ruler*). The webpage, states that implementation needs to be led by a team, that the team needs to receive comprehensive training from the Center, that ongoing coaching support is provided by the Center, and that including families in the work is valued. This type of approach suggests that the program's developers understand the complexity of bullying prevention.

One common approach to avoid that schools may use to address bullying includes having one-off assemblies or events. These events can serve well to raise awareness and jump-start more systemic bullying prevention efforts, but they have very limited long-term effects on improving student behavior (Farrington & Ttofi, 2009). You may have had a similar experience as an educator if you have ever gone to a conference. While at the conference, you are learning about exciting new strategies, research, and programs. Your conference program is filled with notes, and you have already started thinking about all the new ideas that will be put into place in your classroom or school. Once you get back into the reality of the day-to-day life in a school, you begin implementing some of the ideas in the first few days. Then, a week or two passes. Crises arise and alter the typical structure of your day. A few more weeks pass, and concerns around test scores become prominent and the fidelity with which you are implementing those great ideas starts to wane. By the start of the next school year, the ideas from that conference you attended last year are more memory than action. The reason that this decline occurs is because the conference is a one-time event that often is not integrated into the systemic approach taken by your school to improve student outcomes. The infrastructure is often not in place to support the ongoing implementation of ideas gathered at a conference. But imagine if that infrastructure *was* there in your school. If the school is using the CBP, the systems are in place to sustainably support new approaches. Educators attending conferences are able to bring new ideas back to their bullying prevention team, and the team is able to consider how to integrate these new practices into existing prevention efforts.

When searching for programs to introduce to your school, check to see how recently the content on the program's webpage has been updated. Knowing that the program's content is current can give you some insight into how much support you will receive once you purchase the program. Imagine if, after spending a good chunk of your school budget on a curriculum, you end up with several questions on how to implement the program. Then, when you reach out to the publisher of the program, you find out that the publisher doesn't provide any coaching, training, or customer service support. Your school would be in the precarious position of making a guess at how to best implement the program, which ultimately could affect the fidelity of your evidence-based curriculum. Unfortunately, this was the case for the program Bully-Proofing Your School. The program is still listed on the NIJ's website as being "promising" based on one research study and you can still purchase materials on *Amazon.com*, but the publishing company no longer provides support for people who have questions. Other practices to avoid when selecting a curriculum are ones that include mediation to solve true bullying concerns, as this has limited evidence supporting its use and may even make the problem worse (Ttofi & Farrington, 2011). Also, grouping students who bully together for treatment only serves to create a social norm for those students that bullying is acceptable, as they can reinforce each other's views and behaviors (see Dodge et al., 2006). Finally, the use of zero-tolerance policies have adverse effects on bullying, discipline, and the overall school climate (Skiba, 2014). We provide a summary of factors to consider in Table 4.3.

TABLE 4.3. Factors to Consider When Examining Programs

Look fors (positives)	Watch outs (red flags)
Strong presence of research	Discussion of research or bullying is vague
Peer-reviewed studies; experimental studies	Overreliance on surveys or testimonials
Clarity on the program	Claims of quick, simple, or easy fixes (i.e., one-off events or assemblies)
Updated information; availability of training and coaching support	Lack of support or training offered to use the program

SELECTING AN EVIDENCE-BASED PROGRAM

Selection of an evidence-based program is an integral part of implementation science. We go into depth on the key theories and activities behind implementation science in the second part of this book, but we focus specifically on the selection of evidence-based curricula in this chapter. There are six areas to review when selecting an evidence-based program for your school: (1) evidence, (2) usability, (3) supports, (4) need, (5) fit, and (6) capacity (see Table 4.4). Together, these six areas are known as The Hexagon Tool (Metz & Louison, 2019). We summarize each factor briefly before discussing each one in detail.

Evidence

We have already shown you several online resources that can jump-start your search for an evidence-based bullying prevention program. These organizations do a fantastic job of letting you know if the program you are selecting has strong evidence; however, when choosing a program for your unique setting, there are some specifics to consider to ensure you are getting a program that meets your needs. First, you can review the sample that was used in the study to see if the students represented are similar to the students you serve. What is the age or grade range? Were the students from a rural, urban, or suburban area? In what part of the country did implementation of the program occur? Was the program even administered in the United States? For example, prior to research being conducted in the United States, the research showing the effectiveness of the Olweus Bullying Prevention Program was solely conducted with students in Norway. The program may be effective for your school, but it does put an asterisk next to the program as you're determining what is best for your students. This is especially true given the fact that bullying prevention programs are more effective in countries other than the United States (Gaffney, Farrington, & Ttofi, 2019). If after examining these and other questions, you notice that the sample of students is very different from your own, take this information into consideration as you move through the selection process. Although having a starkly different sample is not a deal breaker, it may contribute to the decision to choose a program more reflective of your students' experiences.

As we have written about earlier in the book, the definition of bullying is fraught with academic and real-world problems. Even so, it is important to look at what studies are actually measuring and to decide if what is being assessed is truly bullying. There is an entire field of research on bullying, but programs may actually be measuring something else. For example, if you were reviewing the most recent CASEL guide, *Effective Social and Emotional Learning Programs: Preschool and Elementary School Edition* (CASEL, 2013), you would learn that the Caring School Community program has multiple rigorous studies that show it increased positive social behavior and "reduced conduct problems." The question for us, though, is what is meant by "conduct problems?" Bullying certainly qualifies as a conduct problem, but so do behaviors like fighting, repeated defiance of teachers, and throwing chairs. To truly understand if the program measured bullying, we have to dig a little deeper. In looking at the studies CASEL references for the Caring School Community program, none highlight bullying as an outcome that was measured. Instead, terms like "fighting" are more prevalent. Again, knowing this information does not mean that you should avoid the program, but you should take it into consideration with other programmatic factors.

Usability

The second area that your team should examine when selecting an evidence-based program is its usability. In other words, how clear and easy is the program to use? An example of a program that

TABLE 4.4. Factors to Consider When Selecting a Curriculum

Factor	Description	Key questions
Evidence	The strength of the evidence showing the curriculum to be effective.	• Number of studies • Similarity between your school and the population in the study
Usability	The degree to which the curriculum is well defined, has mature examples to observe, and allows for adaptation.	• Is the curriculum easily teachable and doable? • Are the core features of the curriculum operationally defined?
Supports	The availability of expert assistance (training, coaching) and technology support.	• Is there a qualified expert who can support implementation over time? • Are training and coaching available?
Need	The degree to which the curriculum directly addresses bullying for the identified student population and gaps in school systems.	• Who is the student population of concern? • Is there evidence that the curriculum specifically addresses that student population?
Fit	The degree to which the curriculum aligns with current school priorities, school culture, other initiatives, and organizational structure.	• How well does the curriculum fit with current school priorities? • What other programs or practices align with the curriculum?
Capacity	The degree to which the school is able to sustain efforts, including financial, structural, and cultural capacity.	• Typically, how much does it cost to implement the curriculum each year? • What are the staffing requirements for the curriculum?

has great usability is Second Step. In the Second Step curriculum, materials are grouped together by grade levels so that teachers receive their own developmentally appropriate set of lessons. There is also a principal toolkit that is specifically designed to support administrators in successfully training and implementing the program. All training for the program is completed online through a system that tracks each individual's progress (this could be a pro or con for usability depending on your setting and access to high-speed Internet). Where Second Step really shines is in how easy it is for teachers to administer lessons to students. Teachers are given scripts that they can read verbatim during lessons, greatly reducing the burden of lesson planning. If teachers feel comfortable with administering their own lessons, they are free to adapt the language.

The clarity with which a program is defined allows a school to more easily measure the fidelity of the program. As you know, programs have to be implemented with fidelity if schools are to reap their benefits. They should provide a clear description (i.e., operational definitions) of the key components that are the most important pieces of the intervention. For example, practice profiles, like the one we shared in Figure 2.3, indicate the acceptable to unacceptable variations of an intervention or innovation. It outlines what the intervention looks like in use; consequently, schools can use the practice profile to know exactly what to implement. Usability is also enhanced when there are observable, mature examples of what the curriculum looks like in practice. These examples provide educators with the ability to see the program in action and consider how it can be used in their school.

Supports

Supports relates back to one of our "watch outs" from earlier in this chapter: the availability of experts who can train, coach, and offer guidance on how to effectively implement the program. You may be able to have success by choosing a program that claims to have everything you need "right in the box," but you are much more likely to get results with the appropriate training and coaching. This advantage needs to be balanced, of course, with cost. For example, the Olweus Bullying Prevention Program (OBPP) issues a formal certificate for those who complete their intensive training program. To become a certified trainer, though, you must either travel to receive the training or pay for a trainer to visit you. Either way, it will cost several thousands of dollars. If you have the adequate funding, either through a grant or other means, then this program can be a great way to build the skills of your staff; however, it can be cost prohibitive for many schools.

The ability for a curriculum to use and manage data is a support that aligns with a comprehensive approach to bullying prevention. Some programs directly connect to existing school data systems (think Tableau or Infinite Campus). Others have developed their own data systems to support their programs. An example of the latter is the PBIS framework. The School-Wide Information System (SWIS) is a standalone online data management system for schools using PBIS (PBIS Apps, 2011). SWIS provides schools with a formal way to track office discipline referrals that then allows teams to dig into the data in a way that supports problem solving. For example, using SWIS, schools could filter all of their bullying reports to find out that, although it seems like a lot of bullying is going on around the school, the majority of incidents occur between fourth-grade girls during recess. Having this information would then allow the bullying prevention team to provide interventions at a more targeted, Tier 2 support level, rather than spending a lot of resources attempting to shore up their Tier 1 supports.

Need

When discussing need related to selecting an evidence-based program, we are talking about how well the program meets the need for your specific population. For example, imagine that a school has a high prevalence of cyberbullying, yet the school selected a curriculum that doesn't address cyberbullying directly. The mismatch between what the curriculum offers and the need within the school would lead to a waste of resources. Although the vast majority of evidence-based programs focus on providing Tier 1 supports, some are more nuanced and can align to your school's needs more closely. For example, the Facing History and Ourselves program serves middle and high school students. The lessons from Facing History and Ourselves are designed to be integrated into the school's social studies curriculum. Much of the focus of the lessons is on discrimination, racism, and prejudice. The program not only discusses the social history of these constructs, but also how students today can be active participants in eradicating them. Using a data-based approach, a high school that has identified an increase in bullying specifically related to students' race, ethnicity, and/or nationality may find a program like Facing History and Ourselves meeting its needs much more effectively than other programs.

Fit

When determining how well a program fits your school, there are several factors that should be considered. First, how does the program fit with your student and family population? There are simple answers for some of these questions. For example, is the program designed for the grade levels that your school serves? There are many universal programs for bullying prevention that are geared toward students in elementary school. Far fewer are evidence based for students attending high school. Another consideration is how many languages are supported through the program. If your school has a large number of second-language learners, it may be prudent for your school to put a higher priority on programs that provide materials for students and families in multiple languages.

Another part of fit is the extent to which the curriculum aligns with current initiatives. For example, imagine that a school has an initiative around family partnering and concerted efforts to communicate and partner with families regarding their child's performance in school. However, the bullying curriculum chosen doesn't discuss or address family involvement in relation to bullying. Consequently, the curriculum would be out of alignment with the school's family-partnering initiative. More so, any time that a new program or initiative is introduced, there is risk of it being seen as "just one more thing I have to do" by the teachers and staff. Buy-in from staff can be very difficult if your school has a history of introducing new programs at the beginning of the year, partially implementing them, and then fading them away when the year ends. This "initiative fatigue" can breed outright dread. So how can you avoid such a response?

Capacity

The final area of consideration for selecting an evidence-based bullying prevention curriculum is capacity. Here, capacity refers to a school's ability to support the use of the curriculum with fidelity. There are several facets to examining your capacity to implement the program. The most common considerations related to capacity are those of money and time. If you are selecting a program that has recurring costs each year, either to purchase refresher materials or because the lessons are subscription-based, then you need to determine if those costs can be covered year after year. Should more funding be needed, the bullying prevention team can determine the potential grants and other resources that would provide the required funds. Concerns about the time required for effective implementation also align with available staffing at the school. Are there enough staff members who are willing to engage in bullying prevention best practices? Is there a passionate member of the staff who can take charge of the work? Does this person or others at the school have the appropriate training and education to support the bullying prevention program?

Questions about having adequate staff with appropriate training need to be answered prior to purchasing of any program. Common skill sets that should be accounted for include data systems experience and technology experience. For working with data systems, having someone on staff who is knowledgeable about how to effectively collect, analyze, and use data for problem solving is required for being able to demonstrate your successes and continue effective implementation. This point person is responsible for organizing an efficient survey-implementation process, for collecting ongoing behavior data, and for supporting others in their ability to use data to make decisions. If there are additional technological requirements for your evidence-based program, identifying a technology lead who can support the other staff members who are not as fluent with technology can help alleviate concerns or gaps that may arise.

Using the Selection Factors

Having covered selection, let's look at an example of how schools can evaluate programs for their use. Implementation teams can review a given program and then rate each factor on a scale of 1 to 5 (cf. Metz & Louison, 2019). Imagine that a middle school is determining a Tier 1 curriculum for their students. Table 4.5 shows the reviews for two programs, Expect Respect and Second Step. The school team rated each program after reviewing its needs in relation to the program. Although the team liked the comprehensiveness of Second Step, one can see in the rating that the resources needed and the fit of the program with its intended goal wasn't a great match. As a result of rating the dimensions, the team was able to choose a more affordable and less time intensive program that aligned with their goal of reducing bullying in their school.

TABLE 4.5. Example: Factors Considered When Selecting a Curriculum

	Expect Respect	Second Step
Evidence	4	4
Usability	5	5
Supports	4	5
Need	5	4
Fit	5	3
Capacity	5	3
Total	28	24

MTSS AND CURRICULA

Now that you know how to select a curriculum for your site, we discuss how to use curricula within the context of an MTSS. As you may be aware, MTSS includes a multilevel prevention system that consists of 3 tiers (see *mtss4success.org*). Tier 1 is provided to all students and supports the learning of grade-level content and standards (McIntosh & Goodman, 2016). At Tier 1 for bullying prevention, schools use a curriculum that supports their schoolwide expectations and school climate efforts, as well as provides more direct instruction on bullying prevention. Schools can coordinate their school climate efforts and curricula with one another to provide a strong foundation to curb bullying and to support all students with school connectedness, relationships, and prosocial behavior. Within this section, we describe commonly used curriculum at Tier 1.

Commonly Used Bullying Prevention Curricula at Tier 1

To assist readers with understanding possible options for evidence-based curricula, we have summarized examples of curricula in Table 4.6. However, this summary is not an exhaustive review, as we chose to highlight popular options for our readers to consider. In determining which curricula to include, we searched for ones that were designed to reduce bullying within schools and ones that included specific lessons for students on bullying. There are various programs that address factors or skills related to bullying, but we excluded such curricula if they were not designed for bullying prevention or if they did not examine the effects of their curriculum on bullying prevention efforts. When examining the curricula in this section, it's best to use the Hexagon Tool (Metz & Louison, 2019) to identify a curriculum that will fit your school's needs as described earlier.

Bully Prevention in Positive Behavior Support (BP-PBS)

Bully Prevention in Positive Behavior Support (BP-PBS) is a curriculum for elementary-age students that aligns with PBIS. Students are taught a response strategy to use when they experience bullying or witness bullying. The response strategy is a three-step process in which students "stop, walk, and talk." It consists of first telling peers to "stop" and using a hand signal when they witness any problematic behavior. To create even greater buy-in from students, educators can ask the students what phrase and hand signal they want to use. If the behavior continues, students then walk away from the situation. If the stop and walk are not effective, students then tell an adult about the problematic behavior. In teaching all students the response strategy, students are given a tool to respond to problematic behavior, a norm is set in which unwanted behavior is not accepted, and there is no positive reinforcement for bullying. However, the strategy is not taught in isolation and is essentially an extension of PBIS; the school should have schoolwide expectations of behavior for all students as part of the response strategy (as discussed in Chapter 2). The curriculum consists of five lessons for students and one lesson for the staff. The first lesson teaches students the response strategy and takes approximately 50 minutes, with lesson two providing practice for students that takes 30 minutes and ideally occurs on the same day of lesson one. The remaining lessons cover using the strategy for gossip, inappropriate remarks, and cyberbullying; they are taught for 10–15 minutes on a weekly or biweekly subsequent basis. The staff lesson covers how to respond to problematic behavior and when students should use the response strategy (Ross et al., 2012).

TABLE 4.6. Summary of Evidence-Based Bullying Prevention Curricula

Name	Description	Focus	Cost or additional information	Level	Lessons	Bullying-related outcomes
Bully Prevention in Positive Behavior Support (BP-PBS)	Integrated with PBIS; students are taught a response strategy (stop/walk/talk) to use when they experience or witness problematic behavior.	General behavior and bullying	Free www.pbis.org topics/bullying-prevention	Elementary	6 lessons, 15–50 minutes	• Reduction in bullying incidents, office referrals, physical and verbal aggression • Increases in appropriate response to bullying
BP-PBS: Expect Respect	Integrated with PBIS; students are taught a response strategy to use when they experience or witness disrespectful behavior.	Disrespectful or unwanted behavior	Free www.pbis.org/topics/bullying-prevention	Middle, high	3 lessons, 45–60 minutes	• Reductions in physical and verbal aggression
Facing History and Ourselves	Offers curriculum on lessons related to history, justice, and ethics.	Civic education, SEL skills, equity and justice	www.facinghistory.org	Middle, high	Varies	• Increases in SEL skills and more likely to intervene with bullying • Increases in engagement and relationships among students • Increases in school climate ratings
Olweus Bullying Prevention Program (OBPP)	Comprehensive bullying program with schoolwide, classroom, community, and individual-level components.	All forms of bullying	$46 per teacher guide; $79 per schoolwide guide	Elementary, middle, high	No lessons (Teacher Guide offers support and materials for classroom meetings)	• 20–70% reduction in bullying • Increases in empathy, decreases in willingness to join in bullying • Reduction in cyberbullying
Positive Action	Aims to improve social competence by interrupting a negative thoughts-feelings-actions cycle. Based on concept that *"You feel good about yourself when you think and do positive actions, and there is a positive way to do everything"* (Flay & Allred, 2010, p. 475).	Various antisocial or violent behaviors, including forms of bullying	Classroom kits: $400–500; Bullying prevention kit: $250 www.positiveaction. net	Elementary, middle, high	80–140 lessons, taught up to 4 days/ week, 15 minutes each	• Decreases in beliefs that support aggression • Decreases in physical and verbal bullying for fifth-grade students • Decreases in physical and verbal bullying in grades 3–8, though moderated by parent versus self-report and by gender

Program	Description	Focus	Contact/Cost	Grade/Ages	Dosage	Outcomes
Preventing Relational Aggression in Schools Everyday (PRAISE) Program	Targets social cognitions, attributions, and bystander intervention. Designed for African American students. Developed from Friend 2 Friend program.	Physical and relational bullying	Contact *https://violence.chop.edu/preventing-aggression-schools-everyday*	Elementary	20 lessons, twice/week, 40 minutes each	• For girls and relationally aggressive girls, increases in social-information processing knowledge and anger management and decreases in relational aggression • Reductions in overt aggression for relationally aggressive girls • Limited benefit for boys
RULER	Offers training to improve emotional intelligence among students and enhancing school climate.	SEL skills	*www.ycei.org/ruler*	PreK to 12	Offers units that vary based on grade level	• Increases in school climate • Better quality relationships • Less bullying and aggressive behavior
Second Step	PreK to eighth-grade curriculum focused on teaching SEL skills to students. A bullying prevention unit is available for K–5, though lessons in middle school and PreK address bullying prevention.	SEL skills and all forms of bullying	Elementary classroom kits: $409; Middle school classroom kits: $219–$719; BP Unit: $209; *Various bundling and pricing options *secondstep.org*	Early childhood, elementary, middle	22–28 lessons, once/week; (daily activities for PreK); 25–50 minutes each; BP Unit is five lessons	• Reductions in physical bullying, verbal bullying, and sexual violence in middle school • Increase in willingness to intervene in bullying • Increases in empathy and prosocial skills • BP Unit is currently being researched for effectiveness
Words Wound	Offers a book, guide, and structure to educate students about cyberbullying.	Cyberbullying	Book cost approximately $14 (copy needed for each student); Guide is a free download	Ages 8 and up	7 chapters	• Specifically addresses cyberbullying

Note. The outcomes listed are related to bullying specifically; additional outcomes may be available for the curricula summarized. References: Cipriano et al. (2019); Espelage, Low, et al. (2013); Espelage, Low, et al. (2015); Espelage Rose, et al.(2015); Good et al. (2011); Leff et al. (2010); Lewis et al. (2013); Li et al. (2011); Limber, Olweus, Wang, Masiello and Brevik (2018); Nese, Horner, Dickey, Stiller, and Tomlanovich (2014); Reyes et al. (2012); Ross and Horner (2009, 2013).

BP-PBS: Expect Respect

Similar to BP-PBS, Expect Respect builds upon a PBIS framework and teaches students a response strategy when confronted with or witnessing disrespectful behavior from peers. Expect Respect provides middle school and high school students with more socially acceptable and developmentally appropriate ways to respond to peers, but the core concepts are the same as BP-PBS. Students learn to signal to peers to stop disrespectful behavior, use a walking away or ignoring strategy, and then seek social support from a school adult. The curriculum provides a total of six 45–60 minute lessons for 2 years (the initial lesson in year 1 is used again during the second year). Lesson 1 for students covers the response strategy, whereas subsequent lessons focus on perspective taking and practice using the response strategy. Lessons for the staff about responding to students who use the response strategy and about seeking their social support when confronted with disrespectful behavior are also included (Stiller et al., 2013).

Facing History and Ourselves

Facing History and Ourselves (FHO) is 501(c)(3) charity organization that has a mission of empowering students and teachers to stand up against hate. FHO does this through teaching lessons of history that are aligned with social studies courses in secondary schools. The goals are to foster empathy, build safe and inclusive schools, and improve student academic performance. FHO provides classroom resources, training, and coaching for educators to effectively implement the curriculum. The approach is flexible enough to be used schoolwide or at the individual classroom level. Additionally, materials are consistently updated. For example, the organization provided resources on how to hold safe, inclusive conversations about accountability, justice, and healing after the murder of George Floyd in 2020. CASEL deemed FHO as effective for increasing prosocial behavior and for improving the climate in classrooms for middle and high school students. A complete review of the research supporting FHO's effectiveness can be found in their research report, *How Do We Know It Works?* (Facing History and Ourselves [FHO], 2019).

Olweus Bullying Prevention Program

The Olweus Bullying Prevention Program (OBPP) is one of the most researched and well-known bullying programs available. It is a whole-school program for students ages 5–15 designed to improve school climate, strengthen peer relations, and provide support for students who are bullying or targeted (Olweus et al., 2007). It consists of school-, classroom-, individual-, and community-level components. The classroom-level component includes (1) enforcing schoolwide rules against bullying, (2) class meetings, and (3) meetings with students' parents. The materials include a 150-page teacher guide for implementation within the classroom to support teachers with the classroom-level components. Research has suggested the OBPP is generally effective when implemented with fidelity and can even improve school climate (see Rivara & Le Menestrel, 2016). A recent longitudinal study utilizing a sample of majority Black and low-income students found that the OBPP reduced the perpetration and targeting of students for both face-to-face and cyberbullying (Sullivan et al., 2021).

Positive Action

The Positive Action program is a multifaceted program that includes materials for schools, families, and communities (Flay & Allred, 2010). It is based on improving self-concept and on the notion that when people feel good about themselves, they make positive and healthy choices. The program focuses on the *thoughts-feelings-actions* circle: our thoughts can lead to actions, our actions lead to certain feelings, and those feelings can affect our actions. By teaching students to make positive choices, the idea is that they will then have positive feelings and thoughts as a result, creating a self-reinforcing process in which students value "being good" (Flay & Allred, 2010; Patel, Liddell, & Ferreira, 2018; Positive Action, n.d.). The program offers the curriculum and materials for K–12, which consists of 80–140 lessons, depending on the grade level. The lessons are approximately 15 minutes long and intended to be taught by classroom teachers 4 days a week; however, the number of lessons and time length varies, depending on how staff choose to use and implement the content. The lessons are divided across seven units that cover self-concept, positive actions for one's body and mind, self-management, getting along with others, being honest with one's self, continual self-improvement, and a review of the material. Supplemental materials are available for topics that include school climate, substance use prevention, bullying prevention, counseling, family involvement, and community involvement (*www.positiveaction.net*).

Preventing Relational Aggression in Schools Everyday (PRAISE) Program

The Preventing Relational Aggression in Schools Everyday (PRAISE) program is a classroom-based curriculum derived from social-information processing theory and group processes related to bullying. It is a modified version of the Friend 2 Friend (F2F) program, which is a pull-out intervention for relationally aggressive girls (PRAISE is designed for use with all students in a classroom). PRAISE consists of 20 lessons conducted twice weekly, each of which is approximately 40 minutes. The lessons target social-cognitive retraining (i.e., adjusting students' attributions and perceptions of others' behaviors and actions), empathy building, perspective taking, and responding as a bystander. PRAISE is designed specifically to be culturally appropriate for African American students since it was developed for use with third- to fifth-grade students in an urban setting (Leff et al., 2010).

Second Step

Second Step is an SEL curriculum with an extensive evidence-based behind it (see *www.secondstep.org/research*). It offers curricula for PreK to twelfth grade, as well as a bullying prevention unit and a child-protection unit. The bullying prevention unit is only available for K–5; however, bullying prevention skills are included within the PreK and middle school portions of the curriculum. The early childhood/PreK curriculum includes lessons for 28 weeks that are taught in daily, 5–7 minute activities across five units (skills for learning, empathy, emotional management, friendship skills and problem solving, and transitioning to kindergarten). The K–5 curriculum has 25 lessons for kindergarten and 22 lessons for grades 1 to 3 across four units (skills for learning, empathy, emotion management, and problem solving). Grades 4 and 5 have 22 lessons across three units (empathy and skills for learning, emotion management, and problem solving). The elementary school lessons are 25–40 minutes, depending on the grade level, each week. The middle school curriculum offers 26 lessons that are 50 minutes each or two 25-minute blocks across four units (mindsets and goals; values and friendships; thoughts, emotions, and decisions; and serious peer conflicts).

RULER

Offered by the Yale Center for Emotional Intelligence, RULER is a systemic approach to developing SEL competencies among students. RULER is actually an acronym that represents the five skills of emotional intelligence: Recognizing, Understanding, Labeling, Expressing, and Regulating. By teaching students to regulate their emotions using four core tools (i.e., the Charter, Mood Meter, Meta-Moment, and Blueprint), the Yale Center supports school communities in understanding emotions and building positive climates. Learn more about RULER at *www.ycei.org/ ruler*. Schools that have used the RULER approach have experienced positive increases in school climate, improvements in academic performance, improving student relationships and connectedness, and decreases in bullying and aggressive behavior (Cipriano, Barnes, Rivers, & Brackett, 2019; Reyes, Brackett, Rivers, White, & Salovey, 2012; see *www.rulerapproach.org/about/what- is-the-evidence*).

Words Wound Curriculum

The Cyberbullying Research Center offers a curriculum that targets cyberbullying middle and high school students (Patchin & Hindua, 2013). The Center offers the book *Words Wound: Delete Cyberbullying and Make Kindness Go Viral* and a leader's guide that includes instructional activities. The curriculum is easily adaptable and can be adjusted to fit a variety of schedules and student needs. As noted by Gaffney, Farrington, and Ttofi (2019) in their meta-analysis of cyberbullying prevention curricula, despite the increase in research on the causes and impact of cyberbullying, there still remains a lack of studies on effective intervention and prevention. In fact, evaluations of cyberbullying curricula only began in 2012. Despite these concerns, cyberbullying curricula, in general, have been found to be effective at reducing cyberbullying in youth. The Cyberbullying Research Center offers many additional resources to support families and staff with cyberbullying, including a top-10 list of tips for educators to prevent cyberbullying (see Figure 4.1).

Bullying Prevention Curricula at Tier 2

Tier 2 are standard interventions provided to groups of students who need additional support with core instruction (McIntosh & Goodman, 2016). For Tier 2 bullying prevention, schools use interventions to expand and supplement the Tier 1 curriculum (i.e., schoolwide expectations and any evidence-based curriculum used) and to provide additional lessons on bullying prevention and responding to bullying incidents. Generally speaking, a Tier 2 intervention shouldn't take more than 30 minutes of a staff member's time per week (cf. Hawken et al., 2021). In doing so, resources and time can be saved for students who require more intensive supports at Tier 3 (Harlacher & Rodriguez, 2018; McIntosh & Goodman, 2016).

There are a number of steps educators can take to prevent cyberbullying. Here are a few examples:

1. **FORMALLY ASSESS** the extent of the problem within your school district by surveying and/or interviewing your students. Once you have a baseline measure of what is going on in your school, specific strategies can be implemented to educate students and staff about social media safety and Internet use in creative and powerful ways.

2. **EXPLAIN** to students that all forms of bullying are unacceptable, and that cyberbullying behaviors are subject to discipline. Students need to know that even a behavior that occurs away from school could be subject to sanction if it substantially disrupts the school environment or interferes with the rights of other students to feel safe at school.

3. **CULTIVATE** a positive school climate, as research has shown a link between a perceived "negative" environment on campus and an increased prevalence of cyberbullying among students. In general, it is crucial to establish and maintain a school climate marked by connectedness, belongingness, respect, and integrity, where violations result in appropriate sanction.

4. **SPECIFY CLEAR RULES** regarding the use of laptops, phones, and other electronic devices. Acceptable Use Policies tend to be commonplace in school districts, but these must be updated to cover online harassment (and other teen technology issues). Post signs or posters in school computer labs, hallways, and classrooms to remind students about your standards.

5. **CONSULT** with your school attorney BEFORE incidents occur to find out what actions you can or must take in varying situations.

6. **CREATE** a comprehensive formal contract specific to cyberbullying in the school's policy manual, and consider introducing a formal "honor code" that identifies various forms of bullying as examples of inappropriate behaviors.

7. **TEACH** social and emotional learning skills. Research shows that teaching students how to more effectively manage their emotions and relationships with others can be useful in preventing interpersonal conflict. Encourage social awareness and self-management.

8. **USE PEER MENTORING**—where older students informally teach lessons and share learning experiences with younger students—to promote positive online interactions.

9. **DESIGNATE** a "Cyberbullying Expert" at your school who is responsible for educating him/herself about the issues and then passing on important points to other youth-serving adults on campus.

10. **EDUCATE** your community. Utilize specially created cyberbullying curricula, or information sessions such as assemblies and in-class discussions to raise awareness among youth. Invite specialists to come talk to staff and students. Send information out to parents. Sponsor a community education event or town hall. Invite parents and any other relevant adult. Incentivize as necessary.

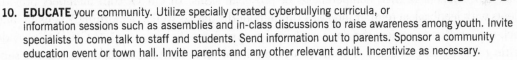

FIGURE 4.1. Preventing cyberbullying: Top 10 tips for educators, by Sameer Hinduja, PhD, and Justin W. Patchin, PhD. Copyright © 2018 Cyberbullying Research Center. Reprinted with permission from the authors and the Cyberbullying Research Center.

Some specific options at Tier 2 include SEL groups, Check-In/Check-Out (Hawken, Crone, Bundock, & Horner, 2021), and Check and Connect (Check & Connect Student Engagement Intervention, Institute on Community Integration, 2020). We briefly describe each of these options in the next sections and how they can be used to support bullying prevention and improve school climate.

SEL Groups

SEL groups offer 20–30 minute lessons each week for students that can expand on the schoolwide expectations and lessons on bullying. The NSSC recommends that all students receive lessons on bullying dynamics and how to respond to bullying incidents, be it as a bystander or as a target (Cohen & Freiberg, 2013). SEL groups can be used to provide more explicit instruction and practice in such skills related to bullying prevention. Other lessons can be crafted around the SEL competencies outlined by CASEL. Schools can identify the needs of their students and then determine the best curriculum to develop. They have the option of creating their own lessons for their SEL groups by following explicit instruction guidelines (cf. Gresham, 2002), but they can also use established curricula. In fact, schools can use lessons from their Tier 1 curriculum, such as Second Step or PRAISE, for their Tier 2 lessons. Of note, schools shouldn't place students who are perpetrators together into SEL groups, because placing all of them into the same group can exacerbate the issues. The perpetrators within the group end up reinforcing each other's bullying behaviors (Dodge et al., 2006; Hess et al., 2017).

Check-In/Check-Out

Check-In/Check-Out (CICO) is designed for students with mild, disruptive behaviors and can be used to reinforce and provide more practice for students with schoolwide expectations (Hawken et al., 2021). For bullying prevention, it can be used to support students who need additional practice and supervision on being respectful or kind toward others. Schools can also use CICO to support further development of SEL competencies or prosocial skills. In CICO, staff members provide students with feedback at regular intervals throughout the day, as well as a morning "check-in" and "check-out" session to review the day's goals and performance. Schools can use CICO to provide specific guidance and feedback to students who are involved in bullying incidents in order to support the prevention and cessation of bullying.

Check and Connect

Check and Connect is another option at Tier 2 in which students are assigned a mentor who meets weekly with them and helps them with problem solving and skill building (Check & Connect Student Engagement Intervention, Institute on Community Integration, 2020). The mentor "checks" with the student by meeting regularly with them and by monitoring the student's progress, for example, in the student's grades, attendance, and performance in school. The mentor also "connects" with the student's family by meeting with them and providing ongoing communication between the school and the family. Overall, Check and Connect increases student engagement with school and builds relationships for students with adults in the school. It can be used to strengthen the connection to school of those students involved in bullying, therein providing a protective factor for them (see Anderson, Christensen, Sinclair, & Lehr, 2004; Decker, Dona, & Christenson, 2007; Zolkoski, 2019). Further, schools can use Check and Connect to provide support and guidance each week for students involved in bullying.

Bullying Prevention Curricula at Tier 3

Tier 3 supports is the most intensive and individualized intervention provided to students, which includes in-depth assessment and the development of an individualized support plan (McIntosh & Goodman, 2016). Tier 3 is comprehensive and long term, and it can consist of significant parental or family involvement, continued interventions from Tier 2, intensive counseling sessions, and connection to community resources (McIntosh & Goodman, 2016). With respect to bullying prevention, schools provide support to ensure that the targets of bullying are able to use the schoolwide bullying prevention response, as well as instruction in any other skills they may be lacking. For perpetrators, schools provide support to ensure that the perpetrator uses other skills to get their needs met rather than bullying others, as well as instruction or psychoeducational groups on relevant topics (e.g., empathy, emotion regulation).

Because Tier 3 is individualized, there are fewer standardized approaches or interventions compared to Tier 2. Rather, schools use extensive problem analysis to develop an individualized support plan (Harlacher & Rodriguez, 2018; McIntosh & Goodman, 2016; O'Neil, Albin, Storey, Horner, & Sprague, 2014). Schools use the individualized support plan to teach students any missing skills that the problem analysis step unveils. This individualized support plan should build upon the previous curricula used at Tier 1 or Tier 2, but can also include prepackaged or individually designed lesson plans to teach the perpetrator or target of bullying certain skills related to social-emotional learning or bullying dynamics. Moreover, some states have supports for youth experiencing mental health concerns that may be utilized at Tier 3. For example, in Colorado, the I Matter program provides three free counseling sessions for youth under the age of 18. We describe problem analysis and the formation of an individualized support plan, including how to structure the environment to prompt and reinforce the taught skills, extensively in Chapter 6 as part of the discussion on problem solving.

Target Bullying Involvement Program (T-BIP)

Although research suggests that there is a lack of targeted approaches to support the targets and perpetrators of bullying (Hess et al., 2017), one promising approach to Tier 3 is the Target Bullying Involvement Program (T-BIP). Developed by Dr. Susan Swearer at the University of Nebraska–Lincoln, the T-BIP is an individualized program for students between the ages of 7 and 18. Implemented by trained specialists, the T-BIP provides a one-on-one cognitive-behavioral intervention for students involved in bullying as a perpetrator, target, or perpetrator-target. As part of the intervention, students complete several assessments that dig into individual factors that may influence their involvement in bullying. Specialists also teach students effective ways to respond to bullying and focus on developing empathy and problem-solving skills. Moreover, by having families and school staff participate throughout the process, the full picture of bullying is taken into account. This involvement includes having parents and appropriate teachers or counselors also complete surveys assessing their impressions of bullying.

As part of the T-BIP, a follow-up meeting with the student, family, school staff, and specialist is held a few weeks after the intervention. During the meeting, the specialist shares the results of the assessments, receives feedback from the other members of the group, and provides a written report with individually tailored recommendations. Research on the outcomes of the T-BIP have suggested it can be effective. In one study by Swearer, Wang, Collins, Strawhun, and Fluke (2014), there was a significant reduction in office referrals after students completed the T-BIP. Moreover, self-reports of bullying also decreased after the T-BIP was implemented (Meints, 2007). You can learn more about the T-BIP at the Nebraska Bullying Prevention and Intervention Initiative website: *cehs.unl.edu/empowerment.*

In Figure 4.2, we provide an evidence-based curricula practice profile to operationally define this component of CBP.

Core Component: Evidence-Based Curricula		
Definition: The intentional selection of evidence-based curricula to teach students bullying prevention strategies and SEL competencies. The curricula are used within a tiered structure.		
Expected Use	**Developmental Use**	**Unacceptable Use**
The school uses a structured selection process to choose the curricula.	The school uses a structured selection process; however, the process may not include all six criteria outlined in the Hexagon Tool.	The school does not use a structured selection process to choose the curricula.
The curriculum is able to be implemented schoolwide.	The curriculum is able to be implemented schoolwide; however, it is currently not being implemented schoolwide.	The curriculum is not able to be implemented schoolwide.
The staff receives ongoing training and coaching for the curriculum.	The staff receives training and coaching for the curriculum; however, they are not delivered using a tiered model of supports or are not continuous.	No training and/or coaching is provided for the curriculum.
The curriculum serves as one part of a layered continuum of supports to prevent bullying.	The curriculum serves as one part of a layered continuum of supports to prevent bullying; however, Tiers 1, 2, and 3 supports are not implemented with fidelity.	Bullying prevention supports do not exist on a layered continuum.

FIGURE 4.2. Evidence-based curricula practice profile.

CHAPTER 5

Family and Community Partnerships

There are dozens of books and standards for family and community partnerships. Typically, experts in the field provide wonderful examples of how a few key components can help a school in developing partnerships that support students academically. In this chapter, the most common approaches to improving and maintaining effective family and community partnerships have emerged from the perspective of implementing bullying prevention best practices.

The National Parent Teacher Association (PTA) published the *PTA National Standards for Family–School Partnerships: An Implementation Guide* in 2009. The PTA guide suggests six standards that, when implemented with fidelity, lead to strong family and community partnerships. Other experts in the field of education have suggested similar best practices. Reviewing the research on family and community partnerships, there are four key components that are represented in almost all of the literature: (1) inclusive school culture, (2) communication, (3) involving all families, and (4) connecting with the community (Constantino, 2015; Henderson, Mapp, Johnson, & Davies, 2007; Redding, Murphy, & Sheley, 2011).

One consideration as you read through the details of these four key components of family and community partnerships is to think about how they may be implemented through a layered continuum of supports. Some strategies that can be implemented as universal supports are those that are best practices for the majority of families and community members. Also consider which strategies would fit well in your school as targeted supports, and may be reserved for a few families who require unique guidance when partnering with the school. For example, families who may have work schedules that rarely allow them to attend conferences or other school events. Finally, consider which strategies may be used for families needing intensive supports, perhaps the small handful of families whose students have been targeted for bullying and are having difficulty responding in an effective manner. Regardless of how intensive the support, families and the community can serve to create a culture of bullying prevention beyond the walls of the classroom.

INCLUSIVE SCHOOL CULTURE

In Chapter 2, we explained how a positive school climate is the foundation of effective bullying prevention. The same is true for partnering with families and the community. Moreover, having an inviting, inclusive school starts before families even walk in the door. The same way we will sometimes drive home on autopilot from work, you have likely become so used to the entrance of your school that you barely even see it anymore. Take a minute to step outside the entrance of your school building and look at it from the perspective of a family member. Ask yourself, "If I were a perspective parent bringing my future kindergartener to this school, would I feel that they are safe?" or "If I had a child with a physical handicap, would I feel welcomed by the ease of access into the building?" If you have ever traveled to a new school to do a training or site visit, you know that it can be difficult to even know which entrance you should try to approach.

Having taken a look at the front of your school, consider some of the solutions that are easily available. Maybe you place a banner above the main entrance to the school saying, "Welcome Families" so that it is clear where families should enter the building. Use positively stated language that demonstrates the safety and security of your school. During one site visit at a middle school, one of us walked up to the front of the building and was greeted with a large red "STOP" sign on both doors. Think of how families may feel when the first message they receive from the school is an order to "STOP. DO NOT ENTER." It is literally the opposite message that we are trying to convey to our families. Instead, think about how our families would feel if they saw a message that read, "Welcome to our school. We are happy you are here. Please press the button below and someone will help you shortly." Nothing about the actual safety of the school has been compromised, but the positive impact on families has been greatly improved.

Using positive language is also paramount when attempting to prevent bullying. We have probably all seen the ubiquitous sign with the word "BULLYING" on it with a circle and cross through it. The message is clear enough: no bullying. But as any educator or parent will tell you, telling children what you *want* them to do rather what you *forbid* them to do typically leads to better outcomes. Many schools take this approach by communicating their anti-bullying message as spreading kindness or being an upstander. Moreover, when adults directly teach students what these behaviors actually look like at school, bullying can become a phenomenon that is less common because students are focused on their expected behaviors.

Beyond considering the language we use in schools, our goal should be to have families feel like they are just as important to the school and its efforts to prevent bullying as the students. This means allowing parents and caregivers to have a tangible impact on the school. Ask any teacher the reason families have told them they don't engage with the school, and you will likely get one of three explanations: (1) their engagement wouldn't have an impact, (2) they don't know how, or (3) they don't have the time. We will discuss reasons two and three later in the chapter, but an awareness that families who understand how their engagement makes a real impact in bullying prevention and the school overall is key to having an inclusive culture.

So how do we help parents and caregivers to understand that they have a real impact in the school? One of the best ways is to show them, not tell them. Too often when we want families to support our school, our effort comes off as trying to "sell" the idea. Instead, schools should do their best to show how families improve the school and *let families realize this on their own*. If a caregiver walks into their child's school and sees an entire wall dedicated to a "Family Wall of Fame" highlighting the ways that families have supported the school over the years, the immediate takeaway is that the school values its families. When a parent attends their child's high school play and hears that a family is recognized for donating supplies or their time to support the school's bullying prevention efforts, it is clear that families have a real impact on the school's success. Having families come to this realization on their own and then be provided with an easy way to be included into this culture is a powerful one-two punch.

One final note on developing an inclusive culture for families at school is that a myriad of opportunities need to be available to ensure equity for all families. Every family in your school is different. Thinking back to the social-ecological model described in Chapter 1, we know that there are countless factors that affect families. They include everything from the makeup of the family itself to laws being passed at the state and federal level that may directly affect them. This is why it is so vital for teachers and the school staff to establish a positive relationship with families from the beginning of the year. When we know more about our families, we are better equipped to be creative about how they can engage with our school. Knowing that a student's mother is a novelist allows a creative writing teacher to extend an invitation for the mother to share her experience with getting published with the class. Being aware that a family member works at a local fast food restaurant may provide you with an opportunity to receive donated food or coupons as incentives for raffles or positive behavior. Every family has something to offer. All we have to do is have a strong enough relationship with families at the outset to know what it is. We offer a summary of examples in Table 5.1 for building an inclusive culture.

BULLYING PREVENTION AND COMMUNICATION

One of the reasons families may not engage with a school is because they simply do not know how. Establishing or reinforcing a strong system of two-way communication in which families have the ability to share their thoughts with staff is vital. Imagine this: a new family moves into your district, and their fourth-grade student is now in your classroom. The father drops off his daughter in the morning just as you are starting to prepare for the beginning of the day. Other students are shuffling in. Marcelo asks you if he can use the bathroom; Daisy is telling you about her grandma's house that she visited over the weekend; two notoriously rambunctious students are engaged in a spirited contest to see who can jump and scream the loudest. You are able to take a brief moment

---

TABLE 5.1. Examples of Building an Inclusive Culture for Families

- Have a welcome banner that hangs in the entryway.
- Include a welcoming message in different languages painted on the walls in the entryway of the school.
- Have a schoolwide expectation that says "Welcome Others."
- Teach students to say hello to adults and to welcome adults when they see them in the school.
- Include family voice when creating schoolwide expectations.
- Include parents as part of a project-based learning assignment.
- Set up a "coffee talk" station where families can gather with staff members to get to know one another in the mornings.

---

to say hello to your new student and her father while gesturing her to her desk. But while you are redirecting the students who are jumping and screaming, you miss the nonverbal cues from the father that he would like to talk just a little bit more.

If your school does not have a strong culture of engaging with every family, you may continue on with the day and rest of the week as you normally do. But let's assume that you and your school consistently make it a priority to partner as much as possible with every family. Instead of continuing to teach as usual, at the end of that first day, you make sure to walk with your new student to where she is picked up by her family. In the 5 minutes you spend speaking with your student's new family, you learn that they just moved from a small town into the much more urban area of your school. Your student's father is an artist who just got a job at the local art museum. He tells you that he meant to talk to you in the morning about the wall in your classroom that has students' artwork hanging up. His art museum is having a showcase of student art in the next few months, and the museum is looking for students under 12 years old to submit their work. When you return to your classroom, you make a note to look into how you can integrate your upcoming lessons and the school's bullying prevention efforts with this potential art museum show.

This is just a brief example of how making a commitment to communicating with every family and having a welcoming culture for families can build partnerships. Now think about how a conversation might go with the parents of your new student if she is the target of bullying at the end of her first month of school. Having started off with a strong partnership with her family through several conversations about organizing the submission of student artwork, you would be able to draw on that connection to empathize and support the family through a difficult situation. If, however, you never had that 5-minute conversation at the end of the first day and never reached out to the family since that point, your first significant conversation with the family is about how their daughter is being bullied at her new school. You not only have to try to sympathize with people you know nothing about, but you have to do it with a family that has not heard anything positive about their daughter's transition to a new school.

Communication is not only important for those times when you have new students, but is also vital as an everyday practice. As Constantino (2015) describes, making just a few small tweaks can significantly improve family engagement with the learning that is happening in the classroom. What's more, this is just as true for SEL topics as it is for academic topics. As an example, a home–school folder is a common communication tool used by teachers. Students are expected to take home their folder each day or at the end of each week. A parent or caregiver is required to "sign off" that the folder has been shown to them. Typically, the material in these folders shows what has been learned in the previous week; however, adding the small change of including what learning will take place in the following week, and how families can reinforce that learning, enables parents and caregivers to supplement their child's engagement with the topics in multiple settings.

To illustrate how this approach can work, let's assume you are a first-grade teacher implementing the Olweus Bullying Prevention Program in your classroom. Your students receive one lesson from the curriculum each week, and the entire scope and sequence of the curriculum is laid out for you in the materials. On Friday, in each student's home–school folder, you include a note that briefly describes the topic that will be taught next week: emotion recognition. In the description, you inform the families that students will learn how to recognize their emotions through how they feel physically and what they look like in others. Four emotions will be discussed in depth, including happiness, anger, sadness, and surprise. At the end of the note, you list a few ideas for how families can further their child's learning at home. They can check out certain books from the library, like *Grumpy Monkey,* or watch the movie *Inside Out,* which is available through the local library or Disney Plus if the family has a subscription. Moreover, instead of having students simply get a signature from their parents attesting that they've been informed about the lessons that were learned on emotion recognition, require them to engage with their family around the lesson. For example, they could be required to ask two family members to show what their faces look like when they are happy, angry, sad, and surprised. What differences are there between the family members? What is the same? Additionally, it's important to keep equity in mind when creating these requirements. Not every family has the financial resources to rent movies or the time to visit the library on a regular basis. We should strive for extended learning that can be accomplished by all students and families.

In the context of bullying prevention and intervention, communication with families is critical in obtaining a positive outcome. Your school could do everything right, but if the family of a targeted students never knows about the incident or the steps your team took to make certain their child felt safe at school, it can easily breed mistrust. When communicating with families about bullying at school, the first outreach should occur before bullying takes place. This can be done in several ways. At back-to-school nights, each teacher could briefly talk about the bullying prevention efforts at the school. The school can highlight its bullying prevention policy in a standalone social media post, newsletter, or email that also provides clear directions on how to contact the school if the family believes their child has been targeted for bullying. Regardless of how it is accomplished, when a school takes the first step in demonstrating its dedication to preventing bullying, rather than having parents or caregivers in effect taking the first step when they allege that bullying has occurred, all those involved will experience better results.

In addition to being the first to communicate with families about bullying, schools should provide multiple pathways for a two-way dialogue. When sending out that first newsletter, social media post, or email, make sure that an email and/or phone number is included in case a family has concerns they would like the school to know about. It can also be valuable to use data-based decision making to determine the best way to provide opportunities for families to contact the school about bullying concerns. Survey your families to ask, "If your child told you that they were bullied at school, where is the first place you would go to find out who to contact at the school about the issue?" Then provide options such as "school's social media pages," "email the teacher," or "the school's webpage." After analyzing the results, review the top answers to see if families would actually get the information they need to feel supported. If the families say that they would first go to the school's webpage, how could you work with the webpage designer to have a highlighted area at the top of the webpage that tells families to "click here" if they have concerns about bullying? If the number-one response is that the family would email the teacher, consider how you can provide support so that all teachers know how to respond to these emails and what procedures they should follow to ensure that a bullying report is completed. To find out more details on how to communicate with families after a bullying report is submitted, see Chapter 3 on Policy.

INVOLVING ALL FAMILIES IN PREVENTING BULLYING

There are three important parts to consider in involving all families: (1) build positive relationships, (2) increase family self-efficacy in helping their children with school-related topics, and (3) include families in the decision-making process.

Building Positive Relationships

Similar to the need for teachers to actively build relationships with their students as part of building a positive school climate, the school staff must actively build positive relationships with families (see Table 5.2). By starting with an understanding that the school strives for inclusivity for all families, the staff has a strong foundation on which to build positive relationships. One of the keys to building these relationships is by creating trust between the school and families. The difficult problem about trust is that it can take weeks and months to cultivate but can be lost in a single moment.

Creating trust in the school's ability to prevent and intervene in bullying situations can be separated into three different time periods: before bullying occurs, during a bullying incident, and after a bullying incident has been resolved. Prior to the beginning of the school year, you will have several opportunities to demonstrate the school's dedication to bullying prevention to new and returning families. Many schools hold back-to-school nights when students and families get to meet their new teachers for the first time in a more informal setting. New families in particular will likely visit the school's website, check social media posts, or look up reviews of the school online to learn about the new school. In states where school choice is available, a school's online presence and word-of-mouth can have an impact on whether families want to attend your school or choose a different one. Knowing these facts, imagine the impression families will receive if there is a consistent kindness, inclusion, and anti-bullying message across all these platforms. The school website has a page dedicated to the kindness campaigns students have initiated over the years as well as support for students and families if they believe their child has been the target of bullying. On the school's social media pages, videos showcase the annual school and community 5K fun run to raise awareness of bullying and the steps needed to stop it. Back-to-school night features a slideshow and 30-second recognition of what every teacher does in their classroom to engage their students in SEL skills so that they grow as people and not just as students.

TABLE 5.2. Building a Positive Relationship with Families

Before a bullying incident occurs	• Communicate to families that bullying is not accepted. • Provide multiple methods for families, students, and staff to report incidents of bullying. • Provide a clear description of your school's plan for when a report of bullying is received. • Ensure that the staff are properly trained on how to intervene in bullying situations. • Have a consistent message of kindness and compassion.
During a bullying incident	• Secure students' safety first. • Avoid trying to mediate the problem in the moment. • Do not force students to apologize to one another.
After a bullying incident occurs	• Communicate with families in a timely manner. • Provide supports to the students who were targeted, perpetrated, and witnessed the bullying as appropriate. • Continue to check in with students to ensure that they feel safe. • Follow the procedures outlined in the bullying prevention policy to reinforce trust with families. • Follow up with families after several days or weeks.

When bullying incidents do occur, trust in the school is immediately tested. What the school staff and administration do in the first moments and hours after becoming aware of an incident are critical in maintaining trust with a family. If a school is following a comprehensive approach to preventing and intervening with bullying, the staff will have already been trained on how to respond to the students and their families. You can find more details and recommendations on how schools should respond when they receive a report of bullying in Chapter 3. With a strong bullying prevention policy in place, the school will be better equipped to respond to a report of bullying in such a way that it maintains trust for all involved. Securing students' immediate safety, communicating directly with families on the process, supplying resources, and providing a layered continuum of supports for targets, bystanders, and perpetrators shows that the school is worthy of being trusted.

After a bullying incident has occurred and been responded to in accordance with the bullying prevention policy, it can be tempting for a school to consider its work done. After all, the report has been filed away, and the students are receiving appropriate supports and consequences. But what about the families of these students? Regardless of the severity or impact of the incident, the family of the student who was targeted needs to know that their child is safe when going to school. As part of the supports that are provided to the targeted student, a safety plan should have been developed, which includes what to do if an incident occurs again and who the student should notify at school. Making a concerted effort to check in with the family as well as the student to see how they feel the safety plan is working after a few days or weeks shows the family how invested the school is in their child's well-being. Even if a safety plan wasn't developed, a simple phone call check-in after a short period of time displays the compassion that the school staff has for their students.

For the family of a student who has perpetrated bullying, it is important for them to know that the school has not given up on their child. Even if the bullying incident was severe, if the school no longer supports the student who perpetrated the bullying, there is no opportunity for that student to learn from their mistakes and grow as a person. By no means does this suggest that the bullying behavior should be dismissed or minimized, but nor should the school define the student as a bully for the rest of their academic career. Students are known to move in and out of bullying roles during their academic career. We should allow students the opportunity to appropriately move into an uninvolved role in bullying as much as possible.

Increasing Family Self-Efficacy to Prevent Bullying

We know from research that families are more likely to be engaged in their child's school when they believe they will have an actual impact (see Hoover-Dempsey et al., 2005). The concept of self-efficacy was first introduced by Albert Bandura in 1997 and, put simply, refers to the degree to which we believe we have the skills and abilities required to obtain the outcomes we want. One of our key tasks as educators then is to support families so that they believe that they have the ability to protect their children from bullying. Because once they believe that their engagement can help, they often choose to do so (Hoover-Dempsey & Sandler, 1997). It is up to us as educators to take the lead in making families feel valuable. Too often when families *don't* feel valued, they stop trying to be valuable.

If your school has been following the guidance we've laid out for engaging families, namely that there should be an inclusive culture, strong two-way communication, and trust, the next step is messaging that families are necessary and valuable partners in the education of their children. As noted earlier, families can be shown their value by highlighting their contributions to student learning visually throughout the school. Sharing research across multiple communication channels that scientifically demonstrates the impact families have in the successful education of their children can also get this message across. Schools can offer training opportunities in different areas for parents and caregivers. The most common way to teach families how to prevent bullying is by holding family education nights. Schools may hold a one-time event or conduct an educational series that includes training on multiple topics. The unfortunate reality is that, if not planned well with consideration given to the ways to include all families, these events can draw just a small handful of attendees.

So what are some effective ways to get families to attend your education nights? First, the messaging needs to make it clear that they have the ability to prevent their children from experiencing bullying. Remember, if families believe that they can have an impact, they are more likely to get involved. For example, sharing scientific research demonstrating that families that directly teach their children how to navigate the Internet safely (versus imposing severe restrictions) reduces their likelihood of being the target of cyberbullying (Elsaesser, Russell, Ohannessian, & Patton, 2017) can create buy-in with families. Testimonials from other families at the school can also paint a concrete picture of how attending the education nights can help caregivers create safety for their children. A second strategy is to lean on our two-way communication. Reach out to families and ask what areas of bullying prevention they want to know more about. By taking this approach, we avoid providing a generic training and instead use data to determine the support we provide. Several other strategies, which are described in more detail later in this chapter, are partnering with the community and using student voice.

One of the biggest barriers for families is time. When we typically hold our family education nights in the evening, there are concerns about child care, dinner, and transportation. Leaning on our partnerships with the local community, schools can solicit donations from a local restaurant to provide dinner for families and their children. Many businesses have budgets set aside specifically for community relations, and providing free meals to a school fits within that budget. This may be an especially enticing option if there is a new restaurant in town that is trying to get its name out in the community. Drawing on a school's relationship with community after-school programs, some of the staff may be willing to volunteer their time in the evening to provide child care during the parent trainings if they can also receive the training themselves at a later date. In terms of transportation, the school can reach out to its local transportation company to determine if there are reduced or free fares that can be provided for the specific purpose of getting families to the training and back home. Many transportation companies in larger metropolitan areas provide these reduced or free fares to 503(c)(3) nonprofits and schools.

Finally, by incorporating student voice into the trainings, we are more likely to get families involved. If your school has developed a kindness club or another school club that has adopted the mission of preventing bullying in school, the students from that club can help provide the training. It can involve something as simple as the students sharing what bullying looks like in their school or what children their age need from their families to support bullying prevention. If you are in a secondary school, one option would be to have the drama club act out scenes of bullying that exist in their school and what effective intervention can look like. Keep in mind though that in an effort to engage all families, we need to understand that not every family has the option of attending a training in the evening. This does not mean that they don't care about preventing bullying, but it does mean that we need to be creative in how we can equitably provide the same training to these families. Here again is an opportunity for student involvement. If your school has a technology class that has access to video cameras and editing software, you can partner with the class teacher to see whether students may be able to record and post the trainings online for all families to access. Not only does providing online access create a more equitable approach to the training, but it can support and further their academic learning through a hands-on project.

Including Families in Decision Making around Bullying Prevention

Many times, the school staff feels a sense of unease when it is suggested that families be included in decision making at the school level. It is not that teachers and staff don't want families involved, it's just that many educators have had tense, difficult conversations with caregivers about how they teach or about a policy decision that is unpopular. The immediate reaction to the idea of including families brings back these past interactions, and instinctively we tend to avoid these more uncomfortable moments in our profession. But that is ultimately the point of including families in the first place. It is easier to have tough conversations with families when they are partners, rather than when they are on the receiving end of decisions with which they don't agree.

One of the first and most impactful ways to include families in decision making is with regard to the school's bullying prevention policy itself. Many components make up an effective policy, and you can read more about these components in Chapter 3. When your school goes through the process of creating or revising the school handbook policy on bullying prevention, having parent and caregiver input is crucial. Family input can provide a quick check on how the policy may be received by the larger population. In certain circumstances, your school may be bound by district-level policy or federal law on some aspects of bullying prevention. For example, many families want to know what punishment the student who bullied their child received. Due to privacy laws, schools are not legally able to disclose this information. Having parents or caregivers truly collaborate in creating language that explains this policy in the handbook may prevent some of the phone calls that school administrators receive in this area. An even greater service that families can offer for many schools is having them read through the policy to catch any jargon that may exist. As educators, it is easy to slip in an acronym or two that is commonplace to us but confusing for families. To put your school in a stronger place regarding the sustainability of family engagement in bullying prevention, your school can also consider adding family engagement to the actual policy. Not only does doing this show your school's dedication to partnering with families in general, it shows that even the most difficult topics have added value when parents and caregivers are included.

Families who are included in the regular staff bullying prevention leadership team meetings can provide numerous benefits to the school. The purpose of this leadership team is to support the implementation of bullying prevention best practices in the school, and families can provide great insights into what impact the policies have on their children outside of the school setting. They can bring back information to the team on how the evidence-based curriculum is being generalized (or not) at home and what they are hearing from other parents and caregivers. Families also have fantastic, creative ideas for events and know the most popular shows, movies, and activities in the community. This input alone can help your school make any purchases for reinforcers to be more informed and likely more reinforcing for your students. The value of the increased capacity and support to the bullying prevention implementation team cannot be overstated. Having families as partners provides additional hands and hours to support the school's efforts in reducing bullying.

Finally, it's always important to remember that when including family members on bullying prevention implementation teams, schools need to honor the privacy and confidentiality of students. This means that any data that are shared during meetings should be de-identified and follow your applicable school board policies.

INVOLVING THE COMMUNITY IN BULLYING PREVENTION

Developing sustainable, ongoing partnerships with the local community is an area that schools often have difficulty realizing. Even though we know including the community–school partnership is important, understanding how to reach out effectively or how to prioritize the community partners we do reach out to can feel daunting. Thankfully, there is an organized approach that can help us identify, select, and connect to these community groups to further our bullying prevention efforts.

Asset mapping is an approach described by Kretzmann and McKnight (1993) as a way of focusing on the assets, as opposed to the deficits, of the community surrounding a school. Although for our purposes we will be speaking about community support around bullying prevention specifically, the same process can be used to map resources for all school learning objectives. Part of what Kretzmann and McKnight (1993) describe in their book are the different types of community supports with which an organization can partner. Two of these specifically relate to schools and how they build relationships with the community.

Types of Community Assets

The first group of community assets are individuals. In the school setting, this means connecting with families in their roles as community members. All families access and engage with the larger community in some way, including through their professions. Our students' caregivers may be nurses, fast-food workers, or stay-at-home parents. Regardless, they have an expertise and connection to the community that we can harness to stop bullying if we make the effort. The first step is gathering information. One of the most effective ways to do this is through a very brief, optional family questionnaire that schools can include in the enrollment packets they provide each year. It can be either a standalone one-page form or included as part of an already existing form. Potential items to include are where family members work, what skills a family member possesses that could support connection to the community (e.g., marketing, graphic design), and what personal or professional connections they may have to the community.

You will also want to make sure that the school is allowed to contact the family if there is an opportunity to partner with the community. Providing an explanation of the value the school places on partnering with families and the community at the top of the questionnaire so that its purpose is clear can help alleviate concerns about providing potentially personal information. Moreover, when families know that they have the opportunity to reduce bullying in their child's school, they are more motivated to support the effort. With these data in hand, the school will have a treasure trove of connections to the community to tap into anytime it is needed.

The second group of assets is the community organizations themselves. A natural partnership for many schools is after-school care. Some elementary schools even have after-school programs within the school building itself. Regardless of the location, reaching out to before- and after-school child care centers to align bullying prevention efforts can further reinforce the lessons students are learning in the classroom. As described in their book *Beyond the Bake Sale*, Henderson et al. (2007) suggest that engaging the leaders of these organizations through observations with the school's teachers, attending professional development sessions to improve their teaching skills, sharing data, and educating the after-school staff on the school's curriculum can lead to greater alignment between in-school and after-school curricula.

Instead of students practicing their social-emotional skills and strategies in just the school setting, there is a continuity of language and practices that extends to child care centers and even the home. This continuity of bullying prevention best practices can lead to students truly having a comprehensive system that protects them from bullying. Practically speaking, including leaders from the child care centers or other youth organizations (e.g., Boys and Girls Club) into your bullying prevention team at the school level can truly be transformational. Child care providers often have a different lens through which they view students. They may have less of a focus on academics and a greater focus on leadership skills, good sportsmanship, and prosocial skills. This being the case, they have insights into strategies that may be more effective for students in your school. It is important to note that when academic or behavioral data on specific students are being discussed, community and family members should not be involved due to privacy concerns.

When students *are* involved in bullying, there are a myriad of resources available to schools as a means of support. Depending on your community, mental health services or offices may be available for more severe cases of bullying. These services can even be covered by Medicaid in certain circumstances. Another potential option for more intensive supports is to research nearby universities and colleges that have child-counseling programs. Advanced-level courses will often require that graduate students receive experience providing mental health services for youth in a supervised setting. The best part about this option is that it is typically free for the school because universities and colleges are in need of youth to serve.

Bullying does not just occur in schools or online, especially so for secondary school students. Access to parks, shopping centers, and other common youth gathering spaces allow for autonomy from adults and thus increased opportunities to engage in bullying that goes unnoticed. So how do you know what businesses or organizations to reach out to? Use your screening survey to ask students where they spend time with friends outside of school and home. Another option is to reach out to your families to get an idea of where their children go during their free time outside the home. Once you know this information, providing something as simple as a 1-hour training on recognizing the signs of bullying and on how to intervene to employees of these businesses and organizations can support greater safety throughout the entire community. Giving employees and security personnel the language and responses used in the school setting can instill greater confidence in how to intervene when bullying occurs. Moreover, there is a greater likelihood that the safety of the target of bullying is supported until they are able to return to a trusted adult.

Finally, there is another way of partnering both with families and the community. This is accomplished by allowing community services to be provided within the school building itself. If you have ever worked at or had a child who attended a community school, this is the model they often adopt. Essentially, any community service that would typically be available by driving to a standalone building is provided to some degree within the school building or campus. These services can include businesses, social service agencies, health agencies, youth development organizations, and support groups. For example, some schools also serve as the community food bank; provide onsite vision, medical, and dental services; and allow donations of school supplies to go directly to their own students. When schools double as a hub for these community needs, it can increase the likelihood that when families enter the school building they will view it as an inviting place. Then, once they are in our buildings, we are able to connect with them to support the academic and behavioral needs of their children.

Mapping Community Assets

In the past several pages, we have given many examples of community assets that may exist and how they can contribute to building a positive, inclusive culture in your school. To begin taking action in your specific setting, it is crucial to engage in a process called asset mapping. The basic idea of asset mapping is take stock of the resources in and around your school. When creating your asset map, keep in mind the core components of CBP. To begin, have your implementation team serve as the group to engage in the asset mapping process. This team will already have knowledge of effective teaming practices and the use of data to inform decision making.

The first step in creating a community asset map is to communicate the purpose and need for the work to the bullying prevention implementation team. As with every large endeavor to prevent bullying, utilizing the broad skillset of your bullying prevention implementation team will support the sustainability and effectiveness of your efforts. Utilizing data, you can demonstrate the need for a community asset map (e.g., families not attending training nights) and explain how creating the map will bridge that gap. Once the asset map is completed, the implementation team can update the map on a regular basis so that when barriers and opportunities arise, the team can quickly access existing community resources.

The second step of developing a community asset map is to brainstorm the categories of resources from which your school could benefit. Again, it is helpful to use the data you have collected to guide some of this brainstorming. For example, if you review your bullying screening data and find that one of the most common reasons students are bullied is because they wear the same, unwashed clothes to school almost every day, the team can begin considering organizations and businesses that could help. They may include clothing donation centers or nonprofits and businesses that make donations of appliances like washers and dryers.

Once you have developed a list of community assets, the third step is to go online to a website like Google Maps or Bing Maps. In the search bar, type in the keywords for these different resources. Check that the current location is centered on your school. What will pop up are all of the nearby community organizations that provide these resources. Using the previous example of clothing, typing "kids clothes" into Google Maps centered in the Denver metro area yields multiple small and chain clothing stores in the area. In a more rural area, the options will likely be more limited; however, even if there is just one chain clothing or big-box store nearby, it may be able to provide resources (see Table 5.3 for an example using a rural location). A search on Google Maps for "appliance donation" in the Denver metro area finds a similar number of results, including popular donation organizations and chain retailers. All of these businesses can be considered when attempting to partner with them to support students.

The fourth step is to document all of the community assets your team finds. Documentation can be done in varying ways. A community asset map does not *have* to be a geographical map. In fact, it is likely easier to search and find potential supporting businesses by organizing the assets in a chart. If you do decide to create a geographic map, Google Maps allows you to save locations with unique labels (e.g., food banks) and access them as bookmarks. It can be helpful to have a map with the school and several community organizations printed as a handout that can quickly

TABLE 5.3. Example of Asset Mapping

School: Paola High School
Location: 401 Angela St., Paola Kansas 66071

Business name	Service	Location	Contact
Agape Christian Church Food Pantry	Food	305 S 2nd St E, Louisburg, KS 66053 (13.4 miles)	(913) 837-5492
Big Brothers Big Sisters	Youth Services	905 E Wea St, Paola, KS 66071	(913) 294-4403
Elizabeth Layton Center	Behavioral Health Services	102 Baptiste Dr, Paola, KS 66071 (1.3 miles)	(913) 557-9096
Family Center Farm & Home	Home goods, clothing, (makes donations to the community)	808 Baptiste Dr, Paola, KS 66071 (0.7 miles)	(913) 370-7479
First Baptist Church Clothes Closet	Clothes	701 Brown Ave, Osawatomie, KS 66064 (8.3 miles)	(913) 755-1892
Miami County Fairgrounds	Space for events	401 Wallace Park Dr, Paola, KS 66071 (2.8 miles)	(913) 294-5090
Paola Pathways	Multi-use trail system for events/fun run/5K	19 E Peoria St, Paola, KS 66071 (1.6 miles)	(913) 259-3600
Two Boys & A Tee	Clothing	29796 Hedge Ln, Paola KS 66071 (1.0 miles)	(913) 259-8432
United Way of Miami County	Financial stability for families, health and education	PO Box 102, Paola, KS 66071	*www. unitedwaypaola.org/ contact-us*
Walmart	Clothing, food, home goods	310 Hedge Ln, Paola, KS 66071 (0.2 miles)	(913) 294-5400

be provided to families. If you opted for a chart of resources, this chart can be also be provided to families in need.

Once you have your list of organizations and their contact information, the fifth step is to use your data-based problem-solving process to determine the current needs in your school. Continuing with our previous example on clothing, a bullying prevention implementation team considers two possible solutions that included groups in the community. First, the team decides that the school could begin the process of soliciting gently used clothes from local donation centers and clothing stores. The second option is to reach out to organizations that may be able to donate a washer and dryer to the school. During the discussion on the second option, the school custodian, who is a member of the implementation team, informs everyone that there is an unused washer and dryer hook-up in the school's basement. So all the team would need to do is to move the donated washer and dryer to the school and make them available to the families of students who are being bullied so that they have the option of washing clothes at the school during the day.

The final step in the process of community asset mapping is to make contact with these community organizations to discuss potential partnerships. Given all of the daily duties that come with working in a school, time is a precious commodity. In an effort to be as efficient as possible, create a form letter from the school that can be emailed to selected organizations and develop talking points for reaching out by phone. Anyone on the bullying prevention implementation team, with just a little bit of practice, can learn the basics of reaching out to the community for support. And sometimes all it takes is one phone call or email to start a long-lasting partnership that can benefit your students for years to come.

STUDENT VOICE IN BULLYING PREVENTION

Students are on the front lines of bullying. They are the ones who see and hear bullying that adults can miss. In fact, some research suggests that even though the classroom is one of the most common locations for bullying to occur, adults often underreport the prevalence rate of bullying compared to their students (Bradshaw, Sawyer, & O'Brennan, 2007) This suggests that there is a gap between what adults see and understand about bullying in our schools and what is actually happening. If we as educators do not include or value the voice of our students in our bullying prevention efforts, then we will continually struggle to bridge this gap.

Developing Bullying Prevention Strategies

Unfortunately, the research on including student voice in bullying prevention is scant at best (Cross, Lester, Barnes, Cardoso, & Hadwen, 2015). A small handful of studies have attempted to implement bullying prevention strategies that focus on elevating student voice. In their study on using student voice to respond to bullying in middle school, Shriberg and colleagues (2017) had seventh-grade students form a student leadership group with the primary purpose of developing bullying prevention solutions for their school. The students partnered with teachers in discuss bullying prevention ideas, such as placing Post-it notes on peers' lockers with a positive message and presenting anti-bullying messages to younger students. At the end of the study, the students who participated in this group reported that they felt the student leadership team was valuable, a finding that aligns with other studies showing that students truly want to be involved in reducing bullying (Berne, Frisén, & Oskarsson, 2020).

Several comments from students involved in the Shriberg and colleagues (2017) study provide a good lesson when considering how to include student voice in your school's bullying prevention best practices. When asked if students in the school are more empowered to make a change when bullying occurs, several students reported that those in the leadership group itself felt more empowered, but that this feeling likely did not extend to the entire school population. This result suggests that when using a student leadership group to prevent bullying, there needs to be a direct connection back to the entire student body, which could include ideas that create a more positive school climate or directly teaching students about bullying prevention. Another common theme from students who participated was that they appreciated the opportunity to partner with their teachers in developing ideas for bullying prevention in the school. It is clear that when we treat students as partners in the fight against bullying, everyone benefits.

The purpose of the student leadership group in the Shriberg and colleagues (2017) study was to support the creation of student-led prevention ideas. Although this approach is fine for getting unique and targeted solutions for a specific school, students can also have an impact in other areas of a CBP approach. Depending on which evidence-based bullying prevention curriculum is being implemented at your school as a universal support, students can partner with teachers to deliver the lessons to their peers or students in lower grades. When students provide appropriate real-life examples, more engaging, tangible connections are created for other students. Although this study focused on students in middle school, students spanning nearly every grade level can contribute their voices to prevent bullying in schools.

To more effectively use student voice, one option is to also have students recognize other students for engaging in positive behaviors that are incompatible with bullying. In fact, there is a program called Stand for Courage that uses this approach. The idea behind Stand for Courage is that students who "stands for courage" are recognized by their peers rather than by adults. A student-led team made up of members nominated by their peers supports the implementation of the work. The student team creates nomination boxes where staff and students are able to nominate another student they have seen engage in prosocial behavior, such as supporting the target of bullying. Positive reinforcement strategies that are developed by the student team are then provided to those students who were nominated on a regular basis. The age range for the Stand for Courage program is grades 6 through 12, a range that is in line with research suggesting that as children mature, they often desire greater autonomy, even when it comes to bullying prevention (Yeager et al., 2015). Although Stand for Courage is not an evidence-based program for bullying prevention, it does provide a wealth of free resources on its website (*www.standforcourage.org*), including an implementation kit.

In Figure 5.1 (on page 94), we provide a family and community partnerships practice profile to operationally define this component of CBP.

Core Component: Family and Community Partnerships		
Definition: The school intentionally builds and maintains partnerships with all families and the community to prevent bullying and support students.		
Expected Use	Developmental Use	Unacceptable Use
The school has an inclusive culture that considers equity when making schoolwide decisions.	The school does not actively create an inclusive culture and/or does not consider equity when making schoolwide decisions.	The school does not have an inclusive culture for families.
The school has multiple methods for two-way communication with families.	The school has limited two-way communication methods with families.	The school engages in one-way communication with families.
The school involves all families by actively working to build their self-efficacy on bullying prevention, including families in decision making, and having a policy on engaging families.	The school involves families; however, it only passively works to build family self-efficacy around bullying prevention, does not include families in decision making, or does not have a policy on engaging families.	The school does not actively involve families.
The school partners with community organizations to strategically support bullying prevention.	The school engages with community organizations but without a clear connection to overall bullying prevention efforts.	The school does not partner with community organizations in a meaningful way.
The school provides structured, meaningful opportunities for students to participate in bullying prevention efforts.	Student perspectives are heard, but not sought out by the school in a structured and meaningful way.	The school rarely seeks out or uses student voice in bullying prevention efforts.

FIGURE 5.1. Family and community partnerships practice profile.

CHAPTER 6

Data-Based Decision Making

We all use data in life to inform decisions we make. Our bank account balance lets us know if we splurge on an item, the speedometer informs us if we should slow down on the road, and our fitness app tells us if we're meeting our daily exercise goal. These data are tied to an outcome we have in mind: we check our account to stay under budget, we watch our speedometer to ensure we get to work safely without a ticket, and so forth. Similarly, school teams use certain data to inform their outcomes related to bullying prevention.

Data-based decision making is defined as a process of using relevant and accurate data to inform important decisions or actions (Kratochwill, Elliott, & Callan-Stoiber, 2002; McIntosh & Goodman, 2016; Shinn, 2008). To guarantee effective data-based decision making, we advocate for the use of the problem-solving model (PSM; Deno, 2016; Good et al., 2002; Harlacher, Potter, & Weber, 2015; Shinn, 2008). The PSM is a four-step process in which educators define a problem clearly and then evaluate the impact of a solution for that defined problem. By using the PSM, schools can rely on objective, rather than subjective, information (Deno, 2003; 2016; Hosp, 2008; Shinn, 2008). Further, the PSM is helpful because it can be applied not only to individual students, but also to groups of students and at a systems or schoolwide level (Harlacher et al., 2015).

THE PROBLEM-SOLVING MODEL

The PSM has four steps: (1) Problem Identification, (2) Problem Analysis, (3) Plan Identification and Implementation, and (4) Plan Evaluation (see Figure 6.1). The PSM can be used by individual educators, but we discuss it here within the context of a team.

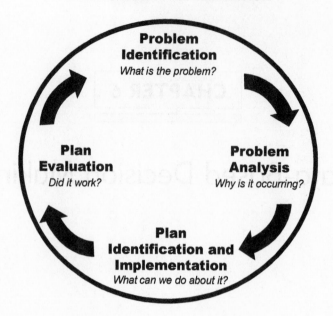

FIGURE 6.1. Problem-solving model.

Step 1: Problem Identification

In Step 1 of the PSM, educators determine if a problem actually exists and if it's significant enough to warrant solving (Harlacher et al., 2015; Hosp, Huddle, Ford, & Hensely, 2016; Shinn, 2008). To do so, educators define problems as the difference between an expected performance and an observed performance (please note that we also refer to *performance* as *result* or *criterion* throughout this chapter). For example, one can compare one's speed while driving, 27 miles per hour (mph), to the speed limit, which is 25 mph. In this example, a gap of 2 mph over the speed limit is likely not a problem; however, if one were driving 15 mph over the limit, this could be a problem (you'd likely know by the sirens and blinking lights behind you!)

Part of identifying if a problem exists is making sure that we collect the correct type of data. In Step 1 of the PSM, teams use screening data or general outcome data. Screening data refer to broad measures that indicate the risk status of students or potential areas of concern for schools (Hosp, 2008; McIntosh & Goodman, 2016). Just as the check-engine light in your car, a fever, or high blood pressure signifies a red flag, teams use similar educational data in Step 1 to alert the school to various issues. If a problem is found, they then proceed to Step 2 of the PSM to dig deeper. It's best to use broader measures in Step 1 to overidentify potential issues, followed by a process of verification to confirm that a problem actually exists. If you've experienced your car's check engine light turning on, you're aware of your own verification processes, such as listening for weird noises or checking for the smell of oil burning, to make sure there's a problem.

For bullying prevention, teams using the PSM can begin with a simple question. For example, *What is the rate of bullying that is occurring?* or *Do we have a positive school climate?* Screening data are gathered to answer the question, and the results are judged against the desired criterion. In this case, a school could administer a bullying survey to students and determine the percentage of students that report being a target of bullying. For example, imagine that 42% of students report being a target in a middle school. That 42% is compared against a desired criterion of "no more than 20% of students will report being a target." With a difference between the observed result (42%) and the expected result (20%) of 22% of students, a team would conclude that a problem does exist, that it's large enough to warrant solving, and then proceed to Step 2.

Step 2: Problem Analysis

In Step 2, teams gather information to understand the context of the problem and determine what factors contribute to the problem. Specifically, they define the problem more clearly, examine and/or gather data about the context, and develop a working hypotheses as to why the problem exists. In short, they answer the question, "Why is the problem occurring?" From the information gathered, school teams develop a solution that is implemented in Step 3 of the PSM. Step 2 involves the "nitty-gritty," as educators use diagnostic measures and other sources of information to understand the nature of the problem. Examples of diagnostic data include specific assessments or tests, reviews of records or archived data, interviews with relevant parties, and observations (Hosp, 2008).

On the basis of the gathered data, teams develop a precise description of the problem (as opposed to the general description in Step 1; Newton, Todd, Algozzine, Horner, & Algozzine, 2009; Newton, Horner, Algozzine, Todd, & Algozzine, 2012). Educators, accordingly, define the problem more precisely by answering *W-questions*: who, what, when, where, and why. For example, a team may identify an increase in referrals for bullying in the problem identification step. In Step 2, they examine existing information and/or gather additional information, including who is being bullied; who is doing the bullying; what type of bullying is occurring; and when, where, and why it is occurring. We offer examples of general versus precise statements in Table 6.1. Although a complete problem statement includes the 5 Ws, in our experience some teams can get stuck trying to define all of the nuances within a statement. If your team finds itself getting stuck for a long

TABLE 6.1. General versus Precise Problem Statements

General problem statement	Precise problem statement
27% of students reported being bullied online.	27% of students in the sixth grade reporting being cyberbullied with negative and crude comments from peers on social media. These posts are made mostly during lunchtime The perpetrators receive likes and comments from peers on the posts.
A student is being bullied once a week.	The student is physically bullied by a classmate while walking home from school, and it occurs on school grounds. The bullying has occurred only on Mondays and Tuesdays. The perpetrator gets personal items from the target, such as a jacket, beanie, or video game.
A group of students are bullying a classmate.	A group of 10 sophomores are spreading rumors about 3 freshmen when talking with peers throughout the day and sending group texts.

time on defining the problem, try moving forward to Step 3 and construct a solution. If the team is unable to do so, the members can return to Step 2 and will likely have a better idea of what additional information to gather. The steps in the PSM are not linear and strict; it's perfectly fine to move back to an earlier step if the team doesn't have enough information to perform the step accurately.

As part of forming a more precise problem statement, teams gather information on alterable variables related to the problem. Alterable variables are variables that educators have the ability to change. To focus on alterable variables that can inform a viable solution, teams will gather data across four specific domains: the *instruction, curriculum, environment,* and *learner* (ICEL; Christ, 2008; Harlacher, Sakelaris, & Kattelman, 2013). Instruction is *how* content is taught; it's the methods used to teach particular content to students, staff, and families. Curriculum refers to *what* is being taught. It may be a boxed curriculum (e.g., Second Step) or a best practice (e.g., schoolwide behavior expectations). The environment is *where* the problem is occurring, including the nature of interactions among the people in the setting and the expectations and routines used in the setting. The learner is the student(s) or broadly, the recipient of the instruction and curriculum. In the context of bullying prevention, the focus is on the students involved in bullying, be they as targets, perpetrators, or bystanders.

The general notion is that bullying within a school can be reduced or effectively eliminated if the instruction, curriculum, and environment all work together to support a positive climate for learners (i.e., students). Accordingly, teams generate questions to identify the domain in which the breakdown exists. Generally speaking, teams want to consider the fidelity of implementation of the universal supports as a reason why bullying may be occurring within a school. For example, if it's found that students are reporting greater rates of bullying in the hallways, is it because further instruction is needed for students to know the difference between bullying and conflict? Is the environment such that there is inadequate adult supervision in the hallway? In asking such questions, educators are generating hypotheses that can be examined. They may collect additional data to confirm or disconfirm their hunches about the problem. We provide a list of possible questions that can be explored when examining the context for bullying prevention in Table 6.2.

We encourage educators to spend sufficient time on Step 2. Rushing to implement a solution may lead to a mismatch between the problem and the solution. How does one know they're done

We frame problems within the structure of ICEL so that we have control over changing it. For example, if we explain that an increase in bullying is due to the media or parents' attitudes, then we are left powerless to change the situation. But if we understand that the increase in bullying is due to a breakdown somewhere between the instruction around school expectations, the curriculum, and/or the environment of the school setting, then we can locate that breakdown, adjust it, and rectify the increase in bullying. It may be tempting to focus on something about the students, such as poor attitudes, judgments on parent involvement, or even the video games that students play. However, these are variables outside of educators' control and thus inalterable by educators. If educators have trouble focusing on alterable variables, it may be helpful for teams to analyze their thinking as they share it by categorizing reasons into "alterable" versus "inalterable." A T-chart (with one column listing unalterable variables and another column listing alterable variables) can be used to organize initial thinking.

TABLE 6.2. Questions and Variables to Assess Within ICEL

Domain	Question	Variable to assess
Instruction	• Were the expectations and response strategy directly taught to students?	Fidelity to lesson plan; Explicitness of skill
	• Do students have fluency with understanding the difference between bullying and conflict?	The number of opportunities to practice
	• Do staff members intervene in aggression and reteach before it rises to the level of bullying?	Corrective feedback provided
Curriculum	• Is the curriculum evidence based?	Score on a formal selection measure for curricula
	• Are skills regularly reviewed with students?	Frequency of reviews
	• Do students have regular times to practice appropriate ways to respond to bullying?	Frequency of repetition with skill
Environment	• Is the environment supportive and positive?	Praise to corrective feedback ratio; Fidelity to use of praise
	• Do adults immediately intervene when they witness bullying?	Fidelity to discipline process; Adult skill demonstration
	• Are there sufficient reminders of bullying prevention and schoolwide expectations? Are expectations and bullying prevention aspects visible and clear?	Precorrection used; Visual prompts used to remind student of expectations
	• Are healthy relationships established among students or among teachers and students?	Quality of relationship; Use of strategies to create relationships
Learner	• Can students verbalize and perform the expectations and respond fluently?	Mastery of skill on instructional hierarchy
	• Were the lesson plans developmentally and culturally appropriate for the student?	Match between cultural background/ student need of instruction
	• Are bullying prevention supports differentiated based on learner characteristics?	Match between supports and need

with this step? Typically, it's when the problem is so well understood that a solution is obvious. A solution should jump out at you and if it doesn't, then continue to gather or review more data until it does.

Step 3: Plan Identification and Implementation

Based on the information gathered in Step 2, teams then work collaboratively to develop and implement a comprehensive solution (also referred to as a plan) to address the problem. Teams anchor their solutions around what skill(s) need to be taught (or retaught) to students, and then adjust the context to ensure use of that skill (Newton et al., 2009; 2012). All solutions include four components: teaching strategies, prevention strategies, response strategies, and evaluation procedures. *Teaching strategies* are the methods used to teach someone a new skill or behavior. *Prevention strategies* are used to prompt the desired skill/behavior and to offset inaccurate use of the skill/behavior. *Response strategies* are used to reinforce the desired skill/behavior and to efficiently correct any misuse or unwanted skill/behavior. *Evaluation procedures* are the methods used to guarantee that fidelity to the plan is achieved and that the solution is beneficial to the staff, students, and/or families (Crone & Horner, 2015; Dunlap et al., 2010; Newton et al., 2009, 2012; Simonsen et al., 2021).

As an example, imagine a school identifies that students are bullying each other frequently during unstructured activities. Teams can first teach students more respectful and safer interactions as well as a way to respond to incidents of bullying (these are the teaching strategies). Educators then modify the environment to support students in using those skills, such as providing reminders or visual prompts (these are prevention strategies), as well as praising students for use of the skill and outlining corrective steps when students use the skills inaccurately (these are the response strategies). By framing the solution around a skill or behavior that needs to be taught or strengthened, the solution follows effective instructional practices (Newton et al., 2009,2012; Simonsen et al., 2021).

This solution frame is most often used for individual students, but we find it's a good instructional approach for the staff as well (Harlacher & Rodriguez, 2018). As one reads the corresponding questions related to the domains in Table 6.2, it's clear that adjustments to the environment and system are critical in developing effective solutions or individualized support plans. Whether it's for one student or all students within a school, the environment is adjusted to prompt and acknowledge use of the taught skill(s) (Crone & Horner, 2015). For schoolwide issues, there's often a need to adjust systems to better support the staff so that they can adopt and implement certain practices and gather relevant data more efficiently (McIntosh & Goodman, 2016; Sugai & Horner, 2006). Additionally, the staff may need training and coaching on new systems or routines. When the PSM is used with one student, there may not need to be wholesale changes to the system, but there are frequently new routines that the staff are asked to implement to support a student (Harlacher et al., 2015). One way to view solutions is that the *prevention* and *response* strategies are the adjustments to systems or routines, whereas the *teaching* strategies indicate what skills are taught to students or what new procedures are asked of staff members (Crone & Horner, 2015). We provide examples in Table 6.3 of how solutions for individual students or systems differ. Notice that within each solution, a skill is taught to a student or group of people, and the environment is adjusted to ensure its use.

Evaluation Procedures

The final piece of any solution is the evaluation procedure that is used. There are generally two types of data to examine: fidelity data and outcome data (Newton et al., 2009; Shinn, 2008). Educators gather fidelity data to determine if the solution is implemented as intended. To accomplish this, educators can use direct measures of fidelity, such as observations, or they can rely on indirect measures, such as self-reports by the staff, attendance, or the completion of work products (Harlacher & Rodriguez, 2018).

When selecting the outcome data used to analyze a solution's progress, educators can use a variety of data, including formative assessments and progress monitoring tools. Formative assessments refer to any assessment that can track progress in a sensitive manner, such as self-reports of

TABLE 6.3. Examples of Solutions for Individual Students versus Systems

Element	Individual Students	Systems
Teaching strategies: What skills need to be used by student(s) or staff to solve the problem?	Student is retaught to use the schoolwide bullying prevention strategy.	Teachers are asked to use active supervision during passing periods to increase supervision and manage bullying. Staff members are taught the method and provided practice opportunities.
Prevention strategies: What can be put in place to prompt the expected skill and prevent the unwanted skill?	Student is verbally reminded of the strategy prior to being in unstructured settings.	Teachers are reminded of the strategy with a morning email and prompt when each bell rings at the end of each period.
Response strategies: How can the new skills be reinforced? How can errors be addressed or corrected?	Student is praised when use of the strategy is witnessed. Student also practices method and receives praise. Misuse of the skill is corrected, and student is asked to repeat the skill.	Administration provides acknowledgment and feedback on the use of active supervision.
Evaluation procedures: What data can be used to examine the fidelity of the plan implementation and its benefit to students or staff?	Student self-reports use of skill as a fidelity measure. Student reports incidents of bullying as measure of outcome.	Fidelity data are the number of staff members observed using active supervision (as part of the observations by administration). Outcome is the number of bullying incidents reported by students.

bullying or teacher-created assessments. Progress monitoring tools have demonstrated reliability and validity and are used to measure progress toward a certain mastery, outcome, or standard, such as curriculum-based measurement (Hosp, 2008). When selecting what data will be used for progress monitoring, we suggest using the data that first indicated a problem in Step 1. Because the problem was quantified as the gap between the expected and observed criterion, it can also be used to check that the problem is resolved. There are times when it makes sense to include additional data beyond the screening data from Step 1, particularly if the problem is more nuanced or isolated than what screening data can capture. For example, educators may identify that the rate of overall bullying has decreased, but they may also want to know if the rate of bullying in a specific location in the school has decreased.

Goals

Educators will want to write specific goals when developing a solution in order to know exactly when the problem is resolved (Deno, 2016; Newton et al., 2012). When a problem is resolved, educators can then reallocate any resources devoted to the solution to other problems or pressing matters. We suggest that each goal include four components: who, what, how much, and when/where (Simonsen & Myers, 2015). The *who* refers to the person or persons meeting the goal. The *what* is the behavior or skill that is being taught or the area of focus. *How much* is the criteria to be reached with the behavior or skill, and the *when/where* are the conditions under which the behavior or skill should be performed. With all four components, educators will know precisely when the goal is reached. Educators will also identify the data source to gauge if the goal is being reached. For example, a school may write goals such as "When confronted with a bullying situation, students will use the bullying response strategy every time (as measured by self-report on a survey)" or "During each passing period, all teachers will stand outside their doorway and use active supervision (as measured by observation by administration)."

Step 4: Plan Evaluation

In this final step of the PSM, educators analyze the gathered fidelity and outcome data to determine if the plan was implemented as intended and if the plan met the identified goal, respectively (Harlacher et al., 2015; McIntosh & Goodman, 2016). Regardless of whether they're working to resolve a problem for one student or an entire system, teams first need to know the extent to which the plan was followed. This allows teams to determine if the results of the plan are due to the plan itself or something else. To illustrate, imagine that your check-engine light came on because your car was leaking oil due to a faulty seal. You bring the car to the shop and are told that their plan is to replace the seal. Despite receiving this information, you want to wait until your next paycheck before implementing this plan. Several days later, the check-engine light turns off even though you never replaced the faulty seal. Given that you didn't implement your plan as intended, it is surprising (and very suspicious) that the light is now off. Is the problem really fixed, or could it show up again later on in an inopportune time? Without having fidelity data to check that the plan was implemented as intended, we can be left feeling unsure as to how a problem was resolved.

Armed with fidelity data, teams can evaluate the outcome of a plan (Harlacher et al., 2013). Fidelity results can be high, indicating a plan was implemented as intended, or low, indicating a plan was not implemented well. Relatedly, outcome data can be categorized as high, indicating the plan was successful in resolving the issue, or low, indicating the plan was not effective in reaching the desired result.

These two dimensions of fidelity and outcome data create four possible results, which we've illustrated in Figure 6.2 (IRIS Center, 2021). If fidelity was high and the goal was reached, then the focus can be on developing a plan to fade out the solution or a way to decrease the use of the plan while maintaining the results. If fidelity was high but the outcome was not reached, then we can be confident the plan didn't work. It's back to Step 2, problem analysis, to gather more information to adjust the plan. Our hypothesis wasn't accurate, so we need to modify the current one. If fidelity was low and the outcome was not reached, this makes sense. It is a logical conclusion since we didn't implement the plan yet, so we need to improve fidelity and implement the plan we had originally intended. Teams can examine barriers to Step 3, plan implementation, and adjust accordingly. Finally, with low fidelity but a successful outcome, we can consider ourselves lucky! We don't know how the problem fixed itself, but it's best for us to consider if the problem still actually exists and to reexamine our use of problem identification or problem analysis to discover where we may have been amiss. As one can see, Step 4 can be a fairly iterative process, as teams consider fidelity and outcome data in tandem. The fidelity assessment for Comprehensive Bullying Prevention related to all five components can be found in Appendix B.

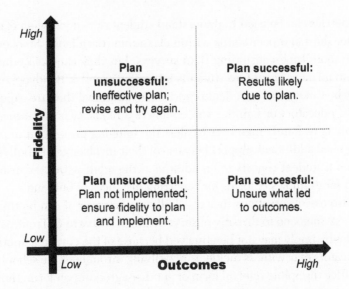

FIGURE 6.2. Using fidelity and outcome data in plan evaluation.

MEASURING BULLYING PREVALENCE

Before we discuss the PSM within the context of bullying prevention, let us first share ways to measure students' involvement with bullying. Schools will want to know which students and what percentage of the student population are involved in bullying. In doing so, they can determine if they have a systemwide issue or if there are individual students that need support. Further, they'll want to identify the data sources most suitable for their questions and their local context.

For measuring students' status with bullying, schools can (1) survey students directly with self-report methods; (2) ask a third party, such as parents, teachers, or classmates; (3) or observe the bullying directly. These methods all have their pros and cons. Surveying students directly is perhaps the most efficient and direct method to determine a student's involvement in bullying (Cornell & Bandyopadhyay, 2009). However, with self-report, students must understand the definition of bullying in order to accurately report it. Without this understanding, targets of bullying may overreport rates of bullying, and perpetrators may underreport their involvement (Branson & Cornell, 2009; Cornell & Bandyopadhyay, 2009). Schools can develop their own surveys, in which they ask students if they are a target or perpetrator and the number of instances they have encountered. The survey can also include questions about specific types of bullying that students experience. Schools can even ask these questions without directly calling it bullying. For example, students can be asked if they have been repeatedly physically assaulted by a peer to assess physical bullying, or they can be asked if they have been called names or made fun of by peers on more than one occasion to assess verbal bullying.

Asking a third party may lead to underreporting of bullying, as teachers or families may not witness certain incidents of bullying and therefore be inaccurate in their reporting (Rupp et al., 2018). This is particularly a consideration for older students for whom the bullying may be more covert and hidden from adults (Juvonen, Nishima, & Graham, 2001). Certain peer nominations methods or sociometrics can be used to understand student dynamics when classmates are asked to report on relationships and peer status within classroom (Bacallao & Smokowski, 2010). Using these methods are more time-consuming than surveys, but they can help educators understand social dynamics and nuances about how students interact (Cornell & Bandyopadhyay, 2009). Additionally, there may be times when a student reports to an adult that they are experiencing bullying. In these situations, educators or families can complete a *request for assistance* form. This form enables staff members or family members to alert the bullying prevention implementation team that a student may need additional support because of their involvement in bullying. This form can be completed when a student reports to an adult or if the adult witnesses instances of bullying. Refer to Chapter 3 for examples of forms for reporting instances of bullying.

Schools can also use observations to assess bullying; however, it can be time-consuming and resource-laden to ask someone to directly observe students (Alberto & Troutman, 2013). As mentioned, some incidents simply may not be observed because of the covert or subtle nature of bullying. That said, educators may witness incidents of bullying throughout the school day. In turn, they can complete an office discipline referral form or another agreed-upon form, thus documenting its occurrence and providing data for school teams to use.

In Table 6.4, we offer a few examples of measures that can be used to screen for bullying as part of the problem identification step in the PSM. We selected these measures for a variety of reasons, including their helpfulness, cost, and ease of use. We do not advocate or endorse any of these tools over other measures and instead encourage schools to use measures that suit the developmental and cultural needs of their students. The Center for Disease Control has an extensive compendium of bullying measures. We encourage our readers to review the compendium, as it provides detailed information on these measures and lists questions to assess victimization, cyberbullying, bystander involvement, conflict, and attitudes toward sexual identity (Hamburger, Basile, & Vivolo, 2011; visit *www.cdc.gov/violenceprevention/pdf/bullycompendium-a.pdf*).

TABLE 6.4. Measures of Involvement in Bullying

Name	Type	Description and considerations
Revised Olweus Bully/Victim Questionnaire[a]	Self-report survey for all grade levels	• 39-item survey that is well established and researched • Requires purchase to use
Youth Risk Behavior Surveillance System[b]	Self-report survey for middle and high school	• Extensive survey of risk behaviors, but schools can select items related to bullying • Free resource • Includes Spanish version
Swearer Bully Survey[c]	Surveys for grades 3–5 and 6–12; teacher and parent surveys also available	• Questions related to victims, witnesses, those who bully others, and attitudes toward bullying • Short forms available
Modified Peer Nomination Survey[d]	Peer-nomination format that measures a range of behaviors for ages 10–14	• 26-item survey that includes a victimization survey and aggression survey

Note. [a]Olweus (2006); [b]CDC (2021); [c]Swearer Bully Survey (2021); [d]Perry, Kusel, and Perry (1988).

Considerations of Confidentiality

One concern when measuring the risk status of students is preserving their anonymity and confidentiality. Schools can survey students, but some students may be hesitant to report or share information accurately if their names are included in the survey (Dillman & Smyth, 2014). Schools can allow for anonymity, which can lead to more accurate rates of bullying and victimization in their sites (Cornell & Bandyopadhyay, 2009). However, anonymity would obviously prevent schools from knowing who is involved in bullying and thus being unable to intervene. To manage this situation, schools can offer students a voluntary option to share their names if they report that they are involved in bullying, whether as a target or perpetrator. They can also offer resources and ways to support students if they identify themselves as being involved in bullying. For example, schools can share information from their policy on how they can seek support from staff members, offer anonymous hotlines to call, or identify staff members they can contact for support. Schools can also use other sources of data (e.g., office referrals, teacher or family requests) to identify and support individual students with bullying. We encourage schools to check with their district office and state department of education regarding policies on surveying students or gathering data on bullying. Some states may have policies detailing what questions can or cannot be asked of students and the use of anonymity and confidentiality.

APPLICATION OF THE PSM

In this section, we illustrate using the PSM for both systems and individual problem solving. When implementing bullying prevention, schools will want to monitor the overall prevalence of bullying in their settings, which allows them to have a pulse on systemic issues related to bullying. Additionally, they can use the PSM to provide support for students who are involved in bullying.

Systems Problem Solving

Let's take the example of a rural middle school that administers a survey to its student population about their experiences with bullying. In Step 1, the bullying prevention implementation team starts with the question "Have you been the target of bullying in the past 2 months?" The team has determined that if it has 15% or fewer students reporting bullying, then it can support individual students with their tiered supports (their rationale is that no more than 15% of students' needs could be managed using their Tier 2 and Tier 3 supports). Twenty-seven percent of students report being the target of bullying, thus indicating that the team has a schoolwide issue on its hands. The team identifies the gap between the observed performance and the expected performance as 27% − 15% = 12%, and determine they have a problem significant enough to address.

In Step 2, the team works to identify a more precise problem statement. They want to know the type of bullying that's occurring, who is being bullied, and where and when it is taking place. After gathering the relevant data, shown in Figure 6.3, the team determines that students primarily experience verbal bullying, that sixth and seventh graders experience bullying most often, and that the bullying occurs primarily in the cafeteria. Students reporting perpetrating bullying are mostly eighth graders (about 70%). Additionally, there is not a consistent time that bullying occurs, other than that it occurs during school hours.

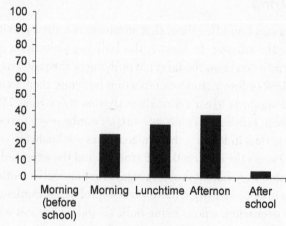

FIGURE 6.3. Reported bullying incidents by type, grade level, location, and time of incident.

In determining why the bullying is occurring, the team theorizes that it is motivated by receiving peer attention. After interviewing students and staff members about what they've witnessed, the team learns that bullying typically involves being called names or insulted, and that it occurs in the presence of other people in the cafeteria. It also includes forms of relational bullying, in which some students are excluded from sitting with others during lunch or during passing periods. The bullying always occurs in the presence of bystanders, and students report that they often laugh and encourage the bullying. The team synthesizes all this information, and develops the following problem statement: *In the cafeteria, eighth graders are verbally bullying younger students and excluding them from sitting with others. Other students observe and laugh/encourage the bullying; thus the function of the bullying appears to be to receive peer attention.*

With a precise problem statement outlined, the team then examines the factors related to the instruction, curriculum, and environment for information that would help in finding a solution. By reviewing various data sources (i.e., lesson plans used to teach students about respect, the schedules of the staff, the response to incidents of bullying), the team determines that students did not receive enough examples of respectful versus disrespectful behavior as part of the teaching of the schoolwide expectations, particularly as they related to the cafeteria setting. It also determines that several students did not use the bullying response strategy when they saw bullying; instead of telling peers to stop targeting others, they nervously laughed. The team also identifies that staff members are providing enough active supervision when they are in the cafeteria (students often use the cafeteria during passing periods or their free period). With a precise statement and enough information related to why the problem is occurring, the team is ready to move to Step 3 and plan the solution.

In Step 3, the team identifies aspects of the solution related to prevention strategies, teaching strategies, response strategies, and data evaluation (recall the frame of solutions in Table 6.3). First, the team identifies that reteaching of respect is important, particularly as it relates to the cafeteria. The school also hypothesizes that students need to use the bullying reponse strategy when others are not respectful of them. The team revises a lesson plan that was previously used and adds examples and nonexamples of respect related to the cafeteria setting, including how to use the response strategy appropriately. Students are taught the lesson in their respective classrooms, after which they are reminded prior to passing periods, lunch, or free periods (during which they may be in the cafeteria) to be respectful and to use the response strategy. In addition to the classroom teaching of respect, the counselors also provide classroom teachers with a 15-minute lesson each week on an aspect related to respect, such as respecting boundaries, respecting the beliefs of others, and respecting personal space. This lesson allows for more nuanced understanding of respect and how actions affect others, which make respect a more salient aspect of the school's culture.

The team also creates and displays new posters that illustrate being respectful and using the response strategy. Students see these posters each time they enter and exit the building. The school administrators also have daily announcements reminding students and the staff about the expectation. The staff follows active supervision strategies, thus providing reinforcement to students in the cafeteria. They also revise the school schedule so that two teachers are present in the cafeteria during lunch and during the afternoon free periods. The two staff members walk in a figure-eight loop in opposite directions, actively looking for respectful behavior and praising students for desired behavior. As an incentive, they meet at the apex of the figure eight, exchange pleasantries and chat, then continue on their loop until meeting again in the middle. Finally, students can earn two tokens for using respectful behavior at any time during their day (often students received one token for displaying any of the schoolwide expectations, but a bonus incentive was provided for the emphasis on respect).

To determine if the solution is being implemented as intended, the team chooses an indirect fidelity assessment in which staff members are asked the extent to which they are completing active supervision. To measure outcomes, the team decides to readminister the survey from Step 1, with a goal of 15% or less of students reporting being bullied. The team also wants to know if the staff feels that the plan is easy to follow and helpful, so they administer a two-item survey asking teachers to rate "How feasible is the plan to implement?" and "How helpful is the plan in reducing incidents of bullying?" The staff rates the plan on a scale of 1 to 5 (1 = not feasible or not helpful, 5 = very feasible or very helpful). With everything set, the team implements the plan as part of Step 3 of the PSM.

After several weeks implementing the plan, it is then evaluated in Step 4. The team examines fidelity data first and finds that 100% of staff are completing the active supervision procedures as outlined. They also note that all students from all grade levels were retaught the expectation of being respectful and the bullying response strategy, so the team is confident that they have implemented their solution. The team examines the results from another administration of the student survey, and finds that bullying rates have reduced to 17% (from 27% previously) after 2 weeks of implementing the plan.

Although the team is proud of its progress, it had not quite reached the goal of a bullying rate of less than 15%. Next, the team examines factors related to instruction, curriculum, and environment. Teachers reported using active supervision and not seeing active bullying or disrespect, so the staff surmises that students were hiding any disrespectful behavior or bullying that was occurring. To enlist more support from students, the team identifies a few students with good social standing to make videos further illustrating being respectful to each other. They also have classes nominate one student each week who is displaying respectful behavior, therein creating a list of students who can be recognized on Fridays by having their names announced schoolwide. The school also creates activities every other Friday in which students are paired up for 15–20 minutes with a student they do not know to interview one another and start a friendly relationship. The intention is to create a more accepting and prosocial culture in which respect and relationships among students are strengthened. The staff takes care that those students with known histories of bullying are not paired. These modifications result in less than 2% of students reporting bullying after 1 month with the plan. Table 6.5, summarizes the factors involved in the PSM when applied to systems-level bullying prevention.

Individual Student Problem Solving

In Step 1 of the PSM, schools assess students for their involvement in bullying to determine if they are in need of support. As an example, a high school surveys its students using questions similar to those in the Youth Risk Behavior Surveillance System questionnaire. In the survey, students are provided a code number to keep their responses confidential. In addition to questions about relationships among students, the survey asks the extent to which students are bullied on school property and via electronic methods (see Figure 6.4 for the questions used). Those students marking "yes" to either question then meet briefly with a counselor or teacher to confirm that they marked the survey accurately and to verify their involvement in bullying. The counselor is the sole staff person with access to the code numbers and is able to identify students who marked "yes."

TABLE 6.5. Use of PSM for Systems/Schoolwide Issues and Bullying Prevention

Step	Question	Data sources or action
Problem Identification	What is the percentage of students reporting being a target of bullying?	Examine indicators of bullying. Clarify if the issue is related to a few students or is reflective of a systems issue.
Problem Analysis	Why is the bullying occurring? What is the degree to which universal supports are used as intended?	Form a more precise problem statement and analyze the context, including the instruction, curriculum, environment, and learners (ICEL). Consider fidelity to universal supports as part of why the problem is occurring. Evaluate the extent to which universal supports are taught to and used by students.
Plan Identification and Implementation	What adjustments to instruction, curriculum, and environment will support learners/students? What can we do to resolve the problem?	Develop and implement a plan based on the hypothesis developed in the previous step. Adjust factors related to ICEL to reduce incidents of bullying, improve climate, and increase use of schoolwide expectations and bullying response strategy.
Plan Evaluation	Did we follow the plan? Did it work?	Examine fidelity to the plan. Administer initial indicator of bullying and check if problem is resolved.

The counselor also asks the student to identify the perpetrator if they are comfortable doing so, so that appropriate action can be taken for the perpetrator.

Once the team documents that students are involved in bullying, Step 2 of the PSM, problem analysis, begins. In this step, the bullying prevention implementation team examines the context and nature of the bullying. In determining why the bullying is occurring, the team gathers and reviews more information. Additionally, the team evaluates the extent to which the target uses the schoolwide response to bullying. The information gathered is then used to inform an individual-

---

The next two questions ask about bullying. Bullying is when one or more students tease, threaten, spread rumors about, hit, shove, or hurt another student over and over again. It is not bullying when two students of about the same strength or power argue or fight or tease each other in a friendly way.

During the past 12 months, have you ever been bullied on school property?

A. Yes   B. No

During the past 12 months, have you ever been electronically bullied? (Count being bullied through texting, Instagram, Facebook, or other social media.)

A. Yes   B. No

Note: Rather than use code numbers, schools can add language to anonymous surveys that asks students to share their names if they report being a target (e.g., "If you marked yes to either question, please write your name below if you would like to be contacted by a staff member").

FIGURE 6.4. Example of a bullying survey item for students.

ized support plan for the target in Step 3 of the PSM. In this step, the team can also develop an individualized support plan for the perpetrator and prevent future occurrences of bullying for both the target and the perpetrator. In Table 6.6 we offer questions for teams to explore in understanding the nature of why bullying is occurring for a given student. One can see that the questions involve assessing the degree to which the universal supports are used by the student and the extent to which they benefit the student. To be clear, if the target of bullying is not using the universal supports for bullying prevention, it does not mean that the bullying is their fault. The staff should be vigilant in ensuring that students who are targeted understand that they do not deserve to be bullied and the school can support them in protecting themselves.

To continue with our example of individual student bullying, the counselor interviews a sophomore, Jessie, who reports being bullied on the school survey. Once the student confirms she was a target of bullying, the counselor interviews Jessie using an interview form the school developed. The form has questions asking about the frequency, nature, and extent of the bullying, including support the student has or has not received. The school team learns that Jessie was bullied in the morning on a daily basis by another student, a junior named Scott. Scott followed and verbally taunted the younger Jessie the entire way to her first class. The counselor sets up a quick plan to have Jessie meet her the next morning at her office so they can walk together to her first class. Afterward, the counselor checks that Jessie feels safe enough to return to class.

Following up on this report, the team interviews both Scott and the teachers who have classrooms near Jessie's locker. The team asks the teachers specifically about witnessing any bullying and their responses to seeing such incidents. Results of these interviews reveal that Jessie did not

TABLE 6.6. Possible Questions for Assessing Why a Student Is Being Bullied

Source	Questions
Instruction	• To what extent has the schoolwide response been taught to the target student? • To what extent has the perpetrator been taught how to respond accordingly when the schoolwide response is used toward them? • To what extent have the schoolwide expectations been taught to the target student and the perpetrator? • Has the target student sufficiently practiced using the schoolwide response? • Has the perpetrator sufficiently practiced responding when someone uses the schoolwide response?
Curriculum	• Are the lesson plans used in teaching schoolwide expectations and response appropriate for the student's age, background, and culture? • Are the examples and nonexamples sufficient for the student's age, background, and culture?
Environment	• Is sufficient adult supervision available when and where the bullying occurs? • Is there sufficient feedback provided to students on using the schoolwide response and expectations?
Learner	• Are there student characteristics that prevent the target student from using the schoolwide response or expectations well? • Does the target student lack certain assertive skills or emotion regulation skills? • What is the reason the target student perceives they are a target?

use the bullying response strategy, and the teachers thought that the two students were friends so they did not intervene during the incidents. There is also a lack of active supervision during the morning passing period, which gave Scott an opportunity to commit the bullying without adults realizing what was truly happening. Possessing all this information, the team forms a precise statement: *Jessie is verbally bullied by Scott on a daily basis in the morning before first period in the sophomore hallway.*

After gathering data on the problem, the team implements a solution (i.e., individualized support plan) for Jessie in Step 3 of the PSM. Because Jessie wasn't using the bullying response strategy, the counselor meets with her to reteach the strategy. Also, a team member reteaches the appropriate staff the agreed-upon response strategy for adults in the school. In terms of supporting Scott, the school counselor adds him to one of her small groups to learn new ways to express himself and be respectful to classmates. Finally, the team teaches relevant staff members to use active supervision in the morning and during passing periods in order to increase awareness and adult supervision of student behavior.

To measure the degree to which the plan is implemented, the team selects an observation measure. Specifically, a school administrator will walk down the sophomore hall in the mornings and witness staff using active supervision. The team chooses self-report as the measure of outcome data by verbally checking in with Jessie each week about the frequency of her being the target of bullying. In Step 4 of the PSM, the team evaluates the implementation and success of the plan, finding that the plan was implemented as intended. Moreover, Jessie is no longer a target of bullying. We summarize the steps of bullying prevention for individual students in Table 6.7.

An Accessible Data Warehouse

When using the PSM and making data-based decisions, school teams will need a data warehouse that is manageable and easy to access (Newton et al., 2009). The warehouse should be a simple,

TABLE 6.7. Use of PSM for Individual Students and Bullying Prevention

Step	Question	Data sources or action
1	Is a student indicating that they are being bullied?	Examine responses to bullying target survey. Clarify that bullying is not a systemwide issue and is instead an individual student issue.
2	Why is the student being bullied, or what is the reason the student perceives they are being targeted?	Survey or interview the student on why they believe they are being bullied. Examine the context and nature of bullying. Assess the extent to which the student uses the schoolwide response to bullying (e.g., stop, walk, talk).
3	What can we do to resolve the bullying?	Develop a plan that may include reteaching/ensuring that the student can use the schoolwide response effectively. Adjust the environment as needed to prevent and manage incidents of bullying. Teach any necessary skills or coping responses to the student. Provide the perpetrator with necessary intervention.
4	Did we follow the plan? Did it work?	Examine fidelity to the plan. Readminister survey to determine if the student is still targeted.

user-friendly database in which teams can access the data in graphical form quickly and efficiently. Consider Figure 6.5 as an example. The data are displayed in tabular form, so if team members want to know where most of bullying occurs, they would have to scan the table, count the number of bullying instances in each location, and compare the number of instances in each location. This is an inefficient process and requires more mental math. However, when the same data are visualized in a bar graph, as shown in Figure 6.6, teams have a much more efficient method for analyzing data. When team members ask "Where do students report that bullying occurs the most frequently?" they can easily determine it's the hallway because it's the longest bar. No scanning, no mental math, and the team can move onto other problem-analysis questions. Not having a data warehouse that can quickly graph the data can stall the data-based decision-making process.

There are various data warehouses that are available; the most obvious are word processing spreadsheets, such as Microsoft Excel or Google Sheets. These are accessible with just about any electronic device, but they do require someone with expertise to craft the data into graphs once they are entered. One common data warehouse is the School-Wide Information System (SWIS; PBIS Apps, 2011). SWIS is a warehouse in which schools enter discipline referral data and Tier 2 and Tier 3 data. Educators can then examine referrals and incidents by location, time, and behavior(s), and determine who committed the behavior or incident and the perceived function of the behavior. Schools can drill down to specific system issues or concerns with individual students with a few clicks; thus it fits well with a problem-solving model (Eliason & Morris, 2015; Horner et al., 2005; Chaparro, Horner, Algozzine, Daily, & Nese, 2022).

For interventions and for monitoring the progress of individual students, many assessment companies offer a data warehouse and visualization of data as part of their package. For example, Pearson and FastBridge offer a variety of assessments and graphing of the reports, including academic, behavioral, and social and emotional (see *pearsonassessment.com* and *fastbridge.org*, respectively). Intervention Central offers a free data entry and graphing tool (see *www.interventioncentral.org/teacher-resources/graph-maker-free-online*). Educators can use this tool to monitor progress of a student's intervention or support. Additionally, sites such as the National Center for Intensive Intervention (*https://intensiveintervention.org/resource/monitoring-student-progress-behavioral-interventions-dbi-training-series-module-3*), offer free downloadable templates for interventions that can be customized for a variety of behaviors or skills that students are learning.

Incident	Location	Time	Student Involved
Physical bullying	Hallway	8:30 A.M.	Britta
Verbal bullying	Classroom	9:00 A.M.	Jeff
Verbal bullying	Main entry	2:15 P.M.	Annie
Physical bullying	Hallway	1:15 P.M.	Troy
Exclusion/relational bullying	Cafeteria	11:30 A.M.	Abed
Exclusion/relational bullying	Hallway	11:30 A.M.	Ben
Verbal bullying	Hallway	2:30 P.M.	Ben
Physical bullying	Classroom	1:00 P.M.	Craig

FIGURE 6.5. Tabular display of data to illustrate inefficiency with problem analysis.

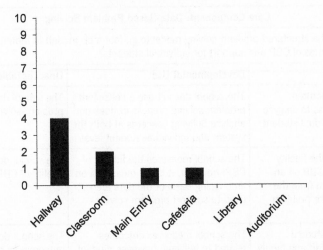

FIGURE 6.6. Visual display of data to illustrate efficiency with problem analysis.

Student Interpretation of Data

Students, even as young as late-elementary school age, can contribute their voices to improving the bullying prevention efforts of a school. For example, teams can involve students by including them in the bullying prevention implementation team that analyzes data. Of course, all students on the data team are allowed to review the needs to be de-identified so that the privacy of students is protected. Teams that include students in their problem-solving process can address one of the gaps we mentioned earlier: students experience bullying more than adults realize (Cornell & Bandyopadhyay, 2009). Further, although data may tell the adults in the school that the most common location bullying occurs is in the hallway, the students can tell the adults *which* hallway and *what* circumstances make it more likely that bullying will take place. Without input from students, for example, teams may see in their data that eighth-grade females experience bullying online more frequently than males and decide to reinforce our digital citizenship lessons. But if we include students in the meeting, they may be able to tell teams the specific apps or social media channels that are being used to engage in cyberbullying. From there, the staff and students can work together to get information from the social media site or app on how to report bullying and think of an engaging way to provide the information to students in the school. Gathering student input into the data can be achieved by having students attend meetings with the bullying prevention team at certain times, creating a student panel to allow students to provide insight, or by conducting focus groups with groups of students.

In Figure 6.7 (on page 114), we provide a data-based decision-making practice profile to operationally define this component of CBP.

Core Component: Data-Based Problem Solving		
Definition: The use of a structured problem-solving model (e.g., four-step model) to monitor the implementation and outcomes of CBP and support for individual students.		
Expected Use	**Developmental Use**	**Unacceptable Use**
The school uses a structured problem-solving process to analyze system-level and individual student bullying concerns.	The school doesn't use a consistent problem-solving process or does not analyze bullying concerns at both the system and individual-student level.	The school does not use a structured problem-solving process.
The school measures the fidelity of implementation for CBP on an ongoing basis, and data from the assessment are used for problem solving.	The school measures the fidelity of CBP; however, it is not measured on an ongoing basis or the data are not used to support problem solving.	The school does not measure the fidelity of CBP.
The school measures student outcomes as well as staff and family perceptions related to bullying at least once each year.	The school measures outcomes related to bullying; however, student reports of the frequency of bullying are not measured at least once each year, or staff and family perceptions of bullying are not measured at least once each year.	The school does not measure outcomes or perceptions related to bullying.
An accessible data warehouse is available for all staff and is used to support data-based decision making.	A data warehouse exists; however, it is not easily accessible, usable, or utilized to inform data-based decision making.	The school does not have a data warehouse.

FIGURE 6.7. Data-based decision-making practice profile.

CHAPTER 7

Implementation Science, Usable Innovations, and Improvement Cycles

In the first part of this book, we provided the *what* of bullying prevention. Having read the first six chapters, you now know what CBP comprises and the associated practices that can be implemented in your setting. They include your bullying prevention policy, strategies to engage families and the community, the needed features to create a positive school climate, and evidence-based programs. But as researchers have suggested, the gap between research and practice is one of the most difficult to bridge (Rogers, 1995; Simpson, 2002; Swearer et al., 2009). Despite having knowledge of *what* works in CBP, schools continue to have difficulty actually implementing these best practices effectively.

In the second part of the book, we focus specifically on the *how* of CBP, and we do so through implementation science. The field of implementation science has been providing guidance on how to effectively implement programs and practices for decades (Fixsen et al., 2005). There is agreement among researchers that implementation science is very complex, and entire books have been written on the topic (Fixsen et al., 2005). This being the case, our goal is to provide you with information and tools on the core features of implementation science to support effective bullying prevention in your school setting as simply as possible.

In the following chapters, we provide a broad introduction to the core components of implementation science through the lens of the five components of CBP. Much of the research supporting these components comes from the work of the National Implementation Science Research Network (NIRN). Part of NIRN's work entailed developing five Active Implementation Frameworks (AIFs): (1) usable innovations, (2) improvement cycles, (3) implementation teams, (4) implementation drivers, and (5) implementation stages. Additional resources are provided for each of the AIFs throughout the second half of this book to provide concrete direction for bullying prevention implementation teams as they begin their work. Following Chapters 7–9 on AIFs, the remaining chapters are dedicated to what implementation of CBP looks like when structured through the stages of implementation.

The good news about the first AIF, usable innovations, is that you have been reading about one since you picked up this book. In simple terms, a usable innovation is the program, practice, or curriculum that you are trying to implement. It is the *what*. For the sake of this book, it is CBP. As described by the NIRN, there are four criteria that separate a usable innovation from just any off-the-shelf program your school may select: (1) the program has a clear description, (2) core components of the program are described, (3) the core components are operationally defined, and (4) assessments measure the effectiveness and fidelity of the program. Although it may seem daunting, selecting your program or approach to prevent bullying is truly a make-or-break moment. Even if you implement a program to perfection, have strong staff buy-in, and do everything else right, if the program you selected doesn't meet these four criteria well, it can be the difference between success and failure. See Figure 7.1 for an example of how the Olweus Bullying Prevention Program meets the criteria of a usable innovation.

Program: Olweus Bullying Prevention Program (OBPP)	
Description of Program	A schoolwide, comprehensive framework focused on systemic change to create a safe and positive school climate.
Description of Core Components	(1) Schoolwide approach (2) Classroom implementation (3) Individual actions (4) Engaging the community
Definition of Core Components	(1) Schoolwide approach includes establishing a Bullying Prevention Coordinating Committee (BPCC), conducting staff trainings, administering the Olweus Bullying Questionnaire, holding staff discussion groups, introducing school rules against bullying, refining the school's supervisory system, holding a school kick-off event, and involving parents. (2) Classroom implementation includes posting and enforcing schoolwide rules against bullying, holding regular class meetings, and holding meetings with students' parents. (3) Individual actions include ensuring supervision of student activities, ensuring that staff members intervene on the spot when bullying occurs, holding meetings with students involved in bullying, holding meetings with families of involved students, and developing individual intervention plans for involved students. (4) Community engagement includes involving community members on the BPCC, developing partnerships to support your program, and helping spread anti-bullying messages throughout the community.
Outcome and Fidelity Assessments	Outcome assessment: Olweus Bullying Questionnaire Fidelity assessment: None publicly available

FIGURE 7.1. Usable innovation example.

PROGRAM DESCRIPTION

The first criterion present in a usable innovation is a clear description of the program. This description goes beyond a brief explanation of what the program intends to accomplish. It demonstrates the values and philosophy behind the program as well as the specific population for whom the program is intended. Our description of the five components of CBP in the first part of this book is a good example. As another example, Second Step is an evidence-based bullying prevention curriculum that has an additional Bullying Prevention Unit that can be purchased. When you visit the Second Step website, the values of the Second Step program are clear in its motto: "Not just better students, better people." This value is part of their philosophy of supporting the development of better students and people through the implementation of SEL curricula. Compare these values to other bullying prevention programs that claim bullying "disappears almost immediately" when their program is implemented, or state that their philosophy is that students cannot rely on "outside authorities" to stop bullying. Taking just a few minutes to understand what values a program supports can help you know if they align with the values of your school.

If you visit the website for the Bullying Prevention Unit in particular, there is a clear description of the population for whom the program is intended: students in kindergarten through fifth grade. As we described in more depth in Chapter 3, when selecting an evidence-based bullying prevention curriculum, it is important to know more details about the research that makes the program evidence based. For example, if a program is evidence based, but the studies demonstrating its effectiveness were only conducted in metropolitan cities, schools in rural areas of the country may want to take a closer look at how applicable the program is to their settings. Perhaps the program relies heavily on high-speed Internet access, or its surveys assume a large population of students for anonymity. These conditions may not apply to schools in more rural areas of the country.

CORE COMPONENTS

The second criterion for usable innovations is the description of the core components of the program. Core components are the key features that truly drive the outcomes that result from the program. When these core components are in place, we can say that the program is being implemented. For example, the core components of CBP are the five components we have described in the first part of this book. Beyond knowing if we are implementing the program, having knowledge of the core components allows us to be as efficient with our time and efforts as possible. Imagine spending hours of time with students and the staff designing and printing anti-bullying posters to display around the school when, in fact, this effort is not essential to the reduction of bullying. Not only would the time and effort spent be frustrating, but it can lead to reduced buy-in from the staff and students and can make implementing the essential components of the program even more difficult. By having the components clearly outlined, we know that we are implementing the most crucial elements of a usable innovation.

Defining Core Components

Identifying the core components is a great start, but to truly be able to have a usable innovation, these core components need to be operationally defined, by which we mean that the core components should be defined in a way that they are teachable, learnable, doable, and assessible (Blase, Fixsen, & Van Dyke, 2018). Many evidence-based programs have these core components baked into their curriculum. Training in the program focuses on *teaching* the core components so that the staff *learns* them and are able to *do* them in their setting. Then, using surveys, the staff is able to determine the degree to which the curriculum has been implemented with fidelity. One method for defining these core components in implementation science is through the use of practice profiles. A practice profile lists the core components of a program and then provides a description of the features of the component when implemented with (1) expected use, (2) developmental use, and (3) unacceptable use. When the component is considered implemented as desired, it means that educators consistently demonstrate the skills and abilities necessary to complete the activities making up the component. For example, one of the core features of a positive school climate (as we discussed in Chapter 2) is that students are directly taught prosocial skills (Sugai & Horner, 2009). Describing one feature of the desired implementation of this core component could be "Staff teach expected schoolwide behaviors to students once at the beginning of the school year and once after winter break." Often several features of a core component help to define what the component looks like in practice. For a core component to be considered implemented with fidelity, it is important to note the degree to which desired implementation has occurred for all of the features.

The *developmental use* descriptor is helpful because it provides an explanation of what it looks like to implement features somewhat inconsistently or in a limited range of contexts. For example, one of the core components of CBP is engaging families, students, and the community in the work. As we described in Chapter 5, a key feature of engaging families is that the school include them in decision making. While the desired implementation of this feature would be that a diverse range of families are included as *active partners* in all appropriate bullying prevention decisions, the developmental use of this feature would be more limited in scope: "families are asked to *provide feedback* on decisions the school has made about the bullying prevention practices."

The final descriptor is for unacceptable use. You can think of this category as nonexamples of implementation or as evidence that the desired activities are simply not occurring. In the example on engaging families, unacceptable use could state, "No family members are included in decision making at the school level." When your evidence-based bullying prevention curriculum provides clear descriptions of what it looks like to implement the program as intended, it gives your school the data needed to problem-solve future bumps in the road.

ASSESSING EFFECTIVENESS AND FIDELITY

The fourth criterion for a usable innovation is having assessments that determine both the effectiveness and the fidelity of the innovation. If we are not able to demonstrate that our approach to preventing bullying is having an impact, the likelihood that it survives inevitable hurdles, such as budget cuts or initiative fatigue, decreases. Assessing effectiveness is relatively straightforward. The most pertinent question is, "Did this approach reduce bullying?" Many innovations come with assessments included; for example, the Olweus Bullying Prevention Program has its own survey to measure the prevalence of bullying. See Chapter 6 for a detailed discussion on how a school can measure the impact of bullying at its site.

Assessing fidelity can be more difficult. When determining the degree to which the program is implemented as intended, some assessments are more surface level (e.g., did the teacher implement the lesson?), whereas others are more in-depth (e.g., observations of the program being implemented). The amount of time and effort a school puts forth in determining the level of implementation fidelity is ultimately up to the staff; however, if you are not seeing the results you expect, your school will want to know if it is because the curriculum is not effective or if it is because the program was not implemented the way it was intended. We discuss ways to measure fidelity more fully in Chapter 6.

INITIATIVE INVENTORY

To give yourself the best chance to obtain buy-in from the school staff, have principal leadership acknowledge and jointly work toward streamlining initiatives through an initiative inventory. The purpose of an initiative inventory is to take stock of all the programs being implemented at the school. Once that list is developed, leadership is able to see patterns and gaps that help to determine the best fit for an evidence-based bullying prevention program.

It can be even more effective to have teachers and other staff members be the ones who help brainstorm the initiatives currently in place (even if it is an initiative that has faded into nonexistence without a formal declaration that it is no longer being required). These initiatives should include both academic, behavioral, and staff (e.g., peer coaching) initiatives, and they can be conducted during an all-staff meeting or by having staff members submit their responses prior to an all-staff meeting. It is often cathartic for frustrated teachers to have the opportunity to share all of their responsibilities, especially if they include initiatives that have fallen by the wayside.

Once this basic list of programs and approaches has been developed, several factors should be examined to help determine redundancies and gaps. Determining the intended outcomes of each initiative will help your school to find out how many programs are in place that overlap with one another. The worst-case scenario is finding out that you have multiple initiatives, all of which are only partly implemented, and all of which are supposed to specifically prevent bullying. The good news is that you are now aware of these fledgling programs and are able to move forward by coalescing your efforts around one approach. Another possible scenario is that you have one or no bullying prevention curriculum, but have a hodgepodge of other SEL curricula. If this is the case, the selection process becomes more nuanced. You need to examine the evidence of the existing program's ability to reduce bullying and determine if it is being implemented with fidelity.

There are a few ways to approach continuing with the initiative inventory process. If buy-in is already high for implementing a bullying prevention program, you may decide to focus only on those programs in your school. Bring the results of the initiative inventory (in this case just bullying prevention related programs) to the bullying prevention implementation team to guide the selection process. If buy-in is low among your staff, expanding the process so that all the school's initiatives are documented may improve buy-in down the road. Have your staff discuss all of them so that everything is on the table. In addition to reviewing initiatives based on intended outcome, you can include other important information as well. You can find a template for completing an initiative inventory in Figure 7.2.

Let's take a look at some of the factors listed in Figure 7.2 and review why they are important. Listing the staff members who are involved in the initiative is vital because by the end of your initiative inventory you can easily analyze the distribution of responsibilities among the school staff. If after completing the inventory you notice that the people involved in the implementation

Initiative	Purpose	Measurement of Outcomes	Team Membership	Training	Coaching	Intended Audience	Measurement of Fidelity
Name of initiative	The key outcomes or focus of the initiative	The data gathered to determine if the initiative is achieving the goal	Staff members that are involved or the staff that make up the team that oversees the initiative	The initial and ongoing training provided to the staff to implement the initiative	The ongoing coaching and support provided to the staff to implement the initiative	The students or stakeholders supported by the initiative	How fidelity of implementation for the initiative is being measured
Systematic supervision	To reduce bullying in the school	Student survey (Youth Risk Behavior Surveillance System)	Michael, George, Tobias, Lindsay, Lucille	1-hour training provided to staff for initial introduction; monthly staff updates	None provided	All students, but particularly those involved as targets or perpetrators	Self-report (questionnaire given to staff members)

FIGURE 7.2. Initiative Inventory template. Adapted from McIntosh and Goodman (2016) and Sugai (2004).

are a diverse, equitable range of staff members, then you are in good shape. On the other hand, if you notice that one group is taking the responsibility for implementing the majority of initiatives, it may be time to consider how this is affecting the buy-in from the rest of the staff, and can be a powerful opportunity to connect with staff members. Bringing to light all of the pressures and responsibilities that they have on a day-to-day basis, acknowledging these hardships, and then working together to reduce the burden can lead to staff being more willing to engage in bullying prevention.

Training and coaching support are key factors in understanding why some initiatives are not being implemented well. When filling in information on these factors, you will want to focus on all forms of training and coaching that are provided for the initiative. For training in particular, consider what initial, refresher, and onboarding training is available. Many bullying prevention programs focus heavily on initial training so that the entire staff understands the purpose and practicalities of implementing the program. A question that is not asked as often is: What happens after the initial training to support ongoing effective implementation? Providing the staff with a specific time dedicated to follow-up training each year helps ensure that their skills and knowledge stay sharp. Additionally, including training as part of the onboarding process for new staff members is vital for consistency.

Once your training systems are in place, the next step is to consider what coaching supports, if any, are available. Ongoing coaching fills the gap between training opportunities and allows staff members to feel supported when problems arise. It may be the case that all initiatives do not have coaching support because resources are limited; schools and districts often have to prioritize funding and salaries above coaching support. There are several different approaches to coaching, and some curricula have coaching built into their costs. This support could look like a 1-hour phone conference each month or the option to have a customer service representative provide solutions. One of the most sustainable methods is to have a resident expert on the staff who serves as a coach for the program. More information on what effective coaching systems look like is available in Chapter 9.

The remaining areas of focus for your initiative inventory include examining who the intended audience is for the initiative and how to measure the outcomes and implementation of the initiative. The intended audience refers to who is receiving the benefits of the initiative, which will typically be your students but in some cases may be students' families or the staff members themselves. By examining the list of intended recipients, the team can determine if one group (e.g., third-grade students) are receiving an inequitable amount of services. Of course, if your data suggest that this specific group is in need of additional supports, there may be a valid reason for them to have a disproportionate amount of services. This brings us to the final area of focus, which is how data are collected for both outcome and implementation effectiveness.

As we mentioned earlier, implementing evidence-based programs with fidelity can be the difference between reducing bullying and, potentially, even increasing bullying. The good news is that most bullying prevention curricula include some form of a fidelity measure. Even if the measure is broad and focuses only on whether or not lessons are being implemented, it can still serve as a metric to determine if additional training or coaching is needed. Analyzing the tools used to measure outcome data can provide additional opportunities for improving efficiency. Many of the academic outcome measures in your implementation inventory will likely be state-mandated tests in addition to more formative assessments that show progress more frequently. What can be helpful is finding common expected outcomes that are measured by different outcome tools. Ask yourself if there is a way to combine or align these tools in some way so that students are only taking one assessment. Finding these hidden efficiencies can go a long way toward increasing buy-in from the school staff.

IMPROVEMENT CYCLES

At the heart of using improvement cycles is a shift in thinking. Instead of approaching a CBP initiative with the idea that there may be bumps in the road (there definitely will be) and the school will simply have to solve those problems, improvement cycles provide a concrete strategy for understanding and resolving problems when they inevitably arise. For the purposes of bullying prevention at the school level, there are two improvement cycles on which we should focus: (1) rapid-cycle problem solving and (2) usability testing.

Rapid-Cycle Problem Solving

Rapid-cycle problem solving is used for barriers that arise and can be adjusted to quickly. One of the key factors to remember in this approach to problem solving is that the goal is not to craft a perfect solution. The types of problems that rapid-cycle problem solving is meant to address are those that typically come about during the installation and initial implementation stages, though it can be used in any stage. Again, the baseline understanding of improvement cycles is that there will be problems, and those problems will be addressed when they occur.

For a consistent, evidence-based approach to problem solving, the four-step problem-solving model can be used. This model is described in greater detail in Chapter 6. The flexibility of this model lends it its sustainability. Not only can it be used for long-term issues, but it can be used for rapid-cycle problem solving as well. In general, rapid-cycle problem solving is best used when looking at a relatively simple problem for which the data are collected quickly.

To illustrate use of the PSM with rapid-cycle problem solving, consider the following example depicted in Table 7.1. The bullying prevention implementation team finds that only 15% of stu-

TABLE 7.1. Example of PSM with Rapid-Cycle Problem Solving

Step	Example
Problem Identification	Only 15% of students know how to make an anonymous report of bullying (goal is to have at least 90% of students).
Problem Analysis	Students are only taught at the beginning of the year about how to report bullying.
Plan Identification and Implementation	Students were retaught how to make an anonymous report.
	Posters and weekly announcements were used to prompt and remind students about how to report.
Plan Evaluation	A random group of students were surveyed to see if they knew how to report.

dents are able to describe how to make an anonymous report of bullying in the school. The goal for the school is that at least 90% of students are able to describe how to report bullying. Examining the reasons for why this problem is occurring, the implementation team determines that the frequency with which students are presented these methods is limited (e.g., there is no signage in highly visible areas of the school, how to report bullying is only taught at the beginning of the year). Now that the team has a description of the problem and an informed hypothesis for why the problem is occurring, a plan is made and executed to alleviate the problem.

To begin, teachers reteach students how to make reports of bullying. To provide prompts and reminders, posters with clear information on how to make an anonymous report of bullying are created and placed in several high-traffic areas in the school. Additionally, each week during morning announcements, the principal takes 30 seconds to remind students about how to make anonymous bullying reports. After a few weeks, a random collection of students are surveyed to determine if the solutions put into place are having an effect. If they are, then the intervention continues as described. If they are not having an impact, the bullying prevention implementation team returns to the rapid-cycle problem-solving process to develop new solutions based on this information. This example illustrates using the PSM shared in Chapter 6 applied to rapid-cycle problem solving. In Chapter 6, we describe a more extensive problem analysis phase, but here, we hope our readers see that the steps can be applied in a more immediate and short-term process.

Usability Testing

The second approach to improvement cycles is usability testing. In short, the purpose of usability testing is to pilot a new initiative on a small scale to determine if it is feasible and gets the results you desire. If the new work is indeed feasible and gets positive results, then the implementation team can begin taking steps to broaden the initiative to support a greater number of students. The steps in usability testing involve utilizing several iterations of the rapid-cycle problem-solving approach. The first cohort of testers try out the innovation or new process and provide data on its successes and problems. Based on this feedback, a new usability test is implemented with a greater number of implementers. This process continues until most of the kinks have been worked out of the approach.

To be clear, usability testing does not need to occur for every single part of a program or approach. In fact, you should be selective about which innovations, processes, or components you test, such that only those you believe will lead to the greatest impact are selected. The implementation team can determine what needs to be tested organically as consistent problems arise with a component of your bullying prevention efforts, or it may be brought to the attention of the team as a possible way to improve bullying prevention efforts. Regardless of the genesis for the selected area to be tested, your team will want to ensure that it is likely to have a significant, positive impact on your students.

Once you have selected the process or component that you want to test, it's vital to plan how you want the test to proceed. First, the bullying prevention implementation team needs to decide who will be the first cohort of testers. Sometimes, an idea for a new approach or innovation may come from staff members themselves, which makes this a simple process. If, however, there are no immediate champions among the staff, the implementation team should consider selecting testers who would have the highest likelihood of success and/or those who realize the greatest impact. For example, research by de Vries, Kaufman, Veenstra, Laninga-Wijnen, and Huitsing (2021) found that adolescents who are in secondary school attach importance to attaining strong social status. What's more, bullying is one method that some students use to achieve this goal. In their study, over the course of the first few years in secondary school, the social standing for these students did not significantly change. As a result, the authors suggest that bullying prevention efforts in secondary schools will have the best chance of succeeding if they are implemented with students immediately during their first year. Based on these findings, implementation teams in secondary schools would be justified in considering testing a new bullying prevention approach specifically with first-year students.

Once the first cohort of testers has been selected, the implementation team will want to define the scope of the test and what data will be collected. When will the test begin and for how long will it run? What type of data should be collected to demonstrate that the feasibility and impact of the new work is a success?

To provide a more concrete understanding of what usability testing can look like in practice, consider the following example. Based on data from recent family surveys, a school wants to improve its connection to the community and build positive relationships between the school and its students and families. The school decides to have an event that involves sharing ideas for acts of kindness in the school, for celebrating family culture, and for favorite hobbies and activities. Local businesses and organizations that students and their families frequent are contacted to be part of a day celebrating the uniqueness and commonalities between students. Since this is a complex, multifaceted endeavor, the bullying prevention implementation team reaches out to a small handful of classrooms that are interested in being the first ones to try this approach for creating greater connectedness between stakeholders and students. One classroom each from the sixth, seventh, and eighth grades agrees to work together to plan and execute the one-day event. Additionally, staff members, students, families, and community members who are involved provide feedback to the implementation team on what was successful and what areas need to be refined for greater impact. After the event, the implementation team reviews the feedback provided by all stakeholders and makes adjustments to the planning and day-of-event activities.

The following semester, an additional three classrooms agree to participate and provide feedback. As these iterations continue, the planning and execution of the single-day event becomes more efficient and effective. Eventually, more people on the staff and other classes begin to hear about the events. The students are interested because of the chance to connect with classmates around shared interests, and staff members are interested because most of the kinks in planning and executing the event have already been worked out. Within a short amount of time, the one-day event that started with just three classrooms has grown to a schoolwide event that includes dozens of families and community organizations highlighting a day of kindness and connectedness.

CHAPTER 8

Implementation Teams

One of the first tasks for schools that decide to implement CBP is developing an implementation team. With so many teams in schools already, the responsibilities of a bullying prevention implementation team may be adopted by a similarly focused existing team (e.g., school climate team, school discipline team) since these teams already have the time and resources dedicated to such work. The purpose of this team is to implement CBP effectively. This entails supporting the implementation drivers described in Chapter 9, engaging with families and the community, and creating an overall supportive environment for bullying prevention to take hold in the school. The members that make up the team are fluent in CBP as well as in the five AIFs that support its implementation. But why use a team at all? Why not have just one or two champions of bullying prevention in the school spearhead the work?

Research on implementation suggests that when an initiative is implemented through a team, it is more likely to be implemented well and efficiently (Fixsen, Blase, Timbers, & Wolf, 2001). As Fixsen and colleagues (2001) found, a well-run implementation team is associated with implementing a program with 80% fidelity, compared to 30% fidelity for teams that are not well run. Moreover, the amount of time it took for the program to be implemented with fidelity was reduced nearly in half. To assist with creating a high-functioning team, we outline five strategies: (1) team formation, (2) collaborative decision making, (3) vision, (4) norms, and (5) standard meeting formats.

TEAM FORMATION

Selecting Team Members

Who you have on your team is almost as important as having a team in the first place. On your bullying prevention implementation team, you want to have people who can speak to all aspects of school management and make decisions. In most schools, this means that your team should include an administrator. Administrators do not have to lead the team, but the team needs someone who is able to make relatively quick budget decisions and provide vocal support to the school staff on the decisions made by the team. When selecting other members of the team, it is imperative to have people with strong skills in problem solving, data-based decision making, and knowledge of bullying, including bullying dynamics and bullying prevention best practices. Additionally, the implementation team should include representation from different grade levels, specialists, non-classroom staff, students' families, community members, and students. In a traditional high school, this team may consist of a freshman teacher, a senior teacher, a band teacher, a basketball coach, a parent, a Boys and Girls Club director, and two upperclassmen, all as active participants on the team. At a rural elementary school, this team may include the principal (who is also the fifth-grade teacher), a first-grade teacher, a physical education teacher, a grandparent, an after-school care director, and two fifth-grade students. Each of these individuals will have a different role and perspective, which is invaluable to successfully reducing bullying.

Teams can easily increase in size so much that the number of members feels overwhelming, but in general implementation teams should have a minimum of 3 members and a maximum of 15 (Smith et al., 2018). The goal is to have enough people to get diverse perspectives, while maintaining few enough members to foster relationship building and efficient decision making. Moreover, maintaining a smaller, core group of team members allows the team to be more sustainable. As turnover inevitably occurs, this core group of members can bring new members up to speed at the beginning of each year.

Team Member Roles

Within each team, there are roles and responsibilities that, when clearly defined and adhered to consistently, support its success (Newton et al., 2012). One of the most central roles is that of a *facilitator*. The facilitator is responsible for drafting the agenda, leading the team through the agenda, guiding the decision-making processes, and evaluating the meeting. It is the job of the facilitator to make sure all voices are heard during the meeting and that the action items from previous meetings are reviewed. Another common role in effective teams is a *note taker*. This is the person responsible for documenting the discussions, decisions, and future action items throughout the meeting. Notes do not have to be exhaustive to the point of becoming a transcription, but having a record of what decisions were made, the rationale behind those decisions, and alternative proposals can be beneficial after several weeks or months.

For example, let's assume an implementation team is going through the problem-solving process because of a drastic increase in bullying reports in the cafeteria. After going through the four-step problem-solving model by reviewing data and determining a likely cause for the higher rates of bullying in this specific area of the school, the team discusses possible solutions. Several options are presented with pros and cons for each one documented by the note taker in the meeting notes. During one of the next meetings, the data are reviewed by the team, and it is clear that bullying has not been reduced as desired in the cafeteria. Instead of the team trying to recollect what they had discussed one or several months ago, the facilitator returns to the notes from the meeting when problem solving was originally discussed. Reviewing the pros and cons of the different options again, the team can efficiently determine a new approach to reducing bullying in the cafeteria. By doing this, the team is able to stay focused on possible solutions instead of being sidetracked about all of the potential reasons the first solution did not work.

Having a dedicated *timekeeper* can be beneficial if a team has difficulty staying on track during meetings. Obviously, the need for a timekeeper also assumes that there are dedicated sections of time for each agenda item. Agendas that simply list topics that will be discussed are a good start, but without specific time frames for each discussion topic, one topic can easily dominate the meeting. This approach results in topics being tabled for future meetings or attempting to rush through topics at the end of the meeting. Specifying the amount of time each topic will take when drafting the agenda for a future meeting also forces the facilitator to prioritize the topics for discussion. What may begin as a list of 10 topics that would be nice to discuss likely gets whittled down to the top 4 or 5 once the facilitator is required to include time limits for each topic. Another benefit of having a dedicated timekeeper is that it provides stability and efficiency. When teammates know that they have a certain amount of time to discuss a topic before they move on to others, it helps them avoid going off track with side conversations or tangents. Additionally, since time is such a precious commodity for the school staff, families, and community members, knowing that meetings will end when scheduled, while also accomplishing the objectives of the meeting, makes the meeting feel valuable.

Being an *active participant* in the meeting is in and of itself an important role. The expectation for each meeting should be that all voices are valid and that all team members make an effort to share their views. Depending on the context, additional roles may be needed. For example, if there are team members attending virtually, designating someone as the *chat monitor* could be a good idea. This ensures virtual attendees will have their voices amplified to the entire team despite not attending in person. The facilitator should also keep in mind that different people have different needs when it comes to contributing to a meeting. Some people thrive on an open dialogue in which ideas and thoughts are shared quickly with the opportunity to revise, review, and move forward. Others do their best when given time to process information and bring more fully formed thoughts to the team. Understanding the different working styles of the active participants on a team, and truly meeting the needs of all members so that they are most effective, is necessary to ensure equitable participation.

Selecting team members for these roles based on their strengths can help support a healthy, functioning team. Some teams choose to have rotating role assignments. Others opt for consistency in roles. Regardless of the approach, the team should ensure that members have a strength in their assigned roles. For example, some team members may type quickly and can continue being engaged as participants in the meeting while taking notes. Others may find it almost impossible to take effective notes and still be engaged in the meeting. In this case, it may be prudent to have just those participants who have strong note taking skills rotate the role between meetings. A summary of team member roles is found in Table 8.1.

TABLE 8.1. Summary of Possible Team Member Roles

Role	Responsibilities
Facilitator	Drafts agenda and leads team through it.
Note taker	Documents the discussions, decisions, and future action items.
Timekeeper	Tracks time spent on items; provides stability and efficiency.
Active participant	Actively participates and provides their viewpoint.

COLLABORATIVE DECISION MAKING

For a team to truly feel like a team, decisions need to be made using a collaborative process (see Table 8.2). As the saying goes, "If you want to go fast, go alone. If you want to go far, go together" (Goldberg, 2016). The same is true for CBP. The last thing we want to do is put a plan together quickly, push it out to the entire student body, then have it fade away within a few months. By making decisions in a collaborative way, we create greater buy-in among team members, which can increase the likelihood that everyone is willing to go the extra mile to ensure its success. Entire books have been written on how to effectively collaborate, but for our purposes, we will focus on a more common approach.

Before diving into specific steps, it's first important to know that true collaborative decision making takes time. This fact means that it may not be the right tactic for every choice that needs to be made. Collaborative decision making should be reserved for higher-impact decisions that play a greater role in the sustainability and impact of the school's bullying prevention efforts. The team should also have a common understanding of what the process looks like. To do this, some teams include the process on their agenda as a reminder or provide a brief overview of the process before beginning. Finally, a collaborative decision needs to be just that: collaborative. If everyone on the team is not engaged or agreeing to use the process, then it is not truly collaborative.

There are several different models for making collaborative decisions, but we focus here on a simplified version applicable to meetings in an educational setting. The steps in making collaborative decisions are (1) have clarity on the goal, (2) explore possible solutions, (3) propose a potential

TABLE 8.2. Collaborative Decision-Making Process with Example

Step	Description	Example
Goal clarity	Statement of the goal to ensure everyone understands it and is on the same page.	To identify a way to engage with families regarding bullying prevention.
Explore possible solutions	The team generates solutions (i.e., brainstorming) and discusses the pros/cons of each one.	1. Hold an open family night. 2. Hold various before- and after-school "open chats" with families.
Propose a solution	The team agrees on one solution to use for the problem.	Hold "open chats."
Clarify unresolved questions	Once a solution is chosen, the team clarifies any questions related to the solution.	Open chats are offered two times each week for 3 weeks.
Share concerns	Any concerns about the solution being unsuccessful are addressed.	There is a time constraint on the staff to have the open chats. The staff will rotate who facilitates them to reduce the burden.
Agree to a solution	The final proposal/solution is read aloud and formally agreed to.	Agree to open chats.

solution, (4) clarify unresolved questions, (5) share concerns, and (6) agree to the solution as a team. (Note that this process is intended to be used when the team needs to make decisions and reach consensus. Similar steps are used in the problem-solving model, which is reserved for identifying and resolving problems in the school related to staff or student outcomes.)

Have Clarity on the Goal

Beginning with the end in mind, the first step in the process is to ensure that everyone on the team has clarity on the purpose for making the decision. For example, let's assume that a middle school bullying prevention implementation team is using the collaborative decision-making process to select an annual event to raise awareness of bullying and how to prevent it. During the team meeting, the facilitator describes the purpose by stating that the school wants to create greater sustainability of the bullying prevention efforts by having an annual event that becomes a school tradition. The event should include as many students, families, and members of the community as possible, and everyone should leave the event with a better understanding of how they can prevent bullying and spread kindness.

Explore Possible Solutions

Once the goal has been clearly explained, the team can begin exploring possible solutions. There are many ways to facilitate such brainstorming, including breaking into small groups, "popcorning" ideas around the room, or posting sticky notes to create a wall of ideas. Regardless of the method used, during this phase the team should focus solely on generating ideas and avoid second-guessing or challenging any ideas. Thinking back to team members' roles on an implementation team, it is important for all members to be active participants during this phase of the process to better achieve buy-in once a solution is proposed.

Propose a Solution

After solutions have been brainstormed, one of the possible solutions needs to be proposed as *the* solution. At this point, the proposed solution may not end up being selected, but a proposal does need to be made so the process can continue. Often, there is one proposal that seems to have greater merit with the team than others. If the team is having a hard time deciding on which solution should be proposed, each member can rank order their top three solutions. Once this is complete, the solution with the best score can be proposed. To apply the process to the example of an annual event to raise awareness of bullying, the implementation team proposes several solutions. The top three ideas, in order, are (1) having a 1-mile and 5K kindness run; (2) having a welcome-back barbecue for students, the staff, families, and the community; and (3) holding an assembly at the beginning of the year.

After deciding on the solution to be proposed, the next step is to clearly state what the solution is. For our example, the solution being proposed is written down in the implementation team's notes as, "To create a new tradition at our school that focuses on raising awareness of bullying, how to combat it effectively, and partnering with families and the community, we will hold a 1-mile and 5K kindness run each year."

Clarify Unresolved Questions

Once the proposal has been clearly stated, the next step is to ask clarifying questions. Examples of clarifying questions for the 1-mile and 5K kindness run could include: "Do just students participate in the run or are families able to run as well?" "Does the whole school participate at once or is the run done by grade level? By homeroom class?" "What community organizations would we partner with for the event?" Obviously, the team won't be able to provide all the necessary details and specifics during the clarifying-questions part of the process; however, documenting some of the areas that need to be clarified if the proposal is accepted can serve to jump-start action planning.

It is also important to note that any concerns should not be voiced during the clarifying-questions part of the process. Sharing concerns, some of which may arise from this part of the process, takes place after all clarifying questions have been addressed. Clearly separating these two parts of the process is vital because it prevents derailing conversations about the proposal. Not starting with clarifying questions may lead to concerns being raised that would have already been addressed if the team had more knowledge about the proposal that comes with the clarifying questions part of the process. It is the facilitator's responsibility to pause any concerns that are raised during the clarifying questions phase of the process and ask that they be presented during the concerns phase.

Continuing with the previous example, the bullying prevention implementation team answers the three clarifying questions that arise. The team decides that both students and families will be able to run during the event. Since all students are required to do a 1-mile run each semester as part of their physical education curriculum, the 1-mile run will serve as the fall semester's requirement. The team agrees that details on the logistics of when students run can be figured out at a later date. Finally, it is decided that since all students will be running the 1-mile, the 5K kindness run will be open to students' families and the community. The 5K event will take place after school hours to allow for more families to attend. Community organizations that could possibly sponsor the event are proposed, including a local running store that sells shoes and other running equipment. The team agrees that other community sponsors could be determined at a later date.

Share Concerns

The next phase of the process is to share concerns about the proposal. The goal of this phase is to bring up legitimate concerns that may lead to the proposal being unsuccessful as planned. Returning to our example, the main concern raised is that the attendance of a large number of community members would distract from the purpose of raising awareness for bullying prevention at the school. Having shared this concern, team members discuss potential solutions. It is agreed that in an effort to focus on raising awareness of bullying and how to prevent it at the school, the 5K kindness run will not be open to the community but that community members can volunteer to support the event.

Agree to a Solution

With a decision that effectively addresses the only concern raised, the proposal is redrafted. This final proposal is read to the team, and everyone is given a chance to ask clarifying questions and express concerns. No questions or concerns are raised, and the facilitator states that the proposal is adopted. The note taker clearly describes the final decision, and the team moves on to drafting the immediate next steps to get the ball rolling. Again, the collaborative decision-making process can be lengthy, which is the reason that it should only be reserved for the most consequential decisions. Once it is used, though, the buy-in from the entire team is almost always higher than it would be for decisions made outside of the meeting or unilaterally.

VISION

Hellen Keller is quoted as saying, "The only thing worse than being blind is having sight but no vision." As a team that is focused on preventing some of the most traumatic experiences children can have, we owe it to ourselves to envision our ideal state. The vision statement of a bullying prevention implementation team focuses on what the future looks like for the school when all of its goals are achieved. Its purpose is to be both inspiring and aspirational. Most important, your vision statement should be something that all team members believe in. Because this statement serves as the guiding light for your team, everyone needs to understand where this light leads.

It is also important to understand what a vision statement is not. Often, vision statements are mentioned alongside mission statements. Their purposes are very different. A vision statement is meant to show where the team wants to be in the future, whereas a mission statement is meant to show how the team will get there in the present. Moreover, vision statements should be dynamic. For example, the original vision statement for Microsoft was "a computer on every desk and in every home." Now that Microsoft has grown to be a global company producing much more than just computers, its vision statement has evolved: "to help people and businesses throughout the world realize their full potential." Instead of focusing just on having their products in every "home" the company's vision is now more global in scale.

So how can your team develop a vision statement? Start by asking yourself the magic wand question: "What would the team ask for if it had a magic wand that could make anything they want to accomplish a reality?" The easy answer for a bullying prevention team is that their vision is a school with no bullying; however, there are a few points to keep in mind with drafting your vision statement. In general, the best vision statements are those that are positively stated. Microsoft's original vision statement was "a computer on every desk and in every home," not, "no desks or homes without a computer." Positively stated visions provide direction on what we are striving to do. Additionally, strong vision statements are short; they convey what the team is striving for within one or two sentences.

Finally, a consideration in developing a vision statement for the bullying prevention implementation team is that it should be aligned with the vision and culture of the school itself. For example, the vision statements of an elementary school and a high school bullying prevention team will likely look different simply because of their students' developmental differences. A vocational high school would likely have a vision statement that differs from a community high school. Although both statements might focus on kindness and respect, the vocational high school may do so within the framework of how it supports being a strong employee. A positively stated vision statement for a bullying prevention team could be something like, "All students' first instinct is kindness." For a vocational high school, a vision statement could reflect the school's unique purpose: "Future workers leading through inclusivity." A community school's vision statement may be "Every student an upstander citizen," which draws on the idea of standing up to bullying and of their role as a citizen in the community. Regardless of what a team decides its vision should be, when it is in place, every team member knows why they are engaging in the work.

NORMS

Team norms are the rules by which all members abide. They provide the foundation for the culture of the team. We have all been part of a team with varying levels of success. Often, the norms that were established, either purposefully or organically, play a significant role in the success of a team. Bullying prevention implementation team norms are somewhat like schoolwide expectations. At the beginning of each school year, staff members explicitly state and show students their expectations for both behavior and academics. Then, if an expectation is not followed, we have a common language and understanding to fall back on when providing corrections. Obviously, professional teams typically don't use a token economy strategy for reinforcement, and no one is sent to the principal's office if they break a rule. It is also true, however, that when norms are disregarded, it can create instability that undermines the ability of a team to effectively make gains.

When developing norms for your bullying prevention implementation team, it's important to include the entire team. In fact, to increase staff buy-in, a collaborative decision-making process can be helpful so that all members feel like their voices are heard. One of the most common ways to develop team norms is to ask everyone to individually think about the *worst* team they have ever been on. It could be a school-level team, sports team, or any other team. Ask each person to write down what made that team so miserable. Next, give each person a chance to quickly describe to the group what they wrote down. The note taker for the meeting should document the comments and group similar themes. Once this activity has been accomplished, repeat the same activity, but have each person describe the *best* team they have been on. At this point, there should be a list of common themes for effective and ineffective teams. To develop the team norms, consider the themes of the best teams and the opposites of the worst-team themes. The discussion among teammates should be geared toward short, simple norms that dictate how the work will be accomplished and how team members will behave. For a list of example norms, see Table 8.3.

If you are part of a school that has clearly defined schoolwide expectations, it may make sense to use those schoolwide behaviors as the "big buckets" for your norms. For example, a common schoolwide expectation acronym is PAWS: Positive Attitude, Act Responsibly, Work toward Success, Show Respect. These expectations are not only appropriate for your students, but can be more concretely defined for team meetings. Possible norms for expressing a positive attitude include using a four-to-one ratio of positive to negative comments, asking clarifying questions before sharing concerns, and providing possible solutions when raising concerns. "Act Responsibly" could

TABLE 8.3. Example Norms

- Communication, collaboration, respect
- Professional, esteem, action, knowledge
- Respectful, responsible
- On time, present, responsible

easily translate to team meetings, with norms reflecting being accountable for completing tasks and upholding the norms that are agreed upon. Team norms that meet the "Work toward Success" expectation could be staying on task and including family voice in decisions. Respect is already a popular norm for adult teams. Common norms for "Show Respect" include arriving to meetings on time, seeking first to understand another's point of view, and allowing all team members to share their views.

A final note on norms is that they are meaningless if they are not enforced. As Gruenert and Whitaker (2015) wrote, "The culture of any organization is shaped by the worst behavior the leader is willing to tolerate." In the case of norms for your bullying prevention implementation team, this quote could be adapted to "The culture of any *team* is shaped by the worst behavior *its members* are willing to tolerate." It is the responsibility of all team members to be self-reflective and recognize when norms are violated. Many books have been written on effective processes for having constructive dialogue between team members so that everyone leaves feeling valued or heard. It is almost impossible for a team to thrive and reach its goals without having mutually agreed upon and enforced norms.

STANDARD MEETING FORMAT

As educators, we know the importance of providing stability for our students. When children have predictable and consistent routines, they are better able to perform academically and behaviorally. This is also true for adults. When we as adults have predictable and consistent routines for our meetings, we are better able to accomplish our goals. This being the case, it is important to provide members of the bullying prevention implementation team with standard meeting formats.

These standard formats have several components. We have already reviewed a few of the most common: member roles and norms. Having consistency in roles during the meeting lets members know how they should be preparing. If you are the note taker, for example, you know that you may need to arrive a little early so that everything is set up prior to the start of the meeting. Norms also ensure that there is consistency in how team members interact with one another, accomplish goals, and communicate to the rest of the school.

In addition to what has already been covered, a key standard to adhere to is having a consistent meeting time and place. One of the most difficult decisions that a team makes is finding a time that works for everyone to meet. Members have to juggle multiple schedules that include after-school clubs, morning family meetings, and a host of other responsibilities. When the implementation-team meeting time is consistent, then members can plan other obligations around that meeting. Moreover, as the years progress, the bullying prevention implementation team meeting will become viewed as a standard "how-we-do-business" meeting.

The meeting agenda can be a place where multiple standards are observed with consistency. To begin with, the format of the agenda itself can be standardized. Take a look at the agenda template in Figure 8.1. You can see that at the top there are some basic facts about the meeting. They include the name of the team, the date of the meeting, the names of members present, the names of members who are filling the roles of the facilitator, timekeeper, and note taker, and meeting objectives and norms. In this example, the roles rotate between members, so that each member is responsible for taking notes and being the timekeeper. The norms that were agreed upon by the team using a shared decision-making process are also included at the top of the agenda. This

Agenda	
Team: Bullying Prevention Implementation Team	**Date:**
Team Lead:	**Time:**
Team Participants:	**Location:**
Norms:	

Objectives:		Facilitator:
1.		Notetaker:
2.		Timekeeper:
3.		

Time	Agenda Item	Notes

Action Steps			
Action Item	Person Responsible	Due Date	Completion looks like?

Meeting Review	
(1 = Strongly Disagree | 5 = Strongly Agree)	
Followed norms?	Average Score:
Met objectives?	Average Score:
What went well?	
What can make the meeting better?	

FIGURE 8.1. Meeting agenda template.

provides a quick reference for the norms, and they are briefly reviewed at the beginning of each meeting. Objectives for each meeting are clearly listed at the top of the agenda as well. You can see that the objectives are concise and measureable. By the end of the meeting, every member of the team should be able to clearly answer whether or not each objective was met.

The heart of the agenda is divided into several parts. On the far left, the start time for each agenda item is listed. This is obviously an important point for the timekeeper, but it also provides some structure for the meeting. Knowing that there are only 5 minutes versus 20 minutes for an agenda item changes the expectations of how the topic will be approached. For example, shared decision making makes more sense for 20 minutes rather than for 5 minutes. Having times listed for agenda items is especially helpful when actually drafting the agenda. Cramming too many items into one meeting without giving the time necessary to fully engage as a team can create tension between members and reduce the likelihood that the objectives for the meeting are met. While the time limits for each agenda item are not set in stone and the team should, at times, be flexible given the circumstances, providing the stability of a well-prioritized agenda is a cornerstone of an effective meeting.

Next to the times for the meeting is the agenda-item section. Prior to the meeting, the agenda should be made available to all teammates so that they know the topics that will be discussed. If your team uses a shared file system, such as Google Drive or Microsoft OneDrive, it is also helpful to provide hyperlinks to any documents or resources that will be discussed. During the meeting itself, the note taker will expand upon the agenda items with pertinent information that supports an understanding of why decisions were made. The next steps can briefly be described in this section as well, although detailed action steps are reserved for a different space at the bottom of the agenda.

These detailed action steps serve to clearly articulate what activities will be completed to move the bullying prevention work of the team forward. It also provides a level of accountability. At the next team meeting, past action steps should be reviewed to determine the degree to which they were successfully completed. The basic outline of an action plan includes the task to be completed, who is responsible for completing the task, the due date, and how one knows that the action is completed. To give an example, a common action step for a bullying prevention implementation team is to review the data on reports of bullying. With limited time in the actual meetings, an action item can be to collect the most recent data, analyze it for trends, and bring the information back to the team for the next meeting, so that decisions can be made on how to adjust the team's efforts as necessary. In this example, one or more volunteers with data analysis experience from the team would offer to complete the task. The due date would be the next team meeting, and the team would know that the action item was completed when the volunteers provide a brief presentation of the data to the team.

The final part that should be included in every meeting is the meeting evaluation. A key component to continually improving as a team is evaluating your effectiveness and addressing concerns. Reviewing the teaming components we have described, several areas are ripe for evaluation. For example, all team members can score the degree to which objectives for the meeting were met, the norms were followed, and actionable next steps were described using a Likert-type scale. Teams can make these surveys anonymous if they like, or have team members share their scores for greater transparency. The drawback with having scores shared publicly is that if there are significant concerns around trust, team members may not provide feedback that is genuine.

The process by which the meeting evaluation is conducted can also be supportive of problem solving. When evaluations are conducted electronically (think Google Forms or SurveyMonkey), the data can easily be tracked over time. These data can then be shared with the team to discern trends and areas for improvement. In addition to quantitative data on the effectiveness of the meeting, qualitative data through the use of consistent open-ended questions can provide fantastic ideas for improvement. Two simple questions that can be asked at the end of every meeting are "what went well?" and "what can make the meeting better?" Not every team member is required to share an answer to both of these questions, but for people who have strong opinions about what they would like to see continue or changes they would like to see made, asking these questions gives them a structured opportunity to have their voices heard.

This discussion of evaluation brings us back to shared decision making and team member selection. Evaluations of meetings are only as good as the tangible changes that come about from their analysis. Collecting quantitative and qualitative data looks great on paper, but if no functional shifts in teaming occur, then the data end up simply being numbers on a page. After evaluating the meeting, the team needs time to consider solutions to alleviate the problem. Given the time constraints at the end of meetings, these solutions may not involve a great deal of analysis at first; however, action steps can be created for work between meetings to find potential causes for lower evaluation scores. For example, if teammates score themselves lower on following norms, a brief discussion could find that members felt like everyone did not have a voice in some of the decisions. The team could then decide that before the next meeting each member will email the facilitator their thinking about why some members did not have a voice and about what a possible solution would be. It's agreed that the facilitator will collect the thoughts and suggestions from the team and implement a change for the next meeting in an effort to ensure that all voices are heard.

CHAPTER 9

Implementation Drivers

Implementation Drivers are the engine that moves a program forward toward successful implementation. There are two implementation drivers: competency drivers and organizational drivers. Both of these drivers are explained in depth in this chapter. In addition to these two drivers, leadership is also a foundational piece that supports the effective implementation of CBP. Poor leadership has caused many initiatives to flounder within schools. We describe some of the key factors that all leaders should attend to when working to implement CBP. A final note on implementation drivers is that in Appendix C we provide an adapted version of the National Implementation Research Network's Drivers Best Practices Assessment. This assessment is specifically tailored to CBP and allows your team to determine the degree to which you are implementing the drivers as expected.

COMPETENCY DRIVERS

Competency drivers support the school staff by providing the knowledge, skills, and abilities to effectively implement CBP. In short, they improve the competency of the staff. Increasing the number of staff members who have the requisite capability for reducing bullying means engaging in the following four competency drivers: (1) fidelity, (2) selection, (3) training, and (4) coaching. Fidelity looks at the degree to which the school staff is implementing the components of CBP as intended. If we don't measure fidelity, we are not able to determine the success or failure of our bullying prevention efforts. We have written about fidelity in greater detail in Chapter 6, and encourage you to review this chapter for more information.

Selection of Team Members

When choosing who will be on the bullying prevention implementation team, the selection driver provides a structured process. We have already discussed the importance of having a wide variety of school staff personnel, family members, and community members on the team. Selection differs in that it focuses on the processes for choosing team members, not simply selecting members based on their role. Depending on your setting, selection may take different forms. For example, if you are in a rural area with relatively few staff personnel who are already taking on multiple roles, being selective is difficult simply because there are limited options. On the other hand, if you are in a suburban high school with 2,000 students, being selective is difficult because you may have to tell passionate teachers that there is not enough space for them on the team.

Regardless of your setting, there are two factors to keep in mind as you select team members. First, the process for selecting members as part of your implementation team should be mutual. By this, we mean that the people who are interested in participating should fully understand their roles and responsibilities as members. A passion for bullying prevention likely led to their initial interest, but they need to understand the expectations that are truly involved. For example, if a math teacher shows interest in being part of the team, they should know that, given their area of expertise, they may be called on to support data analysis for the team. This may seem like a straightforward request, but some teachers may want to have a change of pace from their typical day-to-day responsibilities by joining the team and not realize the commitment that's required.

The second process is more commonly used when hiring new staff but can still be applied to selecting team members. It involves determining how well the team member responds to feedback and is willing to learn. Bullying can be a very emotional and traumatic experience for everyone involved. Ensuring that team members are able to hear differing viewpoints and feedback without becoming defensive goes a long way to avoiding breakdowns in trust and morale later on. You may have experienced this process yourself when applying for a job. Perhaps you were required to role-play how you would present a lesson plan. Then, after you had completed the lesson, you were given feedback on what you could do better. Although part of that selection process was seeing how well you could teach a lesson, what is often just as important is how well you are able to take feedback and apply it so that you continue to improve your skills.

A similar process can be used when selecting members for the bullying prevention implementation team. Although you personally may not be interviewing potential members, the existing knowledge level of the staff, family, and community members who are selected needs to be considered. The goal here is not to exclude specific opinions or approaches, but to ensure that the people who make up the team are able to be open-minded about solutions and are willing to grow.

Training of Staff

Within implementation science, training is distilled down to being skill based and purposeful. As we all know, the amount of time teachers and other school staff have to complete all of their daily responsibilities is extremely limited. This being the case, training on bullying prevention in general, and the evidence-based bullying prevention curriculum in particular, needs to be tightly focused with a clear goal and purpose. The goal of training in schools is to ensure that the entitre staff knows the procedures for addressing reports of bullying, has a basic understanding of bullying and prevention strategies, and is equipped to implement the evidence-based program.

When conducting trainings on the components of CBP, it is vital to have at least one person who is clearly accountable for conducting the training. This is typically a staff member who is on the bullying prevention implementation team. The quality and timeliness of trainings are key responsibilities for this staff member. Also keep in mind that even though there may be one point person for the trainings, this does not mean that all of the trainings must be conducted by that person. For the sake of sustainability, there should be several people able and willing to conduct trainings on the evidence-based bullying prevention curriculum and bullying prevention best practices in general. Moreover, the training materials and resources should be clear enough so that most of the staff are able to use them independently if necessary.

In addition to a point of contact for training, the schedule of trainings should also be defined and included in a school's planning. There are three training plans to develop: (1) initial training, (2) refresher training, and (3) onboarding training. The initial training is designed to provide all staff members with a strong foundation. This training is typically scheduled at the beginning of each school year for new staff members before they are expected to implement best practices. Common topics in initial training include an explanation of the bullying prevention policy, what to do when receiving a report of bullying, and the basics of any evidence-based bullying prevention curriculum that is used at the school. Refresher training is similar to the initial training, but is meant for staff members who have already received the initial training. These trainings occur once at the beginning of the year and once after the winter break. The goal of refresher trainings is to quickly reteach any areas of bullying prevention best practices that the data suggest are not being implemented as intended. For example, if the data are showing that the use of the school's token economy system began to fade near the end of the first semester, refresher training in January could focus on increasing its use. Finally, onboarding training refers to a standardized training that is provided to any staff member who joins the school after the start of the year. This training is very brief, but provides the opportunity for new staff members to gain an awareness of the basic protocols and best practices for bullying prevention used in the school. Additional coaching support is especially important for these staff members to ensure fidelity.

Adult Learning Principles

Research suggests that adults learn differently than children or adolescents and thus require a separate set of adult learning principles to ensure successful outcomes. As outlined by Trivette, Dunst, Hamby, and O'Herin (2009), there are six principles that improve adult learning. The full list of adult learning principles and how they can be applied to bullying prevention is shown in Table 9.1. The first two principles center around planning for the training itself. Specifically, learners should be given a preview of the materials or program prior to the training. This preview gives them the opportunity to enter the training already primed with a baseline of understanding for their learning. In addition to early access to materials, the usability or applicability of the training should be clearly demonstrated. An example of using the first two principles would be providing staff with the presentation slides before the training and explaining how reducing bullying will give them more instructional time in the classroom.

TABLE 9.1. Adult Learning Principles

Principle	Description	Application to Bullying Prevention
Introduce	Give learners a brief preview of the content prior to the training.	Slides of the presentation are sent to all staff members prior to an all-staff training on CBP.
Illustrate	Show how the training topic is helpful to the learner.	During the presentation, time is specifically dedicated to demonstrating how CBP will likely reduce the time spent managing behaviors in the classroom.
Practice	Provide leaners with the chance to use the actual materials or program.	Provide teachers with the evidence-based bullying prevention curriculum that will be used and demonstrate how it is already connected to existing systems in the school.
Evaluate	Support learners in evaluating the outcomes of the program.	The bullying prevention implementation team provides data updates to the staff, including schoolwide fidelity of implementation and bullying outcome data.
Reflection	Use self-assessments to help learners identify their skills and skill gaps.	The bullying prevention implementation team uses data from teacher self-assessments to guide coaching supports.
Mastery	Help learners assess their skills, outcomes, and fidelity to a set of external standards.	Teachers use the CBP Fidelity Assessment to analyze their impact on the system of bullying prevention schoolwide.

Note. From Trivette et al. (2009).

The second set of adult learning principles are used during the training itself. When adults learn new information, it is easier for them to retain that information when it is connected to their existing knowledge and then applied to their own specific circumstances (Donovan & Pelligrino, 1999). Thus, when receiving training on a new bullying prevention program, trainers should clearly connect the program to staff members' current knowledge and actively engage them in applying the new learning to their setting. A trainer explaining how the lessons in the new Second Step curriculum connect to the schoolwide expectations with which all teachers are already familiar is one example. Once training has been completed, the next adult learning principle suggests that participants should be involved in evaluating the impact of the training. In bullying prevention, this could involve the sharing of bullying report data to the entire staff. Over time, the bullying prevention implementation team could show how bullying has been reduced in the school since staff training began.

The final set of adult learning principles reflect a deeper understanding of the content that is being taught. First, participants should be asked to assess the new information and skills they were taught. Entire books have been written on just the topic of measuring professional development (Guskey, 1999). For our purposes, a less-complex process can be conducted. Ultimately, the goal of collecting data on trainings is twofold. Surveys should provide data to the trainer to improve future training opportunities. Additionally, the data can be used to improve staff competencies after the training itself, which typically occurs through coaching support. Do the participants believe they are ready to begin initial implementation of the program or best practice? If not, what are the areas they believe they need to improve? When the staff who are providing coaching services has data that show where additional supports are needed, they are able to provide more efficient services. To be clear, these surveys do not need to be lengthy. The goal is to identify general areas for improvement, not diagnostically determine root causes.

In addition to surveying staff members on their newly acquired knowledge and skills, participants can have the actual implementation of those skills measured, which can often be done through a fidelity assessment. For example, if your school is using PBIS to ensure a positive school climate, it features assessments such as the School-wide Evaluation Tool (SET). The SET includes items that ask staff members to identify the schoolwide expectations and describe their system for collecting and analyzing discipline data. By including adult learning principles in trainings, including refresher and onboarding training, we give ourselves the best chance to effectively implement bullying prevention best practices.

Coaching of Staff

When educators think about coaching, they may initially have visions of district or administrative personnel entering their classrooms to provide support around an academic topic. Indeed, the goal of coaching is to improve the effective use of skills, often learned in trainings, in the actual classroom. There are typically three distinct time frames in coaching support. The first occurs prior to a classroom observation when the coach is planning for the coaching session. The second is the observation of the staff member in the classroom or other appropriate setting where skills will be used. The third is after the observation when the coach and staff member debrief. If your role in a school is one of a counselor, social worker, or school psychologist, it is likely that you have not experienced having a coach provide you with feedback and guidance. However, research has shown that coaching is invaluable for taking the knowledge and skills learned in trainings and actually implementing it in the classroom. In 2002, Joyce and Showers examined the extent to which skills taught during trainings end up being implemented in the classroom. Their results suggested that even if a training is conducted with best practices, only 5% of teachers would apply the skills learned within the classroom. In contrast, when training is accompanied by classroom coaching, they estimate that 95% of the skills taught are implemented.

Given the clear importance that coaching has on implementation, there should be a point person who is accountable for ensuring its effective and timely use in the school. This can be a coach who, for example, observes lessons from the selected evidence-based curriculum being implemented and provides feedback or supports a small group of staff members who are not fully comfortable with intervening in bullying situations. If bullying prevention is a districtwide initiative, the coach may be someone from outside of the school (and should be considered as a member of the school's bullying prevention implementation team if appropriate). Smaller schools or schools that do not currently have district infrastructure for bullying prevention may task one of the bullying prevention implementation team members to lead the coaching for the school. To be clear, coaching is not so much a person as it is a collection of activities. While there may be a point person leading the coaching work, and that person may do some of the actual coaching, anyone with the required knowledge and skills can serve as a coach for the bullying prevention efforts of a school. Indeed, developing the coaching skills of multiple staff members in this area can support the sustainability of the program over time.

Core Components of Coaching

When providing coaching on the components of CBP, such as the bullying prevention policy or the evidence-based bullying prevention curriculum, a clear, written coaching plan should be in place (see Table 9.2). As outlined by Cusumano and Preston (2018), coaching plans should include several essential components, including prompting, performance feedback, creating an enabling and collaborative context, data use, application of content knowledge, continuum of supports, and scaffolding. Regardless of the skill level of the staff member being coached, all of these components can contribute to greater success in implementation.

Prompting refers to the use of discreet cues that remind the staff member how to use a skill before it is needed. For example, if a school is starting a token economy to create a more positive school climate, a simple visual prompt could include placing the tokens on top of the teacher's lesson plan to remind them to praise students who successfully follow the classroom behavior expectations. When providing performance feedback, coaches highlight both the successes and areas of improvement for skills implementation. This feedback should be as specific as possible and focused on the areas that most affect a reduction in bullying.

TABLE 9.2. Summary of Coaching Components

Component	Example
Prompting	Putting a stack of token economy reinforcers on a teacher's desk to remind them to reinforce students for expected behavior.
Performance feedback	The coach praises the teacher for reinforcing students for expected behaviors and suggests increasing their awareness of the number of positive-to-negative comments.
Enabling and collaborative context	The coach spends the first meeting with a teacher by building a relationship with them, getting to know more about their passion for teaching, and connecting it to CBP.
Application of content knowledge	The coach describes a personal example of how they made a mistake when intervening in a bullying situation, how they rectified the mistake, and the lesson they learned from the mistake.
Continuum of supports	The coach uses data to identify a small group of teachers who need targeted supports around implementation of the evidence-based curriculum and meets with this group of teachers once a week to provide support.
Scaffolding	After providing targeted supports to a group of teachers to support their implementation of the evidence-based curriculum, the coach uses data to determine which teachers can begin receiving solely universal coaching supports.

Creating an enabling and collaborative context improves the coaching experience itself. When coaches are able to facilitate a culture that feels supportive, nonpunitive, and collaborative, the likelihood that the staff will embrace the process increases. This means that the coach and the staff jointly agree on the skills that are the focus of coaching, the goals for the coaching, and what data will be used to measure success. Moreover, having a collaborative approach to coaching allows staff members to provide feedback to the coach on what they find most helpful in building their skills. This enables the coach to customize their approach for each individual person they support.

The use of data to inform coaching is vital to demonstrating its success. It may be easy to say that behavior in the classroom "feels" like less of an issue, but when we are able to truly show this changed behavior using data, it can connect the dots between our actions and improved student outcomes. This being the case, it is vital to collect data relevant only to the identified area of need for the staff member. If a teacher has identified her area of need for coaching support as providing students with more opportunities to express empathy for peers, but the coach only measures office discipline referrals (ODRs), the data will not be reflective of the teacher's impact. On the other hand, if the coach is collecting data on the number of opportunities students are given to connect their life experiences with those of their peers, these data can be used to determine progress on improving student empathy.

When coaches are able to use their own experience, knowledge, and expertise during coaching, they are engaging in the application of content knowledge. This past experience of coaches can also support the building of rapport with staff members because coaches are able to demonstrate their own successes and overcoming of barriers. Sharing stories of past experiences in which the desired skills were successfully implemented provides staff members with concrete examples of what implementation looks like. A key criteria when selecting a coach is the degree to which they have knowledge of the subject. Coaches who have extensive experience with the required skills and content are better able to sequence their support based on the needs of the staff and the difficulty of the skill.

Sequencing coaching based on the difficulty of skills aligns with another essential component of coaching: the use of a continuum of supports. Just as students receive a continuum of supports in academics or behavior based on their performance, so too should staff members who are implementing bullying prevention best practices. For staff members who are more efficient and skilled, coaching may follow a universal approach for support. Those who demonstrate greater gaps in their ability to implement skills (e.g., forgetting to reinforce students, not using a 4-to-1 ratio of positive to constructive comments) may receive targeted or intensive coaching supports. These targeted and intensive supports can include strategies like co-teaching with the coach, providing prompts to promote the use of underutilized skills, and increasing the frequency of prompts, feedback, and modeling.

The final essential component of coaching is scaffolding. Similar to how teachers scaffold learning for students based on their skills, coaches should scaffold the support they provide to individuals on the staff. The typical sequence of scaffolding moves from skill acquisition, to obtaining fluency, to generalizing skills to multiple contexts, and finally to adaptation of the skills. Throughout this process, the coach gradually fades the amount of support that is provided. Coaching may begin by modeling skills, including the use of examples and nonexamples, then proceed into practicing the skills with support through role plays or in a natural setting in the school. Once the data suggest that the staff member has become fluent in the use of the skills, they can move into independent practice of the skills before the coaching fades.

ORGANIZATION DRIVERS

Organization drivers differ from competency drivers in that the latter focus on producing skilled staff whereas the former focus on creating a more hospitable environment for implementation. There are three organization drivers: (1) data systems, (2) administrative support, and (3) stakeholder engagement. These drivers specifically focus on the processes, policies, and systems within a school. All three of the drivers work in tandem to develop an environment that is conducive to effective implementation.

Data Systems

The adage "what gets measured gets done" encapsulates the purpose behind data systems. In truth, the adage should be "what gets measured through an effective data system gets done." Data systems are those actions and processes your school actively uses to gather and analyze information that documents student achievement. In Chapter 6 we covered data-based problem solving in detail. Data systems are different, in that they provide the structure for using data. The goal of effective data systems is to make it easy for schools to use their data for decision making. There are several important components of a strong data system in your school.

Similar to other important functions in implementation, there should be a point person for managing the data system. This person leads the coordination of multiple data collections and the use of data to make schoolwide decisions. As an example, a member of the bullying prevention implementation team who is designated as the data system lead collects ODRs, schoolwide behavior screening, and bullying report data on a regular basis. At team meetings, this person provides a summary of the data to help the team determine if Tier 2 or Tier 3 supports are needed for some students to reduce bullying.

In addition to the data systems lead providing a summary of bullying and bullying-related behavior data to the implementation team, an effective data system also provides access to usable data for relevant staff members. Having access to usable data enables the staff to make data-informed decisions on how to support their students. Usable data include data related to the fidelity of bullying prevention best-practices implementation, behavior screening data, and training feedback. Collecting data should be done in a standardized way. Although anecdotal information on the behavior of students can be helpful, relying on this information easily leads to potential discrepancies in how different students are provided supports. Ideally, data are accessible within existing data warehouses used by the school so that the information is easy for staff members to use. The staff member in charge of training can review any feedback on their trainings and plan for improvements, and the staff member in charge of coaching supports can review fidelity data to identify teachers who may need additional support. Taking this approach empowers the staff with the information they need to identify gaps in implementation and move toward improvement.

The final component of a data system is that there be a process for using the data for decision making. This process includes several steps. Bullying prevention data should be analyzed and summarized at least once each quarter. Additionally, these data should be communicated to the staff to provide evidence of the impact their work has in reducing bullying. This reporting can coincide with the traditional staff development days that occur about every 9 weeks. Within the bullying prevention implementation team, data can be used to develop action plans focused on improving implementation and intervening in hot spots. These data-based action plans can also be shared with the school staff so that it is aware of how the bullying data it collects is improving the lives of students.

Administrative Support

Anyone who has worked in a school knows that very little gets done without the support of the administration. The administrative support driver is focused solely on how the school administration facilitates the success of bullying prevention best practices. It includes (1) providing resources; (2) drafting and revising policies; (3) roles, functions, and structures; (4) communication; (5) visible promotion of bullying prevention efforts; (6) problem-solving challenges; and (7) recognition of staff contributions. Examining these supports, the first three can be considered supporting the infrastructure of bullying prevention. When the leadership provides resources to staff members so that they are able to feel confident in their ability to implement the bullying prevention best practices, the task feels less like an add-on to their existing duties. This is further reinforced when the training and coaching provided to the staff are clearly integrated with the work already being done. For example, the Facing History and Ourselves curriculum is designed to be used as part of a secondary school's social studies course. Since some teachers often have reasonable concerns about implementing new programs, strong administrative support can help alleviate these concerns before they become larger barriers. See Table 9.3 for a list of common teacher concerns with new initiatives and solutions for how to support teachers with these concerns (Hall, 1974).

One of the most sustainable approaches school leadership can take to facilitate the implementation of CBP is to develop and/or revise policies at the school level. More detail on what should be included in a bullying prevention policy can be found in Chapter 3, but administrative support that includes annual staff training in bullying prevention shows staff members, students, and families the dedication a school has to preventing bullying. Another component of a school's bullying prevention policy that aligns with the administrative support driver is defining the roles, functions, and structures for bullying prevention implementation. When a school first explores implementing

TABLE 9.3. Common Teacher Concerns and Potential Solutions

Type of concern	Common questions	Potential solution
Self-concerns	Will I have the skills to do this?	• Communicate that support will be provided. • Describe how the lessons are organized and connect the skills needed for bullying prevention to the skills teachers already have and practice well. • Provide sufficient training and coaching.
Task concerns	How should I organize and prepare for this?	• Create buy-in by hearing and addressing staff concerns. • Allocate the appropriate resources for the practices.
Impact concerns	Does this even matter?	• Use data and share testimonies of students to show it is a concern.
	Will this make a difference?	• Share research showing the practices are effective. • Discuss how the practices consider the unique aspect of your site.

a comprehensive approach to bullying prevention, the implementation team in charge may be an existing team (e.g., school climate team). Depending on your school's resources and structures, you may decide to keep this team or to choose a different group of people for the implementation team. The key is to ensure that there is clear communication and that superfluous teams are avoided.

How administrative leaders communicate with staff members, families, and students about bullying prevention initiatives demonstrates their support. Something as simple as providing the implementation team a spot on the agenda at staff meetings to speak about their successes shows that the work of the team is valued. Taking a few minutes during all-school assemblies or pep rallies to talk about the acts of kindness the school administration has seen in the school can reinforce to students the value placed on these actions. This communication also provides visible promotion of the bullying prevention efforts. In addition, leaders who encourage stakeholders to provide feedback on the successes and barriers allow everyone to give voice to their experience.

What is truly important, though, is how leaders respond to this feedback. When families hear that their suggestions were considered and then acted upon by the school's leaders, it shows them that not only are their voices heard, but that they are valued as well. The way in which leadership solicits feedback from the staff, families, and students is important. Simply telling families that you "always have an open door" is a nice sentiment, but requires a lot of initiative on the part of the family. In contrast, school leadership could facilitate the inclusion of a brief, anonymous one-page feedback survey within the handbill of the next school play. As families wait for the show to start, they could complete the surveys and turn them in. This is an easy way for families to contribute their thoughts and opinions.

School leaders who engage in these activities begin to receive positive and constructive feedback from all stakeholders. These data, when combined with other data sources, allow the administration to actively engage in problem-solving challenges with the implementation team. Although the implementation team will be in the role of consistently problem solving concerns, having the engagement and support of the school's administration continues to demonstrate the value placed on their work. Finally, it is the role of the administration to publicly and privately recognize staff contributions to the school's bullying prevention efforts. Some staff members appreciate the public recognition of their hard work in the presence of their peers, while others may find it uncomfortable. This does not mean that recognition in and of itself is not desired, so it is up to the administration to determine what is most meaningful for each staff member. One way that staff members can be recognized is by counting the number of reinforcements given to students for engaging in expected behaviors by each staff member (as discussed in Chapter 2 as part of a positive school climate). The staff member who has given out the greatest number of reinforcements is recognized in the presence of their peers.

Stakeholder Engagement

As we wrote in Chapter 4, multiple stakeholders need to be involved in CBP. This means that families, community members, and the students themselves should have a say in the work. We briefly review the key activities that should take place as part of the stakeholder engagement driver here. More information on how to engage all stakeholders can be found in Chapter 5. The three key activities for stakeholder engagement are (1) developing a shared understanding of the need for bullying prevention, (2) collaborating with stakeholders to learn and design solutions, and (3) communicating with stakeholders about bullying prevention efforts.

Providing a clear description of why bullying prevention is needed to families and community members is one of the first ways a school can create buy-in for its work. As we explained earlier, having data on the prevalence of bullying in the school and on the potential consequences for students involved in bullying is a good starting place. Moreover, demonstrating how behavioral concerns such as bullying can impact the academic performance of students further reinforces the need for staff to be engaged in preventing bullying. Community partners and families can also find value in engaging with the school to prevent bullying. By providing a continuity of language and positive behavior expectations across settings, youth behavior can improve in after-school care programs and in homes as well. The need to improve behavior in after-school care programs and in the home can often be self-identified. Early childhood education centers can also quickly realize a need for partnering with the schools that their children will eventually attend. Not only does this approach provide them with the chance to demonstrate to their paying families that they are preparing their children for school behaviorally, but it also opens to the door for them to potentially partner around academic school readiness too.

Ongoing communication with stakeholders provides opportunities to share successes and receive feedback on challenges. During parent–teacher conferences, sporting events, and other well-attended events at the school, leaders can share the work that is being done to prevent bullying. This outreach also gives schools the chance to hear from families about how bullying prevention in the school could improve. Engaging with after-school and early-childhood education centers, the school can support the sharing of resources and areas of focus for bullying prevention lessons each week. The staff in these programs also have the opportunity to see students in a different environment and from a different perspective. With ongoing communication, the school staff can be more aware of potential difficulties that families are facing that could also influence their children's behavior at school.

LEADERSHIP

This is not a book on leadership, but without effective leadership, bullying prevention efforts will flounder. Administrators are typically thought of as the school leaders. Principals and assistant principals are the face of the school and those to whom the rest of the staff turn when problems arise. The administration may also lead the bullying prevention implementation team, but given their already heavy responsibilities, another staff member may be identified as the lead. Even if you are not leading the implementation team, it is helpful to know about the features of leadership. With this information in mind, you will be able to start identifying when different leadership strategies are needed. For this feature, we review two different leadership challenges and how they should be approached differently.

Technical Problems

The first type of challenge faced by leaders are technical problems (Heifetz, Linsky, & Grashow, 2009). These are the types of challenges that are fairly easy to identify and solve. For example, let's assume the bullying prevention implementation team is discussing its student survey. The survey is conducted online using a third-party survey website, but the team has just found out that it doesn't have the more expensive subscription that would allow them to survey all of their students. As the leader of the team, you speak to the principal, who approves spending the additional $50 to upgrade the subscription. This problem was easy to identify (i.e., the survey subscription plan would not allow every student to take the survey) and solve (i.e., the principal gave approval to upgrade the subscription plan). Additionally, people were generally receptive to the solution, change was only required in an isolated place, and the solution was implemented quickly. All of these factors are hallmarks of technical problems. On the other side of the coin are adaptive challenges.

Adaptive Challenges

As described by Heifetz and Laurie (1997), adaptive challenges are those with no known solutions or no clear options from a myriad of possible solutions. Often, these challenges require changes in values, beliefs, and norms. As a leader, Heifetz and Laurie (1997) recommend six strategies to effectively solve adaptive challenges: (1) identify your adaptive challenge, (2) stand on the balcony, (3) regulate distress, (4) maintain disciplined attention, (5) give the work back to the people, and (6) protect leadership voices from below. As a leader on the bullying prevention implementation team, you have the opportunity to couple these strategies with the consensus-building approaches described earlier to give teammates an opportunity to work through difficult challenges.

Identify Your Adaptive Challenge

The first strategy for tackling adaptive challenges is to be able to identify when you are facing one. To revisit our example about surveying students, an adaptive challenge may arise around the types of questions included in the survey. Do you include questions asking the perceived reason why a student was bullied, such as their sexual orientation, disability status, or race? Some staff members may think that this is valuable information that can inform the direction of intervention efforts. Others may believe that these questions are too invasive and that there will be pushback from families. This is a problem rooted in personal values and beliefs with a myriad of potential solutions but no clear answers; thus, it is an adaptive challenge. It is not a technical problem that can be solved by simply purchasing a more expensive subscription to an online survey platform. At times, challenges that appear to be technical are actually adaptive. This discussion about survey questions may have begun as an agenda item about data collection. What, for all intents and purposes, seemed to be a cut-and-dried part of the meeting morphed into a discussion with political and/or religious undertones. Underlying values and norms end up being discussed, which leads to an adaptive challenge for leaders.

Stand on the Balcony

Once an adaptive challenge has been identified, leaders need to be able to "stand on the balcony." By this, Heifetz and Laurie (1997) mean taking a step back to look at the big picture. If you are someone who likes to get into the weeds working with details on specific problems this stance may not come naturally. When working with students, families, and teammates on preventing bullying, it can be tempting to jump into problem solving and finding solutions for issues that rise to the surface. However, as a leader of the implementation team, it is also vital that you be able to recognize patterns within the team that reflect differences in values, work avoidance, and reactions to change. Being able to both get into the weeds and recognize larger systemic patterns within a team allow a leader to better understand the potential impact of decisions made during a team meeting.

Regulate Distress

The third strategy for resolving adaptive challenges is regulating distress. By their nature, adaptive challenges are stressful. When values and beliefs are part of the reason why disagreements occur within a team, the members of that team naturally feel passionate and express their emotions more readily, which makes it more difficult for members to respond rationally and logically to the challenges. One of the most effective ways to manage distress among teammates is to create a culture and environment within the team that allows for distress to be regulated. Ensuring that a strong set of norms have been implemented and agreed upon by the team is critically important. When dialogue becomes stressful, the leader can lean on these agreed-upon norms to support a discussion that focuses disagreements on ideas and not on the people suggesting them.

Maintain Disciplined Attention

Maintaining disciplined attention, the fourth adaptive strategy, goes hand in hand with regulating distress. In short, a leader who maintains disciplined attention invites differing perspectives because they know that doing so is one of the most valuable contributions that can be made when preventing bullying. Of course, encouraging differences in opinions also means an increase in conflict. Although it may seem counterintuitive at first, conflict is something that leaders should actually *embrace*, not avoid. As Lencioni (2002) describes in great detail in his book, *The Five Dysfunctions of a Team*, when a team does not engage in productive conflict, the voices and perspectives of all the team members will not be heard. Often, avoiding conflict leads to short-term comfort at the cost of long-term success. In contrast, when productive conflict is used effectively, teams are able to strengthen agreement with decisions, and everyone on the team is willing to contribute more to the effective implementation of those decisions.

Using our student survey example again, the differing opinions on whether to include questions about why a student was targeted is a dialogue in which productive conflict should be engaged. Only by airing the perspectives of all implementation team members can there be any sense of buy-in for the decision. The value of having multiple perspectives also reinforces the need for having your implementation team be representative of multiple stakeholders. Regardless of the decision that is ultimately made, families and the community should at least know that they had someone with their viewpoint in the conversation.

Give the Work Back to the People

The final two adaptive strategies, "give the work back to the people" and "protect voices of leadership from below," both speak to the idea of avoiding top-down leadership. If the leader of the bullying prevention implementation team is the principal of the school, these two strategies are even more important. Giving the work back to the people means that the school staff, families, students, and community members should be the ones defining and solving concerns. The role of the team leader is that of supporting rather than controlling others. Part of supporting these individuals is truly believing that they have important perspectives and opinions that can better the school's bullying prevention efforts, even if inviting other viewpoints creates conflict in the short term.

Protect Voices of Leadership from Below

Families, students, and the community may not know the proper channels or methods for communicating their ideas about bullying prevention, but this fact does not mean that their ideas should be summarily dismissed. This is what is meant by protecting voices of leadership from below. Since we are in the school daily and know the traditional ways of communicating our perspectives, we may not immediately understand the value of a family member expressing their opinions if it is done in a nontraditional way. At times, families may be angry because of something that happened at the school. If we only respond to the anger with which they are communicating, even if they are suggesting legitimate concerns that need to be addressed, we will miss an opportunity to improve.

CHAPTER 10

Case Study
Exploration

INTRODUCTION

The rest of this book provides a fictional case study of an elementary school that uses implementation science and its stages of implementation to reach full implementation of CBP. Accompanying this case study in Appendix D is a Stages of Implementation Checklist for Comprehensive Bullying Prevention adapted from the Office of Special Education Programs and NIRN (National Implementation Research Network, 2020). As you read, we point out the items of the checklist so that you can see what they look like in a real-world setting.

EXPLORATION

As implied in its name, the exploration stage of implementation involves gathering information to better inform the upcoming decisions related to bullying prevention in your school. This beginning phase starts when the bullying prevention implementation team is formed or the duties of such a team are integrated into the work of an existing team. Champions for bullying prevention are identified and support the team through communication with stakeholders and assessing current needs and assets. Data should be used to demonstrate the extent of school bullying concerns. Once the team has a strong understanding of the problem, a list of potential practices for preventing bullying is developed. An assessment of the fit and feasibility for implementing bullying prevention practices is made in an effort to select the best approach for your school. Once schools have selected their best practices for preventing bullying and have buy-in from the leadership and stakeholders for the approach, they are close to moving from exploration to installation. Although it is true that a schools can choose a variety of practices to implement, we have outlined this case study to illustrate a school that has selected CBP as the innovation to implement.

Conestoga Elementary School

Conestoga Elementary School serves kindergarten through fifth-grade students in the Portland, Oregon, suburb of Beaverton. There are a total of 526 students attending Conestoga and 29 teachers, with a median class size of 24. Within the student population, there are a total of 26 languages spoken. The majority of students identify as White (70%), then Asian (12%), Latinx (10%), and Black (5%). Only about 15% of students at Conestoga qualify for free and reduced-price lunch. The school has a history of implementing the PBIS framework, though the fidelity with which it is implemented has waned over the past several years. The school was built in the late 1980s and first admitted students in the fall of 1989.

The city of Beaverton has a population of about 100,000, with the majority identifying as White (65%), followed by Latinx (15%), Asian (8%), Other Races (7%), and Black (5%). The median income for a family is over $70,000, suggesting that many families in the city are above the poverty line. The two largest employers in the city are the school district and Nike, which has its world headquarters located in an unincorporated area of Beaverton. In fact, many of the parents of students at Conestoga Elementary School work at the Nike campus.

In October, Conestoga's principal, Mr. Young, begins to anecdotally hear about an uptick in behavior concerns around the school. When checking in with one of his fifth-grade teachers, Mrs. Doran, she is clearly frustrated. "I can't believe how my class is treating my new student," she says. "This girl just moved here and it's almost like the entire class has decided that she is not going to be allowed to join them at recess or at the lunch table. Just this morning when students were sharing their projects from the Oregon Trail unit, I had to write minor referrals for two kids because they laughed and made fun of her project." Talking with one of his second-grade teachers, Mr. Ferris, he described having difficulty managing the physical aggression in his classroom. "I have one student in particular who continually pushes other kids if they are in his way or if he wants something that they have," says Mr. Ferris. "I have tried reteaching more positive behavior, but it doesn't seem to make that big a difference. The thing that's really sad is that he has a target or two that he torments almost every day, and they are two of the sweetest kids."

A week later, it became abundantly clear to Mr. Young that his school had a bullying problem. On the same afternoon, he received three phone calls from three separate families. Every family was frustrated and angry about their child being bullied at Conestoga Elementary School. What made matters even worse was that the students being targeted were students in multiple grade levels. This told Mr. Young that he may be dealing with a systemic issue and not something that could be attributed to just one classroom or grade level. After his last phone call with a parent had ended, Mr. Young went to the behavior records of his school (which took several minutes because they were difficult to find) and saw that his hunch was correct. The number of students reporting incidents of fighting, name calling, and other aggression were obviously higher than in years past. It was then that he decided the first step he would take in tackling the bullying at his school.

Implementation Team

Develop an Implementation Team

Mr. Young knows that to give the school the best chance at reducing bullying he will need to have a representative bullying prevention implementation team. He reaches out to the teachers who have previously described bullying incidents to gauge their interest in joining the team. Both Mr. Ferris and Mrs. Doran agree to join. Once he has teacher representatives from the lower and higher grades, he speaks with the specialists at his school. "We already have several staff members on board, but I want to make sure that we have a specialist join the team as well. You all see every student in the building, so you have a unique perspective that is valuable." Every specialist says they would be interested in joining, including the physical education teacher, Mr. Valenzuela, who also agrees to provide updates to the other specialists. The final group of staff Mr. Young approaches are the support staff. Meeting with the paraprofessionals, cafeteria workers, and custodians, Mr. Young picks up two more staff members for the implementation team: Ms. Pearcy, who is a special education staff member, and Dr. Fluke, who is the school psychologist.

During the next all-staff meeting, Mr. Young takes a few minutes to describe the implementation team that he is forming. He explains the purpose of the team, shares broad details, such as how often the team would meet and the fact that several family members had called him recently to voice their frustration with the bullying going on at Conestoga. "We already have several members of the school staff who have joined the team, but if any other staff members are interested, we have room for probably one more. In the meantime, I would like to hear from you all about what kind of representation we are missing from the team. I am already planning on inviting the families that have reached out to me directly so that we have family members on the team. But who else should we have join our team so that we can give ourselves the best chance of eliminating bullying at our school?"

Looking around the room, Mr. Young begins calling on staff. One person suggests that someone from the after-school program be included. "That's a great idea," says Mr. Young. "They serve a lot of our students, and I know that behavior problems are not isolated to school hours." Mr. Young makes a note to speak with the director of the extended day program that is operated within the school building. Another teacher says that her husband works at the Nike campus, and that he talks a lot about the community relations team that the company has there. "They are always looking for ways to impact the community, so they may be interested in helping out too." The teacher agrees to connect the school to someone from Nike, who can provide more information moving forward. Inspired by the idea of having community members involved, another teacher mentions that a college friend of hers is an associate professor at the University of Oregon and does a lot of work around education. Mr. Young asks the teacher to connect with her friend to find out if she would be interested in joining the team to provide her expertise.

Trying to be mindful of not interrupting families at work, Mr. Young waits until school lets out for the day to call the three families that had concerns about bullying. During each phone call, he reiterates his commitment to reducing bullying at Conestoga Elementary School and tells the families that, if they were willing, he would like to have them be part of their team at the school focused solely on reducing bullying. Every family member Mr. Young speaks with thanks him and admits they are surprised to hear that their concerns are being taken so seriously. After completing the three phone calls, a grandmother, Mrs. Myers, says that she is able and willing to join the team each month.

Over the next 2 weeks, Mr. Young speaks with the director of the extended day program, Ms. Coutts, who agrees to join the team. "I think this would be a great way to make sure we are aligning what we do and what the school does to make sure students are learning SEL skills," she says. A manager from a nearby national sporting goods store also agrees to join the team remotely each month after hearing about the team when dropping off supplies to the extended day program. The manager, Mr. Buck, also says he will keep an eye out for any grant opportunities that may be available from his company's community relations division. The final member of the team to join is Professor Obara from the University of Oregon. During their phone call, Professor Obara tells Mr. Young that even though she would need to join remotely each month, she would love to provide her expertise in the area of research. "It seems like all I get to do anymore is teach and do research, so I'm excited to actually get back to the school level," she says.

With the bullying prevention implementation team members in place (see Table 10.1), Mr. Young schedules the first meeting for the end of the month. For the inaugural meeting, Mr. Young develops the agenda and facilitates the meeting. Topics on the agenda include a meet-and-greet icebreaker, a broad overview of CBP, roles, norms, and vision. During the meet-and-greet, Mr. Young makes sure to include Mr. Buck and Professor Obara since they are joining remotely. He then spends several minutes talking about the purpose of the team and provides a broad overview of CBP. He describes the five components and provides a handout of the Practice Profiles to that all the team members. "In future meetings," Mr. Young says, "we will be diving into each one of the components of CBP in more depth so that we all have a strong understanding of these best practices.

Then Mr. Young transitions into issue of team roles. He makes clear that even though he is the principal and is currently facilitating the meeting, he does not intend for the team to maintain this structure. "This team will be a true team. That means that we are sharing leadership. At times I will facilitate the meeting, and at times I will be an active participant." Starting with these two roles, Mr. Young clearly describes the responsibilities of the facilitator (e.g., develop the agenda and

TABLE 10.1. Bullying Prevention Implementation Team Members

Name	Title	Role	Location
Mr. Young	Principal	School administration	Office
Mr. Ferris	Second-grade teacher	School teacher	Classroom
Mrs. Doran	Fifth-grade teacher	School teacher	Classroom
Mr. Valenzuela	Physical education teacher	School specialist	Gym
Ms. Pearcy	Special education teacher	Special education staff	Special education classroom/ general education classrooms/ recess
Dr. Fluke	School psychologist	School support staff	School campus
Mrs. Myers	Grandparent	Family member	Neighborhood
Ms. Coutts	Director of Extended Day Program	Before- and after-school administration	Before and after school on campus
Mr. Buck	National sporting goods store manager	Community member	Neighborhood shopping district
Professor Obara	Associate Professor	Community member	University of Oregon

send it out prior to the meeting, go through the agenda during the meeting) and those of active participants (e.g., engages with the team during discussion, provides the team with their perspectives). Mr. Young describes the other roles and responsibilities on the team, including that of note taker, timekeeper, and chat monitor. For the first meeting, several volunteers take on the responsibilities of each role, and the team agrees to rotate roles for each meeting.

Moving on to the norms section of the agenda, Mr. Young reminds the team of the schoolwide expectations that they teach students at the beginning of every year: Be Respectful, Be Responsible, Be Safe. The team agrees to the general principle of using these three norms as buckets and that they will further define the meaning of in practice during future meetings. During the final part of the meeting, Mr. Young talks to the team about their vision. "I know that we all, ultimately, want to make Conestoga a school where there is no bullying," Mr. Young says. "But we should also consider what makes our school unique." The team then discusses the differences between a vision and a mission. By the end of the meeting, the action wrangler and note taker have a list of next steps that will be taken prior to the next meeting, which includes reflecting on the team norms and coming to the next meeting with ideas for a vision statement.

Develop Communication Processes and Messages

During the next implementation team meeting, Mr. Young makes sure that developing a communication process is an objective on the agenda. Explaining the situation to the team, he says, "We want to make sure that our work on this team is transparent and includes as many voices as possible. To do this, we need to make sure that we have clear two-way communication pathways. What I want to do during this part of the agenda is to brainstorm all the different ways we communicate with families and the community in our school. Then we will narrow down that list to the most effective communication methods and figure out if it allows our stakeholders an easy way to respond." Over the next 20 minutes, the team shares the different communication methods used by the school. Mr. Valenzuela is the note taker for this meeting and types all of the methods into a spreadsheet that is projected at the front of the room.

When they have exhausted all of the ways the school communicates with families and the community, Mr. Young goes through the list and asks for the team's opinion on how effective each method is at engaging their stakeholders. The review concludes that the three most effective forms of communication with families and the community are (1) home visits, (2) the school's social media pages, and (3) direct emails/phone calls to families. Each of these three methods result in families directly engaging with the school. The team decides that, moving forward, these three methods will be used to communicate the opportunity to be involved in the bullying prevention work at the school. When conducting home visits, teachers will give families a short flyer (Mrs. Doran said she likes to dabble in graphic design and would be happy to create a one-page flyer) and talk briefly about the school's bullying prevention work. At least once a quarter, the school's social media accounts will feature posts about the ongoing bullying prevention efforts and will highlight the acts of kindness that students show toward one another more often. Alongside these posts will be more information on how families can be involved in the bullying prevention work at the school. Last, a schoolwide email will be sent out to all families by Mr. Young describing their new team and asking for volunteers. He will be sure to include the fact that not every family will be able to join the actual team, but the school will have ways for any family that wants to be involved to support the work.

Assess Needs

Identify Changes Needed, Existing Assets, and Potential Root Causes

At one of their first meetings, Mrs. Doran and Dr. Fluke lead an activity around assessing the school's needs for bullying prevention. "We all know that there are a million-and-one programs that we are using across the school, but we are going to focus on the programs and practices that directly affect bullying," says Mrs. Doran. "To do this, we are going to start by figuring out just how bad our bullying situation is here at Conestoga and the potential root causes for bullying." Dr. Fluke then pulls up the data collected by the school for ODRs and projects his screen so everyone can see. "As Mrs. Doran and I were going through our behavior data, we realized that we actually don't collect any data specifically on bullying. We have spaces on our ODR form for physical aggression, destruction of property, and verbal aggression, but nothing for bullying. So, in truth, we don't have a good way of knowing how much bullying is happening at our school." The note taker for the day types in that an identified change that needs to be made is to add bullying as an option for teachers to select when submitting an ODR.

Over the next several minutes, Dr. Fluke shows the team ODR data that they do have that are close approximations to bullying. When he finishes reviewing the data, he transitions the team from discussing ODR data to thinking about the other data collection methods staff use related to bullying. It's determined that there aren't any other ways that data on bullying are gathered other than documenting the phone calls made to families when a student tells a teacher that bullying has occurred. Even the school's annual climate survey does not directly ask about bullying behaviors. Based on the discussion during the meeting, the team members decide that they need to select one or two ways to measure the prevalence of bullying in their school so that they can determine if the plan they will be implementing truly has an impact. "Data collection on bullying" is added by the note taker as an identified need. "ODR form" and "annual climate survey" are added under the "existing assets" header since the process for both are regularly known by the staff.

Even though there are no specific data on bullying in the school, the team agrees that, based on their review of ODR data, it is clear that there are concerns around behavior. In order to measure bullying effectively, the team decides one of the first steps they will take is to add bullying questions to the annual climate survey that will be administered in the spring. The second-grade teacher, Mr. Ferris, volunteers to look into the types of questions that will be most helpful for measuring bullying in a way that also provides data for decision making.

After reviewing the broad behavior data, the team discusses the potential reasons for why physical and verbal aggression are so high and frame those reasons around the five components of CBP. Mr. Ferris tells the team, "I go over our schoolwide expectations with the children at the beginning of the year and do my best throughout the rest of the year to reteach when issues arise." Fifth-grade teacher Mrs. Doran responds, "To be honest, I'm not sure that other teachers at our grade level or the fourth-grade teachers spend more than 10 minutes on behavior expectations the entire year. I guess we have just had the mind-set that as the older students in the school they should already know how to behave the right way." Mr. Young admits, "You know, as an administration, we have been so focused on improving growth on standardized tests, that we probably haven't focused on making sure the staff has the information it needs to effectively understand and manage behaviors. I'm glad we are having this conversation now, because we can start to make up for it." For the next several minutes, the team continues to discuss potential root causes for the high rate of ODRs around bullying-related behavior. They add several potential root causes to their notes, including, "low frequency of directly teaching expected behaviors," and "lack of staff knowledge on the severity of bullying in the school."

Having exhausted the subject of the potential root causes related to the high rates of bullying-related behaviors in the school (see Table 10.2), Mr. Young talks about one of the last root causes mentioned. "You know, Professor Obara," Mr. Young says, "your point about our anti-bullying policy in the school handbook is great. When I was talking with the families of the students who were bullied, several complained about the fact that there was hardly any useful information in our handbook about bullying. We don't even tell families who they should talk to at the school if they think their kid has been bullied." Mr. Young states that he willing to look into how to create a more robust anti-bullying policy for the school. The note taker for the meeting adds this item to the action steps at the bottom of the agenda.

Assess What Is Currently in Place

At a meeting after the one in which the team discussed needed changes and root causes, the team members are excitedly talking about the possibility of creating a comprehensive approach to support their students. A lull in the conversation leads to Ms. Pearcy saying, "I know we are all excited about helping our kids and making sure they are safe. But to be honest, I don't know how I am going to have time for one more thing. I already meet as part of this team once a month, I lead parent trainings each month, serve as the staff liaison for the PTA, and I lead our after-school run club. Oh, and did I mention that I teach special education full time?" There is silence among the team following this brief outburst. Several teammates begin to realize that, despite their enthusiasm for the work, they too are hard-pressed for time.

Mr. Young is the first to respond. "What if we found a way to actually reduce the amount of work we are all doing and still be able to support our students with bullying prevention?" Ms. Pearcy looks incredulously at her principal. "I would say that sounds too good to be true," she says with a slight laugh. "Well," says Mr. Young, "one of our next steps will be to complete an initiative inventory around what we already have in place that supports bullying prevention. And since we know that having a positive school climate is part of effective bullying prevention, that means we will include any work we do in that area as well. To make it more manageable, though, let's try sticking to only the work that we do on a consistent basis. When we are done, we will be able to see everything that we are doing and eliminate those that are redundant so that we have fewer initiatives.

Over the course of the next several minutes, Mr. Young shows the team a blank copy of the initiative inventory they will be using to collection data. Using their schoolwide expectations as an example, he completes one row of the initiative inventory. The team then decides how to approach the task of completing the rest of the initiative inventory, and agree to use a Google Sheet that will allow all team members to enter their information. By the time that the team returns to next month's meeting, they have completed an initiative inventory.

With their first draft of the initiative inventory completed, the team determines what is currently in place to reduce bullying and what needs still exist. The only true program or standardized approach to reducing bullying that was found to exist in the school was PBIS. Reiterating what they had discussed around root causes, team members noted that their implementation of PBIS was poor. Moreover, how teachers administer consequences and reinforcers and respond to reports of bullying are different across grade levels. "It's no wonder we have an issue with bullying," says Ms. Pearcy. "The kids have to relearn what rules are actually enforced every year."

TABLE 10.2. Root Causes for High Rates of Bullying

Component	Needs	Existing assets	Potential root causes
Data-based Decision Making	Data collection specifically on prevalence of bullying	• ODR form • Annual climate survey	• Lack of staff knowledge on the importance of measuring and preventing bullying
School Climate	Improved implementation fidelity of PBIS	• Token economy system as part of PBIS • Schoolwide expectations • School climate team (currently not meeting)	• Outdated and unused behavior matrix • Low frequency of directly teaching expected behaviors • Lack of student and staff knowledge on what constitutes bullying • Lack of staff knowledge on the severity of bullying in the school • Anti-bullying policy in school handbook is limited
Evidence-Based Curricula	Selection of an evidence-based curriculum for bullying prevention	• Hexagon Tool	• Lack of staff awareness on severity of bullying concerns
Policy	More robust anti-bullying policy in school handbook	• Basic outline of anti-bullying policy currently in school handbook	• Lack of staff knowledge on best practices for anti-bullying policy
Family and Community Partnerships	More robust family and community involvement	• Prioritized high-impact communication methods with families • PTA • School volunteer program • Two parents on bullying prevention implementation team	• Lack of dedicated team focused on bullying prevention

Outline a Plan for Readiness, for Developing Staff Capacity, and for Needed System Changes

Having now examined the potential root causes and existing initiatives in place at Conestoga, the implementation team turns to sketching out a plan to create readiness for stakeholders, improve staff capacity, and changes in systems at a schoolwide level. It is the beginning of a new school year, and the team experiences some minor changes. Mr. Valenzuela's wife received a new job offer in the state of Kansas, so he is no longer working at the school. To fill his seat, the music teacher, Mr. Diez, has joined the implementation team. Another change to the team is that the principal, Mr. Young, is no longer facilitating the meetings. Instead, the team has decided to rotate this responsibility from one meeting to the next. The assistant principal, Mrs. Brown, is now attending meetings so that leadership in the school is able to provide quick answers to budgetary and other higher-level decisions that need to be made.

For the first meeting of the new school year, the implementation team catches up with one another, then turns their attention to reviewing what they accomplished by the end of the previous school year. Seeing that the same root causes and existing initiatives are essentially still in place, they agree to move forward in outlining how to create readiness, capacity, and system changes. During the discussion around readying staff members, families, and the community for the bullying prevention efforts, Mrs. Doran expresses a concern that she has run into at a previous school. "At my last school, the principal would bring in a new program basically every year. She would go to a conference over the summer, think what she heard was exactly what the staff need and wanted, then drop it on us at the beginning of the year. I don't want that to happen here. This work is too important."

The team nods in agreement with Mrs. Doran, and starts talking about the best way to make sure that members of the staff don't feel like they have to do just one more thing. The assistant principal then speaks up. "You know, I think what might be helpful is taking some time during our next professional development day, when we have all of the staff together, to show the data that we have started to collect around bullying in our school. Most of the staff have just heard snippets about how bad bullying is, but don't have the full picture." As the team begins to talk about the specifics of what information will be shared during the 15 minutes they are given at the next professional development day, they decide to not only share the school's data, but also what research on bullying shows can be the consequences of students enduring bullying. Then, the team will very briefly describe what the implementation team is working on to reduce bullying in the school. "So, basically, we are going to be showing everyone why the work is important, what we all plan to do about it, and our vision for success," Mrs. Brown concludes.

Reviewing the root-cause data again, Mr. Diez says, "I know this is my first meeting, but, to me, it's pretty obvious where we need to start. For almost every root cause you list, you write that the staff lacks knowledge or understanding of bullying in some way. I know that is definitely true for me. So if we are wanting to make sure that all of us on the staff are ready and have the capacity to reduce bullying, then we need to have a really good plan for how we are going to eliminate those root causes." Mrs. Brown then responds, "You're absolutely right. Mr. Young and I have already begun planning out how we are going to be integrating the basics of bullying prevention into staff professional development. We know that we will be providing training for members of the staff so that we are all on the same page in terms of language, definitions, and the like. But we are also trying to find a way to get some coaching support for staff members when they are giving lessons or responding to incidents. What I can promise you is that, regardless of what direction we go in terms of a curriculum or practice, Mr. Young and I will make sure the entire staff is given enough time to have hands-on learning with the materials."

Turning to a discussion on system changes, the team identifies several areas that need to be addressed and frame the conversation by discussing implementation drivers. They start with data systems. "We talked about this a little last year," says Dr. Fluke, "and when it comes to data, we need to change our system of collecting information on bullying. I was able to collect some of the most useful questions we could use on our spring climate survey at the end of the year. We should definitely get the ball rolling on adding those questions." Mrs. Brown nods in agreement, and says that she will talk with Mr. Young so that they can reach out to the district administration about getting the questions added. "The other piece was around ODRs and making sure that bullying is included as a potential reason for one. And I'm happy to say that we have updated the paper form to include bullying. Since Mrs. Brown is in charge of reviewing ODRs and entering them into our system, we already have someone in place who knows about the changes on that end."

The facilitator brings up the final two systems-change topics before the meeting concludes: administrative support (by modifying the structure of the master schedule) and stakeholder engagement (by reviewing two-way communication). "Okay, we were able to get a lot of these pieces figured out. The last two items we need to talk about is when the staff will have the time to actually administer any lessons from a program that we select and a communication plan, so that we get feedback on how things are going," says Mrs. Doran. Several options are floated as potential times when lessons could be administered, including the first thing in the morning or as part of the weekly "Friday Fun" free time that students receive if they have followed the schoolwide expectations for that week. The team quickly agrees that holding the lessons in the morning would not be a great idea because some students are habitually truant or are consistently tardy at this time. Although the idea of cutting into the time that students receive at the end of the week as an incentive for positive behavior doesn't seem ideal, the team agrees to try it out for the school year and use staff feedback to determine if the time will continue through to the next school year.

Discussions around a communication system that allows for two-way communication and feedback includes a lot of input from Mrs. Myers, who is the grandmother of a third-grade student at Conestoga. "You know, one of the main reasons that I wanted to join this team after I was invited by Principal Young was because of communication. When my granddaughter, Haylie, was being bullied, one of my biggest complaints was that I didn't know who to talk to or what would happen when I *did* talk to someone. I figured I could talk to her teacher, but I didn't know whether she was going to be safe in the meantime while the school was figuring out what to do." The team decides that some basic communication practices will be put into place, so that families and staff receive information on the lessons and responses the school makes to reports of bullying. Part of the information provided around reports of bullying will include the steps the school takes to ensure all students are safe.

Assessment of Program/Practice

Identify Potential Practices or Programs

During one of the next team meetings, the majority of the agenda is dedicated to identifying potential practices or programs that could be used at Conestoga Elementary School to reduce bullying. The school psychologist, Dr. Fluke, suggests several online resources that provide a review of the research supporting the effectiveness of different bullying prevention programs. He also says that he probably has a book or two in his office that describes some of the better programs. Mrs. Brown states that during the next district leaders' meeting she will have Mr. Young, the principal, ask other schools about the practices they use to reduce bullying. Finally, Professor Obara says that she will reach out to several of the local colleges and universities to find out if they have recommendations as well. The team agrees to bring a list of the programs and practices, including as much information that they can find about each program, to the next team meeting so that the entire team can be part of the decision-making process.

Assess Options

The following meeting, the team brings back a collection of different programs and practices. Together, the team lists each option that was brought to the team and groups the options into two different buckets: "curricula" and "practices." Those in the curricula bucket are programs that can be purchased and typically include a set of lessons and training and support tools from a company. The practices bucket includes activities that do not necessarily require purchasing materials, but rather focus on activities that can be implemented with minimal training. Before examining each curricula and practice in depth, the team first reaches consensus on the needs the school has for bullying prevention. The team agrees that the school needs a comprehensive approach that is sustainable, that is aligned with the vision of the school, and that directly addresses the root causes that they identified earlier as contributing to bullying.

Keeping these needs in mind, the team begins reviewing each of the curricula and practices. In order to make the task less overwhelming, a brief description of each program and practice is given by the person who brought it to the team. The team quickly decides if the program or practice should be given further consideration. Once the team has narrowed down the curricula and practices from the initial screening, they begin using the Hexagon Tool to guide their decision-making process (see Chapter 4 for a detailed explanation of how to use the Hexagon Tool).

Selection of Program/Practice

Once the programs and practices are reviewed, the Conestoga Elementary School bullying prevention implementation team makes its decision on how to proceed. Principal Young joins this meeting to hear the results of the team's work. Professor Obara begins by describing how they reached their decision. "We started off with about 20 different curricula and practices. After taking a little time to eliminate the ones that we knew wouldn't work, either because the cost was too high or because they focused more on secondary students, for example, we were left with about 3 curricula and 5 practices. From there, we used the Hexagon Tool to take a deep dive into several factors that would help us decide which curricula would work best for our school. We knew that we could probably only choose one curricula just because of the amount of money, time, and training it would take for our staff to become fluent with how it works. In the end, we decided to select the Second Step curriculum."

Mr. Young says that he is happy that so much thoughtful work was put into the selection of the curriculum, and that he has heard from other principals around the district that their staffs tend to like the Second Step curriculum because it has lessons that are already scripted for them. "So tell me about some of the practices that the team selected," Mr. Young says. Mr. Ferris explains that the team went through a similar approach for selecting practices as they did for selecting the curriculum. "We agreed that we will focus on developing a more robust bullying prevention policy here at the school. Haylie's grandma voiced how important this robust policy would be for other families at the school. They want to know how to make reports of bullying, how often families will be updated on the steps taken, how the school will keep their children safe, and what the potential outcomes will be for students involved. Based on all of this information, we agreed that having a flowchart of the process from the beginning, when we receive a report of bullying, to the end, when an investigation has reached a conclusion about what happened and has determined the consequences." Mr. Young nods in agreement and thanks Mrs. Myers again for her contribution to the team.

Mr. Ferris continues, "Several of the other practices we selected were because they are part of our already existing PBIS framework. We have said it several times, but if we are able to get our PBIS system in a better place, we will make great strides not only in bullying, but also in the overall behavior and the culture of the school l. It also fits right in with the school climate component of CBP. So to start off with, we want to reinvigorate our behavior matrix, our reinforcement system, and our training of staff on how to directly teach desired behaviors." Over the next few minutes, Mr. Ferris explains in greater detail each of the bullying prevention practices that the team wants to implement. By the end of the meeting, the entire team is in agreement that they will move forward with Second Step and the bullying prevention practices aligned with PBIS.

Buy-In of Stakeholders

Grow Relationships with Stakeholders

At the point that the bullying prevention implementation team began to formulate a true vision and plan for their work, team members naturally began talking to their peers about the work they were doing. The lower-grade teachers mentioned the success the team was having in using data to drive decisions. The upper-grade teachers talked to their colleagues about how improving behavior starting in kindergarten means that by the time students get to the upper grades, they will already know many of the skills needed to regulate their emotions and make better choices. When the school specialists met, Mr. Diez talked about the fact that because the approach is schoolwide and all students attend their classes, they would no longer have to figure out different behavioral expectations for students from different classes. At the PTA meetings, Mrs. Myers spoke almost every month about how she truly feels like the teachers and the staff care about making a change for the better. Mr. Buck, the manager at the neighborhood sporting goods store, has been speaking up about the work going on at Conestoga when he attends chamber of commerce meetings.

Each of these connections serves as a starting conversation about bullying prevention. Teachers who are on the implementation team hear both the positive comments about the bullying prevention work as well as the concerns from the staff about the amount of time it will take to learn yet another curriculum. Parents voice their support for reducing bullying, but also want to make sure that their children still get the same amount of instructional time so that they are prepared for the next grade. Other businesses are impressed by the organized approach that the school is taking to reduce bullying and start thinking about how the corporate social responsibility arm of their company could support the work.

Cultivate Champions

In addition to building relationships across multiple stakeholder groups, each member of the bullying prevention implementation team intentionally identifies those individuals who expressed the most interest in the work and those who were leaders of their respective groups. Reaching out to speak specifically with these potential sponsors and champions of bullying prevention, team members begin to cultivate a culture of change. Mr. Diez speaks with the new physical education teacher, Mr. Chalmers, who has quickly become a fan favorite of the students because of his outgoing personality and his ability to make trick shots in basketball. Teachers in younger and older grades who are known to speak out during all-staff meetings are approached by implementation team members to hear about their interest and concerns about the bullying prevention work. When team members assure these teacher leaders that their voices will be heard as the work progresses, they agree to be on board and speak up for the team's efforts during all-staff meetings.

On the family side of the implementation team, Mrs. Myers talks with the president of the PTA. She informs her about Haylie's experience with being bullied at Conestoga and that she did not feel like the school was a safe place for her granddaughter to learn. It was not, until she was asked by Principal Young to join the newly formed bullying prevention implementation team. Mrs. Myers described the ongoing work within the team meetings and that the team planned to roll out bullying prevention supports for all students in the coming months. As the conversation progresses, the president agrees to allow a short amount of time at each PTA meeting for Mrs. Myers to provide updates on the bullying prevention work that is happening at Conestoga and that she will have the support of the PTA behind the rollout.

The two community members on the team, Mr. Buck and Ms. Coutts, also start the process of connecting with potential sponsors and champions in their areas of expertise. Mr. Buck reaches out to the national headquarters' community relations division to see what opportunities exist that could support the bullying prevention work. He finds out that they offer some grants to schools that align with the company's vision and mission. At the next implementation team meeting, Mr. Buck talks about what he has learned, and the assistant principal agrees to be the contact for the school moving forward. Ms. Coutts, the director of the extended day care center, speaks to her team about the partnership with Conestoga at the next all-staff meeting for the organization. Several staff members express their interest in being more involved in bridging behavioral supports from the school to the after-school care center. These two staff members agree to lead the day care center in the work with guidance from Ms. Coutts.

Assess and Create Readiness

Mr. Young sets aside 45 minutes during the next all-staff meeting to talk about the CBP that Conestoga will be implementing in the coming years. Working with the implementation team, he drafts an outline of the topics to be covered:

1. Show data on why bullying and behavior is a concern at Conestoga.
2. Have implementation team teachers share brief stories about how bullying has impacted their classrooms and their students.
3. Describe the work the implementation team has done over the past several months.
4. Tell the staff that Second Step has been chosen as the curriculum and the practices that align with the already existing PBIS framework.
5. Tell the staff that time will be provided to review materials, receive training, and receive coaching.
6. Tell the staff that their instructional time will not be impacted by the addition of Second Step.
7. Provide an opportunity for staff members to ask questions and express concerns.

During the all-staff meeting, Mr. Young and the team use the outline to describe how bullying prevention and behavior in general will be addressed in the coming years. At first, some of the staff seem apprehensive about the idea of needing to be trained and receive coaching on an entirely new curriculum. As the team explains that there would be no loss of instructional time, and that the staff would be provided ample time to review the materials before being asked to implement the curriculum, these concerns appear to abate.

When the time comes to give the staff the chance to ask questions and express concerns, some of the champions that the teachers on the implementation team had spoken with earlier are the first to speak. They express their support for the work and how they believe it will help them, because they will be spending less time addressing behavioral concerns in the classroom and more time connecting with their students and providing direct instruction. These positive comments create a climate that feels supportive of the work. Two staff members raise questions about the specific time line of the work but, in general, there are no major concerns raised. Moreover, there is general agreement that focusing on behavior as a priority is a good choice for the school and that the staff would have the bandwidth to begin training. Concluding the meeting, Mr. Young reiterates that any questions or concerns that come up after the meeting should be emailed to him and he will bring them to the implementation team.

Having provided the school staff with a basic understanding of the work that will be happening around bullying prevention, the implementation team sets out to begin installing the CBP for Conestoga Elementary School.

CHAPTER 11

Case Study
Installation

INTRODUCTION

Once the team has selected the specific practices within CBP to implement, installation of the practices begins. At the beginning of the installation phase, it is important to review the makeup of the implementation team to ensure that the participants still represent varying perspectives (e.g., teachers, specialists). The team members should also have the appropriate knowledge and authority to effectively implement CBP. The bulk of the work during this phase is focused on developing the infrastructure to support implementation, which entails creating an implementation plan with training and coaching systems as well as ensuring resources from those in leadership. In addition to these infrastructure components, the initial trainings for the staff on the bullying prevention practices should take place. Since these trainings and the practices as a whole are in their infancy, it is also imperative that feedback loops be in place to identify and alleviate issues that arise. At this point the bullying prevention policy and procedures should also be reviewed and revised as necessary. By the end of the installation stage, the vast majority of the staff members will be trained in the bullying prevention practice and the infrastructure will be in place to support ongoing coaching.

WELL-FUNCTIONING IMPLEMENTATION TEAM
Ensure That Needed Perspectives Are Present

Given that the next stage of implementation involves putting into place the systems to support CBP, one of the first steps is to ensure that the implementation team is functioning well. Since the team is likely very similar to the one that was assembled during the exploration stage, moving into the installation stage provides an opportunity to reflect on several factors that influence the effectiveness of the team. This means that the issue of implementation team membership should be revisited to ensure that the perspectives of varied stakeholders are being represented.

Following an all-staff meeting, the bullying prevention implementation team meets to discuss the makeup of their team. Looking around the table, Assistant Principal Mrs. Brown sees that multiple grade levels, specialist teachers, families, and community members are represented. "Now that we have selected the program and practices we will be using," says Mrs. Brown, "do we feel like we have representation on this team to consider all the perspectives on bullying in the school?" The team members look around the room and some begin to nod, suggesting that they believe that appropriate representation is present. Then Mrs. Myers speaks up. "I think that we have great representation if you consider the adults in the room. But what we don't have is the perspective of the students," she says.

"You know," responds Dr. Fluke, "that's a great point. We haven't really gotten the perspective of our students yet. All we really have are reports on bullying and the annual school climate survey." Mrs. Brown is next to speak. "Okay, let's think about how this could work. I imagine that we could get a few fourth- and fifth-grade students to join part of our meetings every once in a while." "You know," responds the fifth-grade teacher, Mrs. Doran, "we do project-based learning assignments quite a bit in our class. What if we added bullying prevention as an option for students to choose? Then part of their expectations would be to gather research on bullying, gather data on what bullying looks like at Conestoga, and maybe even interview their peers. It could help us get students' perspective on bullying and students would be able to make a real impact with their project-based learning assignment." The team agrees, and the note taker writes down that Mrs. Doran will speak with the other fifth-grade teachers about the opportunity.

Ensure That the Team Has Appropriate Knowledge and Skills

"A key to us being successful is to make sure that, as a team, we are all skilled enough to support other staff members and families with whatever roadblocks come up," says Mrs. Brown. "Let's say, for example, that one of the paraprofessionals comes up to you and says, 'I saw one of my students yelling names at another third grader. It turns out that it happens a lot, and I think it actually might be bullying, but I'm not sure what to do about it.'" Mrs. Brown pauses. "Each of us in this room should be able to talk to her about how to make sure the other student is safe and show the paraprofessional how to document the incident. As we begin to roll out different parts of our bullying prevention plan, let's also keep track of what an implementation team member should know."

The team begins discussing what knowledge and skills the members currently possess would be necessary for someone new joining the team to learn. They group the knowledge and skills according to the components of comprehensive bullying prevention. As they continue to meet throughout the year, they add new skills to the list when appropriate. By the time the team reaches the full implementation stage, the members will have transformed their initially meager list of knowledge and skills into a clear approach to onboarding new members to the team.

Mrs. Brown then outlines the basics of professional development for the bullying prevention implementation team. "Once we purchase Second Step, we immediately have access to their bullying prevention and SEL online trainings. If we want to be able to support the rest of the staff, we should be the first group to take all of the trainings. That way, we will know both the content and the system so that we can answer any questions staff may have about either one. Do you all think you would be able to do the 3 or 4 hours of training over the course of a month?" The team agrees that they would be able to meet this deadline.

"Great," responds Mrs. Brown. "Mr. Young and I are also looking at how we can get some additional in-person professional development for at least a few team members as well. Professor Obara has talked before about Northwest PBIS training; the organization has an annual conference offering training not only in PBIS, but also in how PBIS can be integrated with bullying prevention efforts. Although we have a strong focus on bullying prevention and Second Step on this team, it's important to remember that we are also working on improving our PBIS implementation too since it also helps prevent bullying by creating a positive school climate. In fact, Mr. Young and I have just recently decided to begin getting our school climate team up and running again. We will be rebranding the team as the school climate team since we want to have a broader focus than just PBIS. However, we want make sure that we are not duplicating efforts between the school climate team and this team. With this in mind, we think it would be a good idea to have someone from this team serve as a liaison between the teams and could speak up if there seems to be duplication of work or if resources from one team could be used for the purposes of the other. Would anyone be interested?"

Dr. Fluke raises his hand. "I feel like I have a good knowledge of how to improve school climate and could contribute to the school climate team," he says. "Great." Responds Mrs. Brown. She pauses, then says, "Now, we don't want to overwhelm the staff or ourselves with too many new endeavors. We are already planning on having them learn the Second Step curriculum, updates to the bullying prevention policy in the student handbook, and a host of other things. We can introduce PBIS more slowly and build on what we already have in place. But if we can secure funding for at least two team members to attend the Northwest PBIS annual conference and bring back some new ideas, we would be able to double dip, so to speak, with our professional development funding for both PBIS and bullying prevention." Table 11.1 summarizes the knowledge and skills for the team.

Regularly Meet and Use Data to Support Implementation

The Conestoga Elementary bullying prevention implementation team meets for 1 hour each month. For the first several meetings that take place during the exploration and installation stages, the team jointly agreed to meet for 90 or 120 minutes, depending on the amount of planning they decide they need to move the work forward. Once the team begins to become comfortable with the rotating roles and how successfully the work being completed in meetings, the meeting times begin to more consistently last for an hour. During the installation phase, after the team has determined its data systems, the members all agree to place a standing item on the agenda called "Data Review."

The time devoted to data review varies depending on the amount of data accumulated in any given month. When the first round of outcome data from the updated annual school climate survey is released, the team spends 40 minutes reviewing the data as a team and analyzing the most important parts of the data. In contrast, during a meeting just after winter break, the team spends 5 minutes reviewing ODR data to see if there are any emerging trends that suggest that interventions need to be adjusted.

TABLE 11.1. Comprehensive Bullying Prevention Implementation Team Knowledge and Skills

Component	Knowledge/skill
School Climate	• Difference between minor and major behavior concerns • The schoolwide expectations • Why climate and culture are vital to bullying prevention • Basic classroom management strategies • Consistently reinforcing students for positive behavior
Policy	• Strong understanding of the school's bullying prevention policy • Able to support the staff with completing a bullying investigation
Evidence-Based Programs	• How to access the online Second Step curriculum • Knowing the difference between Second Step and PBIS
Family and Community Partnerships	• Knowledge of local community resources that may support families in need • Able to provide an "elevator speech" on the bullying prevention efforts of the school so that noneducators can understand them
Data-Based Decision Making	• Knowledge of how to interpret behavior data • Knowledge of the problem-solving process • Able to support other staff members in using the problem- solving process

During one meeting following the collection of exit slip data, the team spends a few minutes reviewing the results. Mrs. Brown pulls up the data results online and projects her screen for the team. "Okay," she begins. "We have our exit-slip survey data from last week's all-staff meeting. If you remember, we presented for 10 minutes on the basic steps the staff should take if a student reports an incident of bullying to them. Here are the results from that survey. As you can see from the scores, on average, staff members agree that they have confidence in their ability to follow the appropriate steps if a student reports bullying. They also, on average, agree that Conestoga takes bullying seriously, that they are well prepared to handle bullying situations, and that the school tries to prevent bullying. The one area that we are still receiving mixed results on is the item 'bullying is a problem at Conestoga.' For this item, we averaged a score of 'Neither agree nor disagree.'"

The team briefly discusses what the data mean for their work. "You know," says Mrs. Myers, "I am a little confused about how the staff can say on one hand that we are doing a lot of great prevention work, but on the other say that bullying is still a problem." Dr. Fluke responds, "Yeah, it is a little confusing. When I think about it, I can see how we are doing some great things, but it just hasn't translated into the feeling that bullying is getting better. Once we get some of our ODR and annual climate survey data back, we will be able to see what the students say as well. I would guess that if the students say that bullying has reduced over time that the lower numbers will begin to climb." Following Dr. Fluke's comments, Mrs. Brown reminds the team about the fact that, according to implementation science, getting a new program or initiative up to full speed often takes several years. "Even though it can feel like our work isn't moving as fast as we would like right now," she adds, "I believe we are doing things the right way and will see the results in due time."

DEVELOP IMPLEMENTATION PLAN

Training Plans

A topic during one of the implementation team meetings focuses on all of the training that is needed for the staff to effectively implement bullying prevention best practices. Similar to the activity in which the implementation team listed the skills and knowledge the team needed, an activity to outline all of the pieces of Conestoga's comprehensive bullying prevention program is created. Although there is some overlap with the knowledge and skills needed by the general staff and the implementation team members, the depth with which the general staff needs to understand key concepts is more limited. The first phase of the activity is led by Dr. Fluke, in which the implementation team brainstorms the different knowledge and skills the staff will need. Additionally, the team considers the best way for the staff to learn each part of the work and indicates what priority to give each skill on a 1–5 scale (where 1 is a low priority and 5 is a high priority; see Table 11.2).

TABLE 11.2. Comprehensive Bullying Prevention Training-Plan Priority Brainstorming List

Knowledge/skill	Training method	Priority
How to intervene when witnessing bullying	All-staff meetings; digital Second Step training	5
General bullying prevention	Digital Second Step training	4
SEL concepts	Digital Second Step training	4
Basics of Second Step lesson administration	Digital Second Step training; grade-level planning time	4
Schoolwide expectations	All-staff meetings	3
Behavior matrix	All-staff meetings	3
General best practices for engaging with families	All-staff meetings	3
Knowledge of what is in the school handbook's anti-bullying policy	All-staff meetings	3
Using student reinforcers	All-staff meetings; grade-level planning time	2
Steps to follow when receiving a report of bullying	All-staff meetings	2
How to complete a bullying report form	All-staff meetings	2
How to submit an ODR form	All-staff meetings	1
Classroom management skills	All-staff meetings; grade-level planning time	1

Once the brainstorming activity is completed, Dr. Fluke brings the team back together to discuss next steps. "Okay, based on what we have all agreed on, our highest training priority right now is teaching all members of the staff how to intervene when they see bullying." Team members nod in agreement, and the general consensus is that one of the worst outcomes is for a staff member to witness bullying and either ignore it or use an approach that makes the situation worse. "We are also saying that the Second Step training will likely have information on the best practices for intervening in the moment, but we also want to address it during an all-staff meeting so that we know that everyone knows how to handle those situations. So our next step is to look at our training plan and begin to fill it out."

Dr. Fluke then has the note taker share her screen so that the entire team can see the training-plan template. The team discusses each prompt column by column, while the note taker enters their decisions. By the time the team completes the training plan, the members have decided that the first training will take place during the next all-staff meeting, with Dr. Fluke and Mr. Diez leading the training. As part of the training, Dr. Fluke and Mr. Diez agree to create a brief exit slip for staff members to complete as a way of determining if they have learned how to intervene when they see bullying. After the training, Dr. Fluke states that he will update the training plan to include the results from the exit slips. The team's goal is that 95% of the staff will accurately describe how to intervene in bullying situations.

The team moves on to discuss the skills they agreed were the next highest priority and follows a similar approach in creating a training plan (see Table 11.3). Using the digital training that is part of the Second Step program, the entire staff is expected to complete training on general bullying prevention and SEL topics by the end of the school year. "I think that asking the staff to complete the digital training by the end of the school year is reasonable," says Ms. Pearcy, "but only if we are able to get access to the Second Step resources soon. Do we have an update on when we will be able to get access to the materials?" Mrs. Brown responds, "Well, we actually have some good news on that front. Mr. Buck, do you want to let everyone know the most recent developments?" Mrs. Brown turns to Mr. Buck, smiling. "Absolutely!" he says. "In talking with some of my colleagues, it looks like the grant application we submitted to my national headquarters is going to be accepted." There is excitement around the room, as most of the staff forgot that they had written a small grant application before winter break. "We should get formal word in the next few days and the money will be disbursed a few weeks after that," concludes Mr. Buck. "And," adds Mrs. Brown, "since so much of Second Step is digital now, we should be able to access the materials right away, including the training."

With the news that materials should be ready within a few weeks, the team continues completing the training plan. The group decides that the training completion date will coincide with the end of the academic year, but to also add a brief refresher training at the beginning of the next academic year for the staff as well. "I know that the principal's priority is to make sure that the staff feels like there is enough time to get comfortable with the materials," says Mrs. Brown. "So we have also decided that during staff meetings, we will provide time for grade levels to meet together and review the Second Step materials once we have access to them." The note taker adds this item to the training plan for the May all-staff meeting. "The other nice thing about the training that is provided by this program is that it includes all-staff meeting presentations as well. There is an all-staff overview, as well as a midyear check-in and end-of-year check-in for the program that the entire staff will receive. Each of these trainings should take about 30 minutes, so we can add them to the training plan as well."

TABLE 11.3. Comprehensive Bullying Prevention Training Plan

Topic	Date	Audience	Trainers	Purpose	Data Collection Method	Goal	Results
Intervening in bullying	March 26	All staff	Dr. Fluke and Mr. Diez	Staff members know the steps to take when they see bullying and know what actions to avoid.	Exit-slip survey at the end of all-staff meeting	95% of the staff members accurately describe how to intervene when witnessing bullying, as measured by exit slips	[To be entered by Dr. Fluke after training]
Second Step overview	April 15	All staff	Mr. Young and Mrs. Brown	Staff members have a general knowledge of the Second Step program and why it is important.	Exit-slip survey at the end of all-staff meeting	85% of staff members agree that they understand the purpose and basics of Second Step	[To be entered by Dr. Fluke after all-staff meeting]
Second Step elementary curriculum	Completed by June 18	Staff members implementing lessons	Digital Second Step training	Introduce core SEL skills, support successful implementation, know how to reinforce skills outside of lesson time.	Second Step formative and summative assessments	90% of staff members complete all of the lessons	[Automatically tallied by Second Step on June 18]
Behavior matrix	April 15	All staff	School climate team and Dr. Fluke	Introduce revised behavior matrix and how it's aligned with bullying prevention.	Exit-slip survey at the end of all-staff meeting	100% of staff members agree to directly teach the new expected behaviors	[To be entered by the school climate team and shared with the bullying prevention implementation team]

Dr. Fluke interjects to talk about training on the behavior matrix. "We have been focused on the Second Step curriculum training for a while now to make sure that staff members are comfortable with a brand new program. As you all know, I am on the school climate team, and right now we are working on updating our behavior matrix for the school. I have been including suggestions that align with the work we are doing as well. So, for example, we added the location of 'online' to the behavior matrix, and are outlining expected behaviors for our three schoolwide expectations. We have also been working with our digital literacy teacher to develop a plan for how students should be directly taught expected behaviors. The school climate team has asked our team to review the new behavior matrix to see if there are areas where we think specific bullying prevention behaviors could be included. Once we give them our feedback, the entire staff will be shown the new behavior matrix and trained on its features by the school climate team." The bullying prevention implementation team begins to review the new behavior matrix and by the end of the meeting have provided several suggestions for the school climate team.

Looking at their training plan for the remainder of the year, the team reflects on the readiness that will be in place at the beginning of the following academic year. "I feel like once staff members know the fundamentals for how to intervene in real-time bullying situations, know the basics of bullying prevention and SEL, and have a plan for how they will administer the lessons, everyone should be in a good place at the start of next year," says Mr. Ferris. "Plus," adds Ms. Coutts, "the training that is left are is the kind that we can include at the beginning of next year or that we can support staff with, like how to submit an ODR form." Looking around the room, Mrs. Brown says, "Okay. I think we have a good start here with training. Let's talk about how we can provide coaching support for the staff after training."

Coaching Plans

The first step the implementation team takes in formulating a coaching plan is talking about needs. "So how do we know which staff members will need coaching?" asks Mrs. Myers. "Well, I think we should approach coaching the same way we approach supports that we provide our students: by using a layered continuum of supports," responds Dr. Fluke. "We should provide the entire staff with some basic coaching supports, but for staff members who need additional supports, we can provide them based on data." The team voices agreement with the approach described by Dr. Fluke. "So what would coaching supports look like for the staff?" asks Professor Obara.

"I think the simplest approach would be to meet with grade-level teams once a quarter or so to check in. We can see what's working well and coach the teams through questions or concerns they may have with certain parts of the program. These check-ins would also give us a chance to start having more structured communication about our work as well," says Ms. Pearcy. "Great idea," responds Mrs. Brown. "Let's look at next year's calendar and schedule out the times we will meet with grade-level teams for 30 minutes for coaching." The note taker projects next year's academic calendar and a blank coaching-plan document. Once an appropriate date is found, the team completes the coaching plan and answers all of the prompts.

For universal coaching supports, the team adds details about quarterly check-ins with grade-level teams. The team also decides to use the information gathered during these check-ins as one possible way that staff members can begin receiving targeted coaching supports. For example, if a teacher says during the coaching session that they don't feel confident in stopping a bullying situation when they see it, that teacher will be offered the chance to join a small group of other teachers needing additional support in this area. The small group of teachers needing targeted supports then would meet to practice the intervention strategies and reinforce their learning. Dr. Fluke agrees to lead the coaching supports for this small group. Once the staff members states that they have confidence in their ability to intervene in bullying situations and can describe to Dr. Fluke how they would approach doing so, the coaching support will fade.

The team agrees to develop a second targeted coaching support, this one focusing on effective implementation of the Second Step lessons. Staff members will be offered coaching if they report not being able to administer the expected lessons when they complete the Second Step fidelity assessment at the end of each module. Another targeted coaching support focuses on staff members who are having difficulty implementing lessons during the quarterly coaching check-ins. Mr. Ferris and Mrs. Doran agree to lead the coaching supports in this area since they will have firsthand experience implementing the lessons. Once the staff reports successful implementation of the expected lessons on the Second Step fidelity assessment, coaching supports will fade. The comprehensive bullying prevention coaching plan is summarized in Table 11.4.

Develop Data Systems

Next, the bullying prevention implementation team turns its attention to the data systems needed to effectively implement comprehensive bullying prevention. "The good news," starts Dr. Fluke, "is that we have already listed some different data that we plan on using to make decisions around training and coaching. Now we just have to make sure that the data we collect are the right data to help us problem-solve down the line." The team then begins to brainstorm the different data that are collected around bullying prevention, starting with the Second Step fidelity measure and the exit slips from all-staff meetings.

With the first two data sources documented (see Table 11.5), the team moves on to talk about outcome measures. Mr. Ferris begins. "If you all remember, several months ago, I looked into the different types of questions that are typically asked on student surveys of bullying. With the help of Professor Obara, we were able to identify several questions that we think would be good to add to the annual culture/climate survey." Mr. Ferris then shares the list of questions with the team. "Well," says Mrs. Brown, "with these questions added, I think we could easily say that we would be able to see our progress in reducing bullying each year." The team adds the annual culture/climate survey to their list of data sources.

"Now that we know we are measuring our overall impact on bullying, it would be helpful to also look into how we can measure behavior concerns on a more regular basis," says Mrs. Brown. "One area that Mr. Young, Dr. Fluke, and I have been looking into is how to use our ODRs in a way that allows us to truly use the data for decision making. We don't want to put too much on the staff's plate right now, but we are thinking about moving forward with a data-management system that allows us to input our ODR information and then creates visuals for us automatically. It also lets us use filters to determine if there are specific grade levels or times of day where more behavior concerns are happening." Dr. Fluke can see some of the worried faces around the room. "As Mrs. Brown said, we don't want to overwhelm people with too many tasks at once. The staff will be learning about Second Step and getting trained in several different areas, so we are just going to keep this work internal to the school climate team for now." Dr. Fluke goes on to describe the potential options they are looking at piloting, and explains that he will be the one who tries out the system first to see if it would make sense for the school.

TABLE 11.4. Comprehensive Bullying Prevention Coaching Plan

Topic	Date	Recipient	Coach(es)	Tier	Entry decision rule	Fading decision rule
General implementation support	September 16	Grade-level teams	All implementation team members	Universal (I)	Completed once each quarter	Completed once each quarter
How to respond to in-the-moment bullying	Ongoing	Small staff groups as identified by data	Dr. Fluke	Targeted (II)	Staff offered coaching if (1) exit-slip scores are below 100% after an all-staff training, (2) staff members voice low self-efficacy in the skills, or (3) incident occurs in which staff members don't follow best practices.	(1) Staff members voice high self-efficacy in the skill, and (2) they can verbally describe to a coach how to respond to in-the-moment bullying.
Second Step lesson implementation	Ongoing	Small staff groups as identified by data	Mr. Ferris and Mrs. Doran	Targeted (II)	Staff members offered coaching if (1) they report not administering expected lessons on the Second Step fidelity assessment or (2) they report difficulty implementing lessons during quarterly coaching check-ins.	Staff members report successful implementation of expected lessons on Second Step fidelity assessment.

TABLE 11.5. Comprehensive Bullying Prevention Data Systems

Data tool	What's Measured	Audience	Administration date	Administrator(s)	Database	Use	Shared
All-staff meeting exit slip	Knowledge of the bullying prevention topic of training during the all-staff meeting	All Conestoga staff	1 time each month	Mr. Young	Google Sheets (link)	To determine immediate knowledge gained on bullying prevention during all-staff meetings	All-staff meeting
Second Step fidelity assessment	Degree to which Second Step lessons are implemented as intended	Grade-level teachers	After each module of lessons (about once every 6 weeks)	Dr. Fluke	Second Step database	Determine if program is implemented as intended and how to improve implementation	Individually for specific scores; all-staff meeting for aggregate
Annual culture/climate survey	Prevalence of bullying, culture of school	Students	Spring of each year	Mr. Ferris	District data warehouse	Measure overall reduction in bullying at Conestoga	All-staff meetings; parent–teacher conferences; PTA meeting;
ODRs	Frequency and type of discipline	Students	Ongoing	Mrs. Brown	Google Sheets (link)	Determine real-time behavior progress	Individual data for parent meetings; all-staff meetings; parent–teacher conferences
Staff feedback form	Buy-in from staff	All school staff	Midyear and end of year	Dr. Fluke	Google Sheets (link)	Receive feedback from staff on bullying prevention efforts	All-staff meetings; parent communications

"There's another piece around data that we don't want to lose sight of," says Mrs. Myers, "and that's feedback from staff." Mrs. Brown adds, "You're absolutely right. If we don't keep an eye on how staff members feel about this work and get their feedback on what would make it better, we run the risk of everything falling apart because they don't feel like we are valuing their opinions." Dr. Fluke states that he would be happy to design a survey that could quickly be created on Google Forms and shared with staff members once or twice a year to get their feedback. "I think it could also be a good idea to share the feedback and how we are using it to inform what we are doing as an implementation team at all staff meetings," says Dr. Fluke. The team agrees and the note taker for the meeting adds that Dr. Fluke will create the staff feedback form and share it with the team at the next meeting.

The team takes a quick break before coming back to review the table they have created showing the data collected as part of bullying prevention at Conestoga. Mr. Buck is the first to talk after the break. "I think we have a pretty comprehensive data system here," he starts, "but one thing that I know about myself is that being able to actually understand what all of the data mean is sometimes a bigger ask than collecting the data in the first place." Several people on the team nod in agreement. "One solution that I have found helpful with my research," says Professor Obara, "is creating templates or protocols to help my graduate students interpret the data we collect. I imagine we could do something like that here." "That would be great." responds Mr. Buck, "So you just create a spreadsheet or checklist or something?"

Professor Obara pulls up some of the templates that she uses with her students and projects her screen for the team to see. "Since we collect the same data and ask the same questions over time, we can now basically use fill-in-the-blank sentences that provide interpretation and put the information into PowerPoint slides." Professor Obara pulls up an example of a PowerPoint template. "This one is looking at youth violence in general, but you can see that we can basically just replace the percentages within the sentences based on the most recent data. We could do the same thing with bullying data for Conestoga. Just off the top of my head, we could probably create an interpretation template for overall bullying rates, types of bullying, and ODRs." Professor Obara begins typing in the following examples on her computer:

<u>Template:</u> *During the [DATE RANGE] school year, [PERCENTAGE OF STUDENTS REPORT-ING BEING THE TARGET OF BULLYING] of students at Conestoga Elementary School reported being the target of bullying. This is a [REDUCTION OR INCREASE] of [PERCENT DECREASE OR INCREASE] from the past year.*

<u>Example:</u> During the 2023–2024 school year, 28% of students at Conestoga Elementary School reported being the target of bullying. This is a reduction of 5% from the past year.

<u>Template:</u> *During the [DATE RANGE] school year, the most common type of bullying students experienced was [MOST COMMON TYPE OF BULLYING], followed by [SECOND MOST COMMON TYPE]. The types of bullying were [SIMILAR OR DIFFERENT] across grade levels. Students in third grade reported [MOST COMMON TYPE OF BUL-LYING IN THIRD GRADE] as the most common type of bullying they experienced. Fourth-grade students said that the most common type of bullying was [MOST COM-MON TYPE OF BULLYING IN FOURTH GRADE], and fifth-grade students reported that [MOST COMMON TYPE OF BULLYING FIFTH GRADE] was the most common.*

<u>Example:</u> During the 2023–2024 school year, the most common type of bullying students experienced was verbal bullying, followed by relational bullying. The types of bullying were different across grade levels. Students in third grade reported physical bullying as the most common type of bullying they experienced. Fourth-grade students said that the most common type of bullying was verbal bullying, and fifth-grade students reported that relational bullying was the most common.

<u>Template:</u> *A total of [TOTAL NUMBER OF ODRs FOR BULLYING] ODRs for bullying were recorded for the [DATE RANGE] school year. This is a [INCREASE OR DECREASE] of [TOTAL NUMBER INCREASE OR DECREASE] over the past year.*

<u>Example:</u> A total of 18 ODRs for bullying were recorded for the 2023–2024 school year. This is a decrease of 2 over the past year.

<u>Template:</u> *On the district's annual school climate survey, [PERCENTAGE OF STUDENTS REPORTING STUDENTS TREAT EACH OTHER WITH RESPECT AT SCHOOL] of students at Conestoga agreed that students at their school treat each other with respect. The average score for elementary schools across the district for this question is [AVERAGE PERCENTAGE OF STUDENTS ACROSS THE DISTRICT REPORTING THAT STUDENT TREAT EACH OTHER WITH RESPECT], which suggests that students at Conestoga treat one another with [MORE OR LESS] respect compared to other schools in the district.*

<u>Example:</u> On the district's annual school climate survey, 82% of students at Conestoga agreed that students at their school treat each other with respect. The average score for elementary schools across the district for this question is 68%, which suggests that students at Conestoga treat one another with more respect compared to other schools in the district.

"These are just a few examples, but you can see how we could easily just put this information in a PowerPoint or in a brief one- or two-page flier that we provide to families and staff." The team agrees to start creating more templates to help make interpreting the data they collect easier for anyone on the team to understand. In addition to Professor Obara, Ms. Coutts says that she would like to help create the templates. "The templates are something I could actually use with my staff in the after-school program, so I would love to learn more about how to work with them in a meaningful way," says Ms. Coutts. Mrs. Doran is the last to join the small workgroup creating the data interpretation templates so that a member of the school staff has input on what information would be valuable from the school perspective. After the work group's task is recorded in the meeting notes, the team next discusses their goals for bullying prevention and how the data they collect can be used to measure progress.

"All right, we know what we are measuring for bullying outcomes and fidelity to Second Step," says Dr. Fluke. "But what are we thinking makes sense for goals?" Dr. Fluke looks around the table and sees that Mr. Buck looks confused. "It looks like you have some thoughts, Mr. Buck," says Dr. Fluke. Mr. Buck raises his eyebrows and responds, "Yeah, it's just that we don't really know where we stand in terms of the amount of bullying that's happening because we haven't really collected good data on it yet. So I'm not sure how we are supposed to set a goal since we don't know how big the problem is yet." "Yeah, I was thinking about that too," says Ms. Pearcy. "Maybe it should be something where, for the percentage of students who say they've been bullied, we can have as our goal reducing bullying from the first year we collect data by 10% the following year?" "That's a good idea," responds Mr. Buck. "That way we can set a goal that's actually attainable since it's relative to our baseline numbers."

The team goes through their list of data sources and begins discussing potential goals for each one. They make sure that the goals feel attainable given the fact that they are just starting out with comprehensive bullying prevention in the school. When looking at the goals for staff training, the team agrees that a goal of 95% of the staff completing the online Second Step training is reasonable and that they will strive for 80% fidelity on the Second Step fidelity tool. The 80% mark is also where the team agrees to the goal of the staff indicating that they have improved their knowledge of how bullying prevention is conducted at Conestoga as measured by the exit slips at all-staff meetings. Due to the fact that bullying was not previously listed as a reason for receiving an ODR, the team agrees to use a relative reduction of 10% of ODRs listing bullying as the reason from the first year of implementing comprehensive bullying prevention to the second. Finally, on the staff feedback form, the team sets the goal that 85% of the staff will report that Conestoga does a good job of preventing bullying.

PROVIDE INITIAL TRAINING

Once the Second Step program is purchased, the bullying prevention implementation team begins following through on their decision to be the first group within the school to take the online training. During the following team meeting after all members have completed the training, the team reviews the training plan that was developed several months earlier. "If you remember," says Mrs. Brown, "we all agreed that once we got the Second Step program that the entire staff will complete the online training by the end of the academic year. That gives everyone a few months to take the training. We will also be giving grade-level teams the chance to look over the materials during the next all-staff meeting so that they become more comfortable with how everything works. Finally, at the beginning of next school year before students arrive, we will have a refresher training for the staff so that everyone is on the same page regarding what implementation will look like."

Dr. Fluke is next to speak. "If you remember from a few months ago, we reviewed the updated behavior matrix that the school climate team had drafted and provided feedback specific to bullying prevention. The school climate team has since finalized the behavior matrix and will be presenting it at the next all-staff meeting. I will be one of the presenters, so I will be sure to mention how the school's focus on bullying prevention is included in the work of PBIS." Mr. Ferris responds, "I'm excited that we are able to actually align the work of these two teams. We all know how important having a foundation of a strong climate and culture is for preventing bullying, and this is a great step in that direction."

Over the remaining months of the academic year, the bullying prevention implementation team members present at all-staff meetings on the topics of bullying prevention and Second Step. Staff members who administer curriculum lessons complete their training using the Second Step digital training. The entire staff receives training on the updated behavior matrix that will be used at the beginning of the next school year. Dr. Fluke continues to serve as a liaison between the PBIS and bullying prevention implementation team. When questions about the curriculum or how to address issues of bullying arise, members of the implementation team are well prepared to provide guidance since they have already completed their training.

REVIEW AND REVISE POLICIES

"A key piece of our infrastructure for preventing bullying is our school and district policies," says Mrs. Brown at the beginning of an implementation team meeting. "The majority of our meeting time today will be dedicated to reviewing our current school handbook policy on bullying and seeing where we can include best practices from comprehensive bullying prevention." Since the team is still in the installation phase regarding policy, its goal is to compare what comprehensive bullying prevention suggests should be included in a school policy compared with their school's actual policy. Using Table 3.1 provided in Chapter 3, the team finds that they have only a few best practices in their existing policy: the definition of bullying, a prohibition against bullying (but no description of how making false statements about bullying is prohibited), and a broad statement that bullying has consequences. The team recognizes that there is clearly a lot of work to be done to revise their school policy to one that includes multiple best practices.

After taking stock of where their current policy stands, the implementation team discusses the best way to approach revising their policy. "I would love to be able to have an updated policy in place at the beginning of the next school year," says Ms. Coutts. "Then we would be able to include it in all the communication to families and in any trainings that we have before the beginning of the school year. Maybe it would be best to look at what we can update most easily, then work on the more in depth changes over time?" The team agrees and discusses the easiest updates that can be made. They include updating the definition of bullying so that it includes cyberbullying, updating the prohibition of bullying language so that it includes making knowingly false statements, and including the work that the team has accomplished around prevention.

Conestoga Elementary School does not have standard bullying reporting, investigation, or record-keeping processes. Mr. Ferris, Dr. Fluke, and Ms. Pearcy agree to review the forms included in Figures 3.2 and 3.4 and the flowchart in Figure 3.3 and see where they may adapt them to better fit their school. Dr. Fluke says that he will also work with the school climate team to discuss the section on consequences that will be included in the bullying prevention policy. "I want to make sure that the consequences that we include in our policy are in line with the work that the school climate team is doing," he says. Mrs. Brown states that once the majority of changes are made to the policy, she and Mr. Young will share the updates with the district and their legal counsel as necessary to make sure that everything in the policy aligns with state law and district policy.

COMMUNICATION

Having made significant progress in their installation of bullying prevention best practices, the implementation team turns its attention to how communication about their work takes place. "Okay, team," says Mrs. Doran. "We are starting to make some great strides with the installation of our bullying prevention work here at Conestoga. So how are we going to make sure that students and families know about what we are doing? And, probably even more important, how do we go about getting their feedback?" The team decides to engage in a brainstorming activity to identify all of the points of contact they have with families and the community during which communication about bullying prevention can take place.

The team discusses the different opportunities throughout the year to discuss bullying prevention with families, the community, and students. In addition, they outline the different types of communication that would be appropriate given the event and how that communication would take place. When they finish, the team has identified about half a dozen opportunities to communicate with stakeholders about bullying prevention.

"As each of these events gets closer, we can take time during our meeting to draft the communication materials," says Mrs. Doran. "The hardest part will be the first time we create them. Next year, we really just have to update the data and any additional work we have put into bullying prevention." Dr. Fluke speaks up next. "It's also important for us to make sure we look at the data collected through some of these events during our dedicated data review time in meetings." The team nods in agreement. "I think what I may be most excited about," he continues, "is the chance to reach out and connect with other community organizations during our end-of-year carnival. This event could be a great opportunity to develop even more relationships like the one we have with Mr. Buck's company." The team's discussion is summarized in Table 11.6.

TABLE 11.6. Communication Efforts of the Implementation Team

Event	Audience	Time of year	Communication opportunities	Communication method
Back-to-school night	Families and students	Before school year begins	Information on anti-bullying curriculum; new anti-bullying policy; new behavior matrix	Handouts
First all-school assembly	Students	First month of school	Introduce new curriculum to students and focus on kindness for the year	In-person presentation
Parent–teacher conferences	Families, students	One each quarter	Review curriculum topics being taught; Reporting procedure if bullying is witnessed or experienced; open conversation about concerns	In-person presentation
Annual school music performance	Families	May each year	Information on reduction in bullying and prevention measures taken by school; brief survey of families on their perspective of bullying prevention at Conestoga	Included as part of handbill; one-page insert within handbill
End-of-year carnival	Families, community, students	June each year	Information on reduction in bullying and prevention measures taken by school; survey for families; connections with community partners	Table during carnival
Social media posts	Families, community	One each week	Data on bullying; feedback on bullying from families; online bullying report form	Social media pages

CHAPTER 12

Case Study
Implementation

INITIAL IMPLEMENTATION

Now that the infrastructure for the evidence-based bullying prevention best practices has been installed and the school staff has been trained, the school can begin its initial implementation. This means that the bullying prevention implementation team is meeting regularly, that teachers have started implementing the evidence-based program, and that data-based decisions are being made on a regular basis to continually improve bullying prevention efforts. Additionally, ongoing coaching support is being provided to teachers and other staff members involved in administering the best practices. By the time the initial implementation is in full swing, the majority of teachers are implementing the bullying prevention program, some are beginning to achieve fidelity, and there is an overall increase in confidence among all stakeholders in the usability and success of the work.

Begin Use of Comprehensive Bullying Prevention

There is excitement in the air. It's just a few days before the beginning of a fresh school year. The bullying prevention implementation team at Conestoga Elementary School has just sat down to an impromptu meeting in between scheduled staff meetings and classroom preparation time. Mr. Ferris begins the conversation in the school library. "I don't know the last time I have been so eager to get kids back in the school," he says. "We have so many great things we are going to be rolling out. In a month from now, things are going to be so different from what has typically gone on here." "And don't forget," adds Dr. Fluke, "that with our help, the school climate team has basically set up an entire lesson plan for the staff to teach our revamped expected behaviors on the first day."

The team begins discussing the sequence of implementation for the CBP components. Dr. Fluke reviews some of the key next steps. "So, looking at the implementation plan, the behavior matrix will be reviewed during the next all-staff meeting. Members of the staff have already seen a draft version that they provided feedback on, but they will be trained on the final version in that meeting. They will also receive the Second Step beginning-of-the-year training before our first day with students. Then, it's show time."

On the school's first day with students, Conestoga begins implementing what has taken most of the previous year to explore, plan, and install. Teachers across the school welcome their new group of students and make sure to connect with the families who accompany their children as well. Most of the first day is typical: students learn where their desks are, get to know their classmates, and meet their teachers. What is different, though, is the beginning of intentional shifts in behavior and focus. Instead of just learning the names of their classmates, students are allowed time to share some of their personal stories. For example, in Mr. Ferris's class, a second-grade student named Zach shares that his family recently moved from Illinois and that he loves the Chicago Cubs baseball team (this was already obvious given the Cubs T-shirt he wore on the first day of school). Tyler, another student in Mr. Ferris's class, who has attended Conestoga since kindergarten, blurts out, "I love the Cubbies!" Despite the fact that Tyler has been at Conestoga for 2 years and that Mr. Ferris has a cursory knowledge of who he is, Mr. Ferris had no idea that he was a Cubs fan.

In addition to students having the space to share their personal stories, teachers are encouraged to begin building stronger relationships with their students this year as well. "Well," responds Mr. Ferris after Tyler's exclamation, "I'm glad that there are two Cubs fans in the class because I think that most of us here are Seattle Mariners' fans." Several other students in the class start to cheer. "In fact," continues Mr. Ferris, "I usually go to several Mariners' games each year with my family." Mr. Ferris then tells the students a little more about himself. In addition to being a fan of baseball, he tells his class that he plays the guitar, that his favorite book is *The Outsiders*, and that he has two cats at home. This leads to a conversation about which students in the class have pets and which don't, and what kinds of pet students wish they could have (tigers and penguins are the runaway winners). By the time Mr. Ferris's class is scheduled to begin reviewing the updated behavior matrix, there is a feeling of connectedness among the students.

Although teachers typically have a very busy first day with students, as the school psychologist, Dr. Fluke's schedule is fairly light. The students with whom he will meet in small groups for academic or behavior support are getting to know their new teachers and, in general, there are not too many crises. Usually, the worst he has to handle are the parents of kindergarten students who don't want to leave after dropping off their kids (despite the fact that their 5-year-old is already doing great in the classroom). So on the first day, Dr. Fluke likes to visit classrooms to find out if the teachers need any support or a quick break. This is what he is doing when he comes across two younger female students standing near the hallway bathroom. The smaller of the two has her back against the wall and her head down looking at her shoes (which Dr. Fluke notices are hand-me-downs and possibly third- or fourth-generation hand-me-downs). The taller of the two students is unusually close to her peer and is also looking down at her shoes.

When Dr. Fluke walks up to the two students, the taller student quickly jerks her head to look at him. The other girl continues looking at her shoes. "Happy first day of school," says Dr. Fluke. "Hi," says the taller girl. "What are you two up to?" asks Dr. Fluke. "We are going to the bathroom. Mrs. Nguyen said that we have to go with a buddy." Mrs. Nguyen is a second-grade teacher new this year to Conestoga. In the limited time that Dr. Fluke has interacted with her, he has found her to be a caring, if not idealistic, teacher just a few years out of college. "Okay. Why don't you go ahead and go to the bathroom," says Dr. Fluke. The taller girl says okay and starts skipping her way into the bathroom. Dr. Fluke sees that the shorter girl is still against the wall and looking down at her shoes. He walks over to her and gets down on one knee so that he is at her eye level.

"Hi there," he says gently. "I'm Dr. Fluke. What's your name?" The girl doesn't respond and keeps looking down. Dr. Fluke lowers his head further to the point of being below the girl's face so he can look up at her and make eye contact. "Hi," he says again. He can see now that the girl has been crying. "I can see that you're sad. Why don't we take a walk?" The girl still doesn't say anything, but does begin to move away from the wall. Dr. Fluke walks slowly next to the girl and leads her toward Mrs. Nguyen's classroom, which is just a few feet away. He opens the classroom door and makes sure to stand where he can also see the entrance to the bathroom in case the second girl leaves.

The opening of the door gets Mrs. Nguyen's attention. When she sees that one of her students is looking down and standing next to Dr. Fluke, she walks over to the two of them. "Hi, Dr. Fluke," she says. "Is everything okay, Chloe?" she asks. Chloe keeps her head down and shakes it to say "No." Dr. Fluke looks over to the bathroom and sees that the other girl has still not left. "I think," Dr. Fluke responds to Mrs. Nguyen, "that there was an issue between Chloe here and the buddy she went to the bathroom with." Looking at Dr. Fluke, Mrs. Nguyen says, "I see. Well, once Akilah returns from the bathroom, we can all talk about what happened."

This comment draws Dr. Fluke's attention. During one of their trainings on the basics of bullying and how to respond, he remembered learning that adults should avoid trying to mediate bullying between students in the moment. Given the fact that Mrs. Nguyen is new to the school this year, Dr. Fluke wonders about the fidelity of their onboarding process and bullying prevention. "Actually, if you don't mind, Mrs. Nguyen, once Akilah gets out of the bathroom, would it be alright if I check in with her?" "Sure, no problem," responds Mrs. Nguyen. "Come on, Chloe," continues Mrs. Nguyen. "We just started decorating the name tags we are going to put on our desks, and I have a special stencil you can use." Chloe lifts her head a little to make eye contact with Mrs. Nguyen and seems to be interested in getting something especially for her. Dr. Fluke makes a mental note to check in with Chloe tomorrow.

Turning back around after watching Chloe and Mrs. Nguyen walk into the classroom, Dr. Fluke is surprised to see Akilah standing right in front of him. "Oh!" says Dr. Fluke. "Akilah, you surprised me." "I want a special stencil," Akilah says. It takes Dr. Fluke a second to realize that Akilah had overheard the conversation between Mrs. Nguyen and Chloe. "Well, I'm sure there are a lot of great stencils you can use in the classroom. Mrs. Nguyen just noticed that Chloe was feeling sad, so she wanted to cheer her up a little bit." Akilah doesn't respond, but continues to stare at Dr. Fluke. "But I want a special stencil," she repeats. "I understand. When you head back in the classroom, you can find a special stencil. First, though, I wanted to talk to you about Chloe. Like I said, she was feeling sad. Why do you think that is?"

Clearly seeing that Dr. Fluke was not understanding the importance of her getting a special stencil, Akilah quickly retorts, "I don't know. Maybe because she has ugly shoes." Then she quickly moves past Dr. Fluke and into the classroom. Dr. Fluke calls her name and Akilah turns around. "Come here for a second, please," he says. Akilah walks over to where Dr. Fluke is standing outside of the classroom entryway. "Tell me what you and Chloe were talking about when I saw you standing in front of the bathroom earlier. Was it about her shoes?" Akilah pauses for a second and says,

"I was showing her my new shoes. They have unicorns on them. See?" Akilah lifts up her foot and shows Dr. Fluke one of her shoes. He can see that they look new and have a unicorn with a horn that lights up when she walks. "Those are very nice shoes," responds Dr. Fluke.

"My mommy bought them for me because it's the first day of school," Akilah says. "Oh, she must love you very much to buy you such great shoes," says Dr. Fluke. "Yeah. She buys me lots of stuff. Ashley and Stephanie's mommies buy them new shoes every school year too. They're my friends. But Chloe never has new shoes, so I guess her mommy doesn't love her very much." Akilah says. Dr. Fluke worries that he may have inadvertently given Akilah another line of attack on Chloe so quickly responds, "Oh, I know Chloe and her mom. And her mom loves her very much. Moms have lots of ways to show that they love their daughters. Tell you what. If it's true that Chloe is feeling sad because she doesn't have new shoes for the first day of school, let's try to be extra nice to her today." Akilah pauses for a second and says, "Okay." Then she skips her way back into Mrs. Nguyen's classroom.

Although Dr. Fluke is worried about such an encounter between two students happening on the very first day of school, he reminds himself that this is the first year in which the school is trying to implement a new culture, a new policy, and new expectations. Thinking back to the definition of bullying, Dr. Fluke is already aware that several of the components are present in what he witnessed. There was a clear power imbalance: Akilah appears to come from a more well-to-do family than Chloe. Dr. Fluke noticed that shoes weren't the only part of Chloe's outfit that were a hand-me-down. He couldn't be sure, but the way Akilah talked about her friends made it seem like she may also have greater social power than Chloe. The other two aspects of bullying were still yet to be determined. Dr. Fluke didn't know if the behavior was going to be repeated, and he didn't know if Akilah was intentionally trying to hurt Chloe. It would seem reasonable that if one student saw that she made another cry because of what she said and didn't apologize or appear to feel bad about hurting the other student, that the behavior may be intentional. Despite this, Dr. Fluke was giving Akilah the benefit of the doubt in that she may just have some gaps in her social skills or felt anxious with adults around to apologize to Chloe. Regardless, he decides to check in with Mrs. Nguyen later that day to find out how Chloe is doing and to give her details about what he saw.

In the staff lounge, Dr. Fluke is able to find Mrs. Nguyen during her lunch period. "Hi, Mrs. Nguyen. Do you mind if I talk to you about Akilah and Chloe from this morning while you're having lunch?" Dr. Fluke asks. "Oh, not at all," Mrs. Nguyen responds. "I have been thinking about what happened all morning. Chloe was able to perk up a little bit, but she still seemed kind of down when our class went to the cafeteria for lunch. I just hate to see a student upset on her first day of school." Dr. Fluke then took several minutes to explain what he had seen before he brought Chloe to Mrs. Nguyen's classroom. He then shares his thinking behind not having the two students together when asking them about what had transpired. "I don't really know Chloe or Akilah that well," says Dr. Fluke. "So I didn't know if there was a history there, or if it could be a bullying situation. Just in case it was bullying, I didn't want to try to mediate what had gone on with both students at the same time since we know that the power imbalance can, and often does, play out even with adults trying to do the right thing."

Mrs. Nguyen tells Dr. Fluke that she appreciates him supporting her with the two students, and asks if there is anything else that he thinks might help the situation. "Right now, I think the best thing we can do is to keep our eye on their interactions. If we see something like what happened today happen again, then we can talk with them in more depth." Mrs. Nguyen nods. "One thing that might be helpful is to talk with Chloe's family today. It could be a simple phone call or, if they pick her up, having a quick chat." Mrs. Nguyen asks, "So, tell them about what happened today? Wouldn't that make them upset?" Dr. Fluke responds, "Well, typically we like to connect with families before a potential bullying incident occurs, but with it being the first day of school, we didn't really get that opportunity. What I like to do if I have a potentially difficult conversation with families is to use a 'sandwich' method. By that, I mean, sandwiching the negative part of the conversation between two positives. So what are a couple of things that went well for Chloe today?" Mrs. Nguyen describes two things she noticed when working with Chloe that stood out as strengths. "Great," says Dr. Fluke. "So you can start out with one of those positives, then talk about the incident with another student and how you helped Chloe feel better, then finish with the second positive." Mrs. Nguyen states that she likes that approach and will let Dr. Fluke know how the conversation goes.

Over the next several weeks, the universal bullying prevention supports are implemented for the first time. In passing conversations, Dr. Fluke hears from staff members that they were initially still nervous about teaching social-emotional skills to students, but after a while they realized that it was similar to teaching academic topics. When checking in with their grade-level colleagues, Mr. Ferris and Mrs. Doran heard similar sentiments. Mrs. Doran was particularly interested in hearing how well Mrs. Nguyen was implementing the Second Step lessons. Mrs. Nguyen admitted that since she was a new teacher she was feeling pretty stressed about getting a handle on all of her responsibilities. Mrs. Doran does her best to empathize with Mrs. Nguyen and tells her to give herself some grace since she is still new and trying to put into practice everything that she has only read in books.

In Mr. Diez's unique role as the music teacher, he is able to build relationships with every student in the school. He sees firsthand how teachers in every class implement the new expected behaviors in the hallways. Some teachers are more effective than others at getting their students to have a quiet voice and stay in line while walking through the hallways. Since the music classroom is one of a kind in the school, he also has the opportunity to try his hand at directly teaching expected behaviors. After the third class, he began to get a feel for how to talk about respecting instruments, for example, and being responsible by making sure to put instruments back at the end of the class. Since he has the benefit of interacting with all of the students, Mr. Diez feels even more confident in his ability to speak to the bullying prevention implementation team about changes in school climate.

Implement Training and Coaching Supports

At the next bullying prevention implementation team meeting, the members begin by talking about how the first few weeks of the school year have gone. In general, everyone has positive news to report. The behavior matrix was introduced to students in every class, and the expected behaviors were directly taught in each of the locations around the school. Teachers introduced the Second Step lessons to students, and most classes had already completed the first few lessons. The team also talks about the success of their start-of-the-year Second Step training with the staff. Dr. Fluke shares the interaction he saw during the first day of school between Akilah and Chloe. He also shares the update that Chloe's family told Mrs. Nguyen that they appreciated her letting them know about what happened.

"Looking at all the training that the staff has received on bullying prevention best practices, we are in a great place to go back and see where we still have work to do in implementing all the pieces of CBP," says Mrs. Doran. The note taker pulls up the most recent iteration of the team's training plan that was first developed the previous year. Looking down the list of different training topics, the updates to the training plan include the results for each topic. The note taker then brings up the brainstorming list the team created the previous year to see what topics the staff still needed to be trained on. "If we are just working off of the priority list here," says Mrs. Brown, "then our next training for the staff would be focused on our school handbook's anti-bullying policy."

"The last I remember, we all reviewed our bullying prevention policy and realized there was a lot of work to do to align it with best practices," says Ms. Coutts. "Then Mr. Ferris, Dr. Fluke, and Ms. Pearcy reviewed some sample investigation and report forms, and we all provided feedback for a final version of the policy." Ms. Pearcy speaks next. "Yes. We were able to get an updated policy created, and I saw that it is now in the school handbook. So I assume that our district gave us the go-ahead to make the changes?" Mrs. Brown responds, "We received formal approval from the district over the summer. Unfortunately, that meant that we were not able to train the staff yet given all the other trainings we had planned. If I'm thinking about the priority list of areas for training that we have, I would be putting this one high on the list." The team agrees and completes a row in their training plan to allow for the introduction of and training on the new bullying prevention policy.

At the next all-staff meeting, 20 minutes is dedicated to sharing the new policy with the entire staff. Mr. Ferris, Dr. Fluke, and Ms. Pearcy lead a conversation about the changes to the policy, about the staff's responsibilities as outlined in the policy, and about how to talk with families about the new policy during parent–teacher conferences. Ms. Pearcy also informs staff members that they don't need to worry about remembering the talking points about the updated policy during parent–teacher conferences because the implementation team will provide a one-page handout with the highlights for all teachers. As part of the implementation team's data system, the exit slip for the all-staff meeting asks everyone about their self-efficacy with the new policy and for any feedback to be included in future revisions. The coaching plan is also updated to include discussions about the new policy.

In early September, the implementation team meets and talks about their upcoming coaching support for grade-level teams. "Next week, we will begin our general implementation support for grade-level teams," says Mrs. Brown. "Looking at our coaching plan, we have said that we would all have a role in providing this coaching. Let's figure out who will be meeting with each grade level, the main topics we will cover, and our approach to make sure we aren't giving the grade-level teams the answers but letting them find their own answers to their questions." The team spends the next several minutes assigning team members to the different grade levels. Mr. Ferris and Mrs. Doran are the coaches for their respective grades, and Dr. Fluke, Mr. Diez, Ms. Pearcy, and Mrs. Myers take up the remaining spots. Mrs. Brown tells the coaches that she is willing to provide support for them on how to effectively coach their grade-level teams if they prefer since she provides coaching to many of the teachers as a regular part of her duties. When the meeting is adjourned, everyone is feeling confident in their ability to provide coaching support to the grade-level teams.

At the next implementation team meeting, the team spends several minutes discussing the data system and coaching supports for the first module of the Second Step lessons. "We are coming up to the end of the first Second Step module of lessons," says Mrs. Brown. "Looking at our data system, we have a fidelity assessment to administer to teachers. This measure will give us our first hard data on how implementation has been going across the school." Dr. Fluke speaks next. "Once we have those data collected, I will put all the information together for us to analyze at our next meeting. We will be able to see what is going well and what areas of support we may need to address in coaching support. Once we get to that point, we will update our coaching plan." "That's where Mr. Ferris and I come in to provide small-group coaching support to those staff members who need it," adds Mrs. Doran.

As planned, the small-group coaching supports begin shortly after the data are returned on the fidelity of implementation of the Second Step lessons. Mr. Ferris and Mrs. Doran meet with a small group of teachers once each week after school to provide support for what areas, as identified by the data, are needed. Specifically, they focus on time management within lessons and how to integrate the lesson concepts outside of the dedicated teaching time. By the end of the first year of implementation, Mr. Ferris and Mrs. Doran are no longer providing coaching support to teachers on lesson implementation because all of them have begun scoring themselves higher on the Second Step fidelity measures.

Over the course of the next several months, implementation team members continue meeting and progressing in their training and coaching plans. The key topics on which they wanted to train the staff are administered, and data related to their effectiveness are collected. Those teachers who indicate that they have less self-efficacy on topics or who report needing more training are provided coaching supports. Dr. Fluke continues working with both the bullying prevention implementation team and the school climate team. Similar training and coaching structures are beginning to be implemented around PBIS, which contribute to building a safer, more welcoming culture at Conestoga.

Use Data to Track and Improve Implementation

The bullying prevention implementation team spends the first couple months of the first year of implementation, in part, by following their data system plan. After each all-staff meeting, Dr. Fluke takes the staff's exit tickets and compiles the data to present at the next implementation team meeting. One of the first all-staff meetings held included time for the staff to be briefly trained on the new bullying prevention policy at Conestoga. Mr. Young asks teachers to bring a laptop or their cell phone with them to the meeting so that they can complete their exit ticket before leaving. Dr. Fluke quickly realized after trying to provide paper exit tickets at staff meetings that the amount of time it took to collect the paper forms and enter the data was too long. So the data collection method was changed to a Google Form that everyone is able to access on their smartphone or laptop.

When Dr. Fluke returns to his office after the staff meeting, he is able to see the results of the exit-slip data from the staff training on the new policy. What he sees is not great. The majority of staff members reported on the exit slip that they "disagree" or "strongly disagree" that they are confident in their ability to follow the policy. In response to a question about reports of bullying, they also said that they "disagree" or "strongly disagree" that they know what to do if a student reports bullying to them (see Figure 12.1). Dr. Fluke begins thinking about how he will present these data to the implementation team at the next meeting. He walks down the hallway to the central office to speak with Mrs. Brown about the agenda for their next meeting. Mrs. Brown agrees to provide some extra time to review the exit-slip data and determine the next steps.

At the implementation team meeting, Dr. Fluke displays the results of the exit-slip survey to the team. He can see from the facial reactions around the room that they understand the results are not what they had hoped. "I know this isn't great feedback," begins Dr. Fluke. "So let's take a

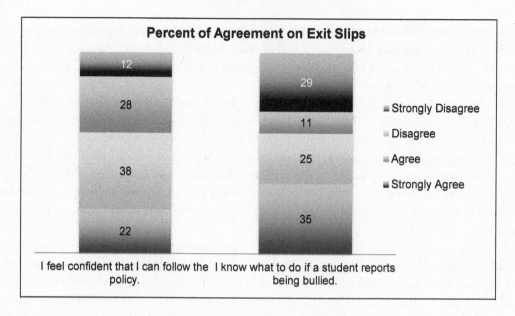

FIGURE 12.1. Data from exit slips.

look at our problem-solving process and figure out what we can do to remedy the situation." The team then begins going through the four-step problem-solving process to find a solution. They begin by clearly defining the problem, and arrive at the fact that staff do not know how to appropriately respond when a student reports bullying. Moving to the second step of the problem-solving process, they eventually determine that the most likely reason that their problem exists is because they did not provide enough time for teachers to review the policy to feel comfortable with it before they were asked to begin using it. The majority of comments on the exit slip mentioned the lack of time devoted to explaining the policy and the specific responsibilities of teachers.

"Alright. Now that we have come to an agreement on why the training didn't go well, let's talk about what we can do to solve the problem," says Mrs. Brown. The team begins brainstorming ways to provide teachers more time to become comfortable with the policy before being asked to implement it. "One point that I can talk with Mr. Young about," says Mrs. Brown, "is if we can hold off on communicating the new policy with families. We can continue operating under our old policy for now to give ourselves more time to properly train the staff. To be honest, I feel bad about how we rolled this out. We basically told teachers that they have new responsibilities without giving them the right amount of time to learn what they are. So we need to make sure that we fail forward and learn from this lesson."

"So if we hold off on rolling out the policy," responds Mr. Ferris, "then that gives us time to go into depth with teachers on the new policy. We should probably add this new step to our training and coaching plan as well." The team agrees and updates both plans to reflect dedicated time for a more in-depth training and coaching experience for teachers. The members also update their data system to include a second administration of the exit-slip survey to determine if they have made adequate progress once the training and coaching has gotten under way. With these changes in place, the team feels confident in continuing to discuss other areas important to the implementation of CBP.

In November of the first year of implementation, the team examines the school's ODR data to check if there are any emerging trends. In reporting the ODR information, Dr. Fluke filters the data by the reason students were disciplined. He begins by showing the team the data for students who received an ODR because of physical aggression. "So far, we haven't received a report of bullying this year," Dr. Fluke begins. "But I think when you look at these ODR data, you will see that it doesn't mean we are bereft of any problems." The data Dr. Fluke displays show that there were six ODRs across the entire school for physical aggression. Filtering these data by grade level, the team sees that half of the ODRs were given to second-grade students. When Dr. Fluke provides details on these three ODRs, a familiar name jumps out.

"Two of those ODRs are for Akilah in Mrs. Nguyen's class," says Mrs. Doran. "I know that Mrs. Nguyen has been having a hard time with her, but I didn't realize that she had been given two ODRs this early into the school year." As the team reads about the incidents of physical aggression, they notice that both were targeting the same student: Chloe. "This is concerning," says Dr. Fluke. "I'm sure you all remember my telling you what I saw the first day of school between Akilah and Chloe." The team nods in recognition. "If this isn't bullying, it sure seems to be on its way to becoming bullying," says Mrs. Doran. "What should we do?"

Mrs. Brown is the first to respond. "It may be a good idea to talk with Mrs. Nguyen to get more information. These two incidents rose to the level of an ODR, but my guess would be that there have been other less-egregious things that have happened as well." Mrs. Doran responds, "Okay. I can talk with her. I have been doing some coaching with her around our Second Step lessons, too, so I already have a pretty good relationship with her." The team next reviews other parts of the ODR data. They see that the fourth grade has the second-highest number of ODRs. Mr. Diez says that he will check in with the fourth-grade team to see if it can provide more information on the overall climate in that grade. Both Mrs. Doran and Mr. Diez agree to email updates to the team once they have had their conversations.

When the two emails come in, Mrs. Brown realizes that the next implementation team meeting will need to focus a significant amount of time on what was reported. Mrs. Doran wrote that she heard from Mrs. Nguyen that Akilah did, in fact, have other behaviors that were concerning towards peers, but that the two ODRs were submitted when Akilah's behavior became "over the top." The other behaviors that Mrs. Nguyen said were concerning included calling students names and excluding them from being part of a class work group or their lunch group. According to Mrs. Nguyen, the reason for much of Akilah's name-calling or exclusionary behavior was that the other students were "too poor" or "didn't have nice-enough clothes." The final point that Mrs. Nguyen mentioned was that Akilah actually seems to be one of the more popular students in the class and has several friends she enjoys playing with at recess.

Mr. Diez's update on the fourth grade included some similar themes. The majority of the ODRs the team found during the meeting occurred during transitions when students were going to recess and during recess itself. One fourth-grade teacher told Mr. Diez that it "always seems like there's an issue with playing soccer during recess." Mr. Diez said that the teacher wasn't sure what the main issue was, but that the recess paraprofessional told him that students were excluding others from joining in the soccer games during recess. When Mr. Diez spoke with the recess paraprofessional, they told him that some of the students tell others that they can only be on their team if they are wearing Nikes. The ODRs are usually written when a student is disrespectful after the paraprofessional tells them that it doesn't matter what shoes someone has, everyone is allowed to play.

During the next team meeting, the first topic on the agenda is about the information that Mrs. Doran and Mr. Diez gathered about ODRs. "Why do all these kids care about shoes so much?" asks Mrs. Myers. "Well, it seems to be shoes, clothes, basically anything that shows you have money," responds Professor Obara. Mrs. Brown is next to speak. "In general, the families in our school live comfortably," she says. "There are some students, though, who qualify for free and reduced-price lunch. Apparently that issue has become somewhat of a social dividing line in our school. Let's talk about how we can solve this problem." The team begins to follow the four-step problem-solving model to identify the problem, the potential reasons the problem exists, and possible solutions.

At the conclusion of the problem-analysis phase, the team has identified several solutions that could lead to resolving the problem. First, the members decide that they need to have more information about the prevalence of socioeconomic status being used as a reason that students are targeting others for exclusion and name calling. Mrs. Brown agrees to speak to the district administration about adding an option to their annual climate survey that allows students to report "my clothes" and "how much money my family has" as options for the reasons that they have been bullied. Another approach that the team decides to discuss with the second- and fourth-grade staff is to align some of their lessons around stories of successful people who come from lower-class upbringings. Mrs. Brown suggests involving the soccer star Abby Wambach in some way. "She is the youngest of seven children, she used to live in Oregon, and she is the most prolific soccer scorer in history." Mr. Diez agreed with Mrs. Brown's decision, especially since soccer was one of the areas that the fourth-grade boys were fighting over. "You know," says Mr. Buck, "I think our company used to do some work with her as well. I can look into that."

As the months of the school year continue to pass, the plans that the implementation team designed based on their data are implemented. Greater time is spent training the staff on the parts of the new bullying prevention policy so that everyone can feel more confident about their ability to implement the policy with fidelity. A second round of exit-slip data are collected, and the data indicate that the staff has greater self-efficacy with the policy. Teachers who still reported that they do not believe they are able to follow the policy in practice receive additional coaching supports. When the first formal bullying incident in the school occurred in early November, the teacher who was notified was able to ensure the student's immediate safety and followed the policy's steps in filing a report. Over time, additional bullying reports were made. Some teachers responded as expected, and those who did not were provided additional coaching and support.

Near the end of the school year during the first year of implementation, the bullying prevention implementation team is operating well. Data are consistently reviewed, problem solving is based on these data, and professional development for the staff is consistently updated based on need. The annual climate and culture survey is administered to students about 6 weeks prior to the end of the school year. When the results came in shortly afterward, the implementation team dedicates the majority of their meeting time to analyzing the data and to determining what steps should be taken to improve bullying prevention at Conestoga for the next school year. Many of the team members are eager to see the results of the survey because Mrs. Brown was able to add the additional items they had asked about to the survey.

"For this meeting," Dr. Fluke says at the team meeting at which the annual climate and culture data are being reviewed, "we are going to start from a high level looking at the results and then narrow down our focus to look at specific trends." He then pulls up slides that he created to share the results of the survey. "First, we can look at the percentage of students who reported that they had experienced bullying this school year. You can see here that 31% of students reported being the target of bullying this past year." Mr. Ferris responds first to this information. "That seems really high compared to the number of bullying reports we actually received," he says. Mrs. Brown comments, "Yes it does. I think this information tells us that we may need to look at our methods for communicating how students and families can report bullying when it happens."

Dr. Fluke says he agrees, then continues showing the team the data from the climate and culture survey. "I know that we are all interested in seeing the specific data around why students believe they were targeted. I have created a bar graph here that shows what students reported." Looking at the graph, the team can see that the top reasons students reported being targeted for bullying was "how much money my family has" followed by "the way I look" and "my clothes." It appears that the hypothesis the team had about the reasons why students were being bullied in their school was at least somewhat accurate. "Well," says Mrs. Doran, "this certainly lines up with what we were hearing anecdotally from the students. So what can we do about it?"

The team begins to use their problem-solving process to examine potential solutions for the top reasons students report being the targets of bullying. Solutions that are discussed include creating clearer expected behaviors on the behavior matrix for recess, reaching out to community organizations that provide supports for low-income families, and working with grade-level teams to discuss how inclusivity can be further integrated into their lessons. The team develops an implementation plan that outlines which members will be responsible for each one of these proposed solutions. The team agrees that updates will be provided prior to the start of the next school year. Mrs. Brown volunteers to look into community supports since she will be working more over the summer and would like to have something set up at the beginning of the year, if possible.

The final meeting of the first year of implementation concludes with a sense of accomplishment among the team members. They were able to begin implementing some of the best practices for bullying prevention over the course of the year. Moreover, when barriers were found or mistakes were made, they worked together as a team to address them. Everyone on the team expressed their gratitude to one another for a great year and their determination to continue the work of implementation in the fall.

FULL IMPLEMENTATION

The ultimate goal of CBP is for schools to reach full implementation, because achieving this goal means that they are giving students the best chance of attending school without experiencing bullying. Schools do not typically reach full implementation within the first several years of starting a new initiative. Full implementation is reached when at least 50% or more of the staff are using bullying prevention best practices with fidelity and outcomes are being achieved. The bullying prevention implementation team still meets regularly, the data are still collected and used for decision making, and feedback loops with stakeholders are still in place to support continuous improvement. The outcomes of this stage are a reduction in the prevalence of bullying in the school and sustaining bullying prevention efforts with fidelity.

Continued Use of Data for Implementation

At the beginning of the new school year, which is the second year of implementation, the bullying prevention implementation team again meets prior to students starting class. Whereas in the previous year the team was anxious to see the work begin, this year there is an air of determined optimism. With 1 year of experience under their belts, the team members fee confident in their ability to provide effective training and coaching, respond to unforeseen circumstances, and quickly problem-solve concerns. When the meeting begins, Mrs. Brown provides an update on the progress that has been made at connecting with community organizations over the summer.

"I am happy to say that we have some good news," she begins. "After our last meeting, I reached out to several local food and clothing banks. There was one food bank and one clothing bank that Mr. Young and I decided to use." "What do you mean use?" asks Ms. Pearcy. "Well," responds Mrs. Brown, "you know how we have portable classrooms off to the side of the school that we had used for overflow classes before the new elementary school in the district was built?" The team nods. "We decided that since we are really just using one of the spaces for storage right now, we will repurpose it as a food and clothing store for families who qualify for free- and reduced-price lunch. Our custodian is finishing up the organization of the space right now, and we should have donations from the two stores arriving later this week." Mrs. Brown goes on to describe the process for communicating with families about the opportunity to shop for free clothing and food.

Everybody decides that they want to take a look at the repurposed portable right away and walk in that direction. As they are walking, Mr. Buck has another update. "So I was talking to the people in the community relations division at my company about all the work we are doing here at Conestoga. I do my best to keep them updated on how we are spending the grant funds they provided us, and I'm always looking out for additional funding sources. Well, when I mentioned that one of the main reasons students were being bullied was because of their clothes and shoes, one of my colleagues said that they might be able to help. Long story short, they are able to donate shoes and some clothing items as well!"

As the teachers are busily discussing this great news about donations from Mr. Buck's company, they arrive at the repurposed portable. When they step inside, they see that Mr. Young is already working at attaching some shelving to a wall. Looking around, they can see that their custodian has done an amazing job of making the space look and feel like an actual store. There are shelves similar to those in a grocery store where canned goods and boxes can be placed. In the area where clothing will be available, there are short tables and even two clothing racks with hangers. "Wow. This is amazing," says Mrs. Myers. "I mean, I was expecting just some long tables where food and clothing would be stacked, but this looks like a place I would actually shop in," she says, laughing. "Yeah, that was our goal," says Mr. Young who had joined the group. "We wanted to make families feel respected and welcome. Hopefully we are able to accomplish that by the time everything is up and running.

Once the school year begins in earnest, the team notices that the comfort level of the staff who are implementing the bullying prevention best practices has increased since the previous year. Teachers are more fluent in their teaching of the behavior matrix in the first few days of school, and the more-specific behavior expectations for recess are explained to every student. Having learned from their mistakes around introducing the new bullying prevention policy, the team provides refresher training on the new policy before students arrive. Data from their exit survey show that the vast majority of the teachers report feeling like they have the ability to follow the policy as written.

In the second year of implementation, the team chooses to focus on gathering more data from students' families. The team made this decision after the opening of the Conestoga Family Store (as it became known). During parent–teacher conferences, larger school performances with families present, and shopping times at the Family Store, families were asked to provide their ideas and feedback on how they should be included at the school. Results from the surveys are analyzed to improve how the school connects with families. Many families report that they feel that Conestoga wants their children to succeed and is responsive to their needs. Suggestions include providing more opportunities for families to connect with the school in informal social ways. Based on this feedback, the implementation team begins working on a way to incorporate social activities into the back-to-school night at the beginning of the next school year. The team also brainstorms other plans, including holding a Kindness Run and Kindness Week at different times in the school year.

Continued Use of Training and Coaching Supports

Near the end of the second year of implementation, the bullying prevention implementation team truly begins to have the sense of running itself. Anyone on the team is able to jump in and facilitate meetings if necessary because the agendas are created ahead of time and the team is becoming more fluent in how to engage in the problem-solving process. At around this time Mr. Young and Mrs. Brown also bring the PBIS and bullying prevention teams together for a joint meeting.

Mr. Young begins the meeting by describing the successes of both teams. "Over the past couple years, our school has made remarkable progress in both our implementation of PBIS and of bullying prevention best practices. As everyone here knows, Dr. Fluke has been a member of both teams during this time. When he and I talked recently about the work of these teams, we realized that there is actually quite a bit of overlap in the work we do. Both teams focus on improving student behavior: the school climate team through direct instruction of expected behaviors throughout the year and the bullying prevention team through supporting social-emotional lessons for students. As Dr. Fluke reminds me often, the foundation of effective bullying prevention is a strong school climate, which is what our school climate team strives to create. So, with these commonalities in mind, we wanted to bring you all here today to discuss combining these two teams into one."

At first, there is silence around the room as everyone takes in this suggestion. Then Mr. Diez quips, "It sounds to me like Dr. Fluke wants to get out of having so many meetings." Everyone laughs, and Dr. Fluke replies, "Actually, even though I would have one less meeting, we are thinking that we may need to extend meetings, at least initially, from our standard 1hour to 90 or 120 minutes. Once we get more comfortable with the work, we can probably drop down to 1-hour meetings again. Like Mr. Young said, there is a lot of overlap in the work, and longer meetings would help make sure both initiatives are as informative as possible to help our students." As the discussion continues, it becomes clear that it would make sense to combine the teams, and the staff makes the decision to begin this new structure at the start of the next school year.

One of the last areas discussed by the bullying prevention implementation team prior to the end of the school year is the onboarding of new staff. "Now that we have our SEL curriculum, specific bullying prevention training from Second Step, a comprehensive policy on preventing bullying, as well as a host of other areas of training, I think it would be a good idea to clearly lay out an onboarding plan for new staff members," says Mrs. Brown. The team uses its past training plan to outline the necessary onboarding activities and trainings of new teachers related to bullying prevention. Having learned their lesson of asking teachers to implement the new policy without enough support and training, the team decides to prioritize certain trainings then spread out other trainings across the school year. Mrs. Brown says that she will also speak with Mr. Young about the possibility of starting a peer mentoring system for new teachers the first year, which would provide a less-intimidating way for them to have their questions addressed.

During one of the first joint meetings of the PBIS and bullying prevention implementation teams (now referred to as the behavior support team), the members discuss the value of having a consistent, predeveloped training for the entire staff at the beginning of the year. The training would cover the basics of culture and climate best practices from PBIS (such as the behavior matrix) as well as how to intervene in bullying situations and the responsibilities of the staff according to the bullying prevention policy. The team develops a new exit-slip survey for this training and pilots the training at the next all-staff meeting. Beginning with the third year of implementing CBP, the behavior support team administers the training to the entire staff prior to students arriving.

In addition to the consistent start-of-the-year staff training, data are used to determine needed supports for staff members for not only bullying prevention efforts, but for PBIS efforts as well. Monthly grade-level coaching meetings serve to broadly support teachers who are implementing the SEL curriculum, and coaching on behavior topics for staff members who are not connected directly to a grade level is provided. In the fourth year of CBP implementation, the behavior support team begins to self-report having more fluency and fidelity with reinforcing students for positive behaviors and using the skills learned from the SEL curriculum. Based on feedback from the staff, the vast majority of teachers agree that they feel supported by the behavior support team and that the amount of training and coaching is appropriate.

Evaluate for Expected Outcomes

"The vision that we have for Conestoga around bullying is that there is none," says Dr. Fluke at the end of the fourth year of CBP implementation. "All of the work that our team has done over the years has been to get closer and closer to this goal. The first time that we truly measured bullying across the entire school was 4 years ago, and 31% of students reported being the target of bullying." Dr. Fluke then pulls up the beginning of a line graph on his computer, which he projects for the entire behavior support team to see. In the second year, we saw a dip, with only 27% of students reporting being the target of bullying. Last year, we saw a smaller decline, with 25% of students reporting being the target of bullying. Which brings us to this year." Dr. Fluke displays the most recent bullying scores from the climate and culture survey that was administered just a few weeks earlier. "This year, only 17% of students reported being the target of bullying. While that is obviously 17% too many, it does represent a 14% decrease in bullying at Conestoga over the past 4 years."

Mrs. Myers, the grandmother of a now former student at Conestoga, is the first to respond to Dr. Fluke. "Five years ago, I remember being surprised that the principal had called me after the mean things I said to him because my granddaughter was being bullied. I was even more surprised when Mr. Young asked me to join a school team to help create real solutions to the problem. I am glad he did and that I said yes. I know that there are still 17% of our students whom we need to continue working to protect, but I also think that we can be proud of the progress we have made over the past 5 years." Dr. Fluke replies, "Well, we are glad that you agreed to join our team too, Mrs. Myers."

Dr. Fluke then displays the data on ODRs, and shares that there have been similar reductions in ODRs over the course of the past 4 years. "So when we think about how we got to this point, we really don't have to look too much farther than our fidelity data." Dr. Fluke then pulls up fidelity data on the implementation of Second Step lessons, the staff reports of completed trainings, the Tiered Fidelity Inventory for PBIS implementation, the staff self-reports of how well the bullying prevention policy has been followed, and the fidelity with which the staff discussed Conestoga's bullying prevention efforts at parent–teacher conferences. Across all areas, the team sees that the fidelity data have improved significantly since the beginning of data collection several years ago. "What I really want people to notice," continues Dr. Fluke, "is that we have over 50% of our staff members reporting that they implement these practices with fidelity. What these data mean is that, for now at least, we are in full implementation."

Over the next several years, members of the behavior support team at Conestoga continue to use the principles of CBP to drive their efforts. The team uses a continuous-improvement cycle to assess and bolster their bullying prevention work. This work leads to more impactful kindness events and a fundraising effort that (thanks to Mr. Buck's connections at his company) included Abby Wambach as a speaker. Students were even able to turn in their PBIS reinforcement tickets for a chance to meet and get a picture with Abby. Families who donated a certain amount of money were also able to meet the soccer star, all while knowing that their money was going toward preventing bullying at Conestoga. When staff turnover inevitably occurs, the systems are in place to continue effective bullying prevention work. The team members have the training and coaching supports in place for onboarding new teammates and staff in general.

Glossary

Social Media, Cyberbullying, and Online Safety Terms to Know

Sameer Hinduja, PhD, and Justin W. Patchin, PhD

In our Glossary below, we define the terms you need to know in the realm of social media, cyberbullying, and online safety, so that you are increasingly informed about technological jargon as you work with the youth under your care.

Acceptable Use Policy (AUP): A policy that schools and other organizations create to define the responsibilities and appropriate behaviors of computer and network users.

Among Us: A murder mystery online game in which you work with other players (Crewmates) to fix a spaceship while trying to determine who the killers (Impostors) are.

Android: Operating system created by Google. Android powers smartphones and tablets.

Anonymizer: An intermediary website that hides or disguises the IP address associated with the Internet user. Generally, these sites allow a person to engage in various Internet activities without leaving an easily traceable digital footprint.

App: Abbreviation for "application," it is a piece of software, primarily referring to those used on smartphones, tablets, and other touch-based devices.

Ask.fm (app): An app (and website) where users can ask and answer others' questions with the option of doing so anonymously.

Bash Board: An online bulletin board on which individuals can post anything they want. Often, posts are malicious and hateful statements directed against another person.

Blocking: The denial of access to particular parts of the Internet. Usually a message will be shown on screen to say that access has been denied. For example, Facebook users can block other users from sending them messages or seeing their posts.

Blog: Interactive Web journal or diary, the contents of which are posted online where they are viewable by some or all individuals. The act of updating a blog is called "blogging." A person who keeps a blog is referred to as a "blogger." The term was created by combining "web" and "log."

Bullicide: Suicide that results directly or indirectly from bullying victimization. The relationship between bullying and suicide is complex and for that and other reasons, many researchers have concerns with the utilization of this term.

Bullying: Repeated and deliberate harassment directed by one in a position of power toward one or more persons. Can involve physical threats or behaviors, including assault, or indirect and subtle forms of aggression, including gossip and rumor spreading. The term bullying is usually reserved for young people and most often refers to these behaviors as they occur at or near school.

Cancelled: When individuals are collectively and very publicly shamed online for disappointing others with their opinions or actions. This often leads to major damage to the cancelled person's reputation when considering the power of vocal groups on social media committed to a cause.

Catfishing: In the online world, catfishing refers to the practice of setting up a fictitious online profile, most often for the purpose of luring another into a fraudulent romantic relationship.

CD9: Used when youth want to convey to others that they can't talk openly because parents, teachers, or other adults are nearby. Short for "Code 9."

Chat: An online real-time conversation, typically carried out by people who use nicknames instead of their real names. A person can continually read messages from others in the "chat room" and then type and send a message reply.

Chat Room: A virtual online room where groups of people send and receive messages on one screen. Popular chat rooms can have hundreds of people all communicating at the same time. Typed messages appears instantly as real-time conversation. All of the people in the room are listed on the side of the screen with their screen names.

Cheesing: In gaming, this means that a player is reducing an opponent's health by forcing them to respond to moves that are difficult or impossible to block. On social media, this involves the juvenile challenge of sticking cheese on cars as an act of vandalism. In photos, it means the subject is grinning widely and without any embarrassment or reservation.

Clubhouse: An audio-based social app where individuals can gather and connect in channels to discuss certain topics on a regular or ad-hoc basis. Each person is represented by an icon-based avatar but shares only their voice with others.

Cookie: A file on a computer or other electronic device that records user information when visiting a website. Cookies are often used to identify the websites that the device has visited, save login information and customization preferences, and enable the presentation of more personalized information or content.

Cuffed: Tied down in a committed relationship. Related to "cuffing szn," which is the season of the year when individuals are looking for new romantic relationships.

Cyberbullicide: Suicide resulting directly or indirectly from cyberbullying victimization. The relationship between cyberbullying and suicide is complex and for that and other reasons, many researchers have concerns with the utilization of this term.

Cyberbullying: Intentional and repeated harm inflicted through the use of computers, cell phones, and other electronic devices.

Cyberspace: The electronic "universe" created by computer networks in which individuals interact.

Cyberstalking: Repeated harassment using electronic devices and networked technology that includes threats of harm, or that is highly intimidating and intrusive upon one's personal privacy.

Cyberthreats: Electronic material that either generally or specifically raises concerns that the creator may intend to inflict harm or violence to others or to himself or herself.

Dashboarding: When online users (usually on gaming consoles) rapidly switch from online in-game play to the home screen for their console or other devices. Gamers do this when they are losing badly, and don't want the game to register their demise, or lack of kills, or another metric that demonstrates poor performance.

Decoy Apps: Apps used to store private information, such as photos, videos, voice recordings, or texts. They look like everyday apps such as a calculator so they offer a secure way to hide certain information. They also are called vault, secret, or ghost apps. A teen may use decoy apps on their phone to secretly store sexual pictures and videos that they don't want their parents seeing.

Diabolical (Devious) Lick: A social media trend where students post videos of themselves perceivably or actually stealing or destroying property from their schools.

Digital Evidence: Tangible signs, proof, information, or data that demonstrate some behavior. This could be a screenshot, a record of Internet activity, a saved piece of content, etc.

Digital Footprint: Evidence of a person's use of the Internet, typically focusing on dates and times of specific websites visited. This includes anything that can be linked to a user's existence, presence, or identity. See also, "cookie."

Digital Immigrant: A person who has not grown up with digital technology, such as smartphones, social media, and the Internet, but has adopted it later. Many adults are referred to as digital immigrants, because they have known a time when these technologies didn't exist.

Digital Native: A person who has grown up with digital technology, such as smartphones, social media, and the Internet. Many adolescents or young adults would be classified as digital natives, because they have not known a time without these technologies.

Discord (app): Discord is an app and website that allows individuals who share an interest (e.g., a specific video game, hobby, or topic) to communicate via video, voice, text chat, and screensharing. You can even integrate it with your gaming console and join others' servers, set up your own, and create channels/categories. While mostly used for gaming, it has communities for tons of other uses, such as Netflix shows, anime, schoolwork, dance, books, and more.

Email: Electronic mail. Allows Internet users to send and receive electronic messages to and from other Internet users.

Fabotage: Slang for "Facebook Sabotage" and used to describe hijacking, and meddling with, someone's Facebook account while it is unattended.

Facebook (app): The most popular social media app with over 3 billion members. Users can create personal "profiles" to represent themselves, listing interests and posting photos and communicating with others through private or public posts and messages. They can also join groups about common interests, play games with friends, buy and sell goods and services, run a business, plan events, and more.

Filtering: The act of restricting access to certain websites or social media platforms. For example, a filter might compare the text on a web page against a list of forbidden words. If a match is found, that web page may be blocked or reported through a monitor-ing process. Generally speaking, a filter allows or denies access based on previously specified rules.

Finsta: Combining the words Fake and Instagram, a finsta is a secondary Instagram account which is usually meant for a smaller, private audience, and allows the user to share pictures and videos in an unfiltered and more natural way without having to make each shot perfect or socially acceptable.

Firewall: Hardware or software that restricts and regulates incoming and outgoing data to or from computer systems. Firewalls allow or disallow accessing certain websites or social media platforms.

Flaming: Sending angry, rude, or obscene messages directed at a person or persons privately or an online group. A "flamewar" erupts when "flames" are sent back and forth between individuals repeatedly.

Following: The act of requesting another person to connect with your online social network (on Twitter, Instagram, and similar sites).

Friending: The act of requesting another person to connect with your online social network (on Facebook).

FYP: "For You Page" is TikTok's home screen and also refers to the feed you see that displays a curated assortment of videos that the app's algorithms believe you will like. Users typically want their TikToks to be featured on the FYP because it increases the chances it will go viral.

Gamergate: Controversy involving issues of sexism and progressivism in video game culture, stemming from a harassment campaign conducted primarily through the use of Twitter (and other platforms).

Gaming: Participation in video (often online) games, which involve individuals adopting roles of fictional characters, thereby directing the outcome.

Gaming Console: A device designed for users to run video games on a television. Popular consoles include the Sony PlayStation, Microsoft Xbox, and Nintendo Wii.

Geolocation: The process or technique of identifying the geographical location of a person or device by means of digital information processed via the Internet.

Geotagging: The process of adding geographical information to various pieces of digital content in the form of metadata. The data usually consist of coordinates like latitude and longitude, but may even include bearing, altitude, distance, and place names. Geotagging is most commonly used for photos and videos and can help people get a lot of specific information about where the shot was taken, or the exact location of a friend who logged on to make a post.

GG: In video game parlance, it means "good game" to convey appreciation to someone else for playing with you.

Ghosting: The act of ignoring someone who has messaged or otherwise reached out to you; disappearing from any interactions with them. Often refers to the context of romantic relationships and/or dating apps.

Griefing: When a player in an online game deliberately irritates and harasses other players within the game.

Grindr: The world's largest online platform for gay, bisexual, transgender, and queer people.

Grooming: Some people use online mediums across the Internet to connect with children so that they can exploit them or even blackmail them for sexual purposes. Befriending a child in this way is called grooming.

GroupMe (app): A group chat app that allows you to create groups (such as family, relatives, friends, team members, whatever you want) and send text, memes, hyperlinks, images, and video. It works on every smartphone and even on the Web, and it allows you to quickly send messages without having to compile a list of addressees.

Hacking: The act of circumventing security and breaking into an authorized location (a network, computer, file, etc.), usually with malicious intent.

Happy Slapping: An extreme form of bullying where physical assaults are recorded on electronic devices like phones, and then sent to others or posted online. This term is more commonly used in the United Kingdom.

Harassment: Unsolicited words or actions intended to annoy, alarm, or abuse another individual. Often based on a protected status (e.g., sex, race, disability, or sexual orientation).

Harm: Physical, psychological, or emotional injury to someone.

Hashtag: A descriptor or label preceded by the pound (#) sign that helps others easily find content related to that word or phrase. Facebook, Twitter, and Instagram, for example, allow users to look up and click through hashtags to find other users' content that are also listed (tagged) with that hashtag.

Hate raids: A phenomena on Twitch where abusive streamers and bots flood a creator's channel with hateful messages. Targets have typically been Black and LGBTQ+ streamers.

Houseparty (app): A video chat app quite popular among teens. You can add friends based on the phone numbers you have stored in your contacts list or search for their usernames. Once you open the app, you can join "rooms" (chats) with other friends who are currently using the app. IYKYK: "If you know, you know."

Influencer: An individual who can sway an audience through a digital platform. This term is often used in relation to social media marketing, promotion, and other related efforts.

Instagram (app): An app where users can apply filters to photos and videos before posting them for others to like and comment on. User can also share their content on other social networks like Facebook and Twitter.

Instant Messaging: The act of real-time messages sent and received between two or more people over a network such as the Internet. This can occur through software such as WeChat, WhatsApp, Snapchat, Viber, and Facebook Messenger.

Internet: A worldwide network of computers communicating with each other via phone lines, satellite links, wireless networks, and cable systems.

iOS: Operating system created by Apple Inc. iOS powers iPods, iPhones, iPads, and Apple TVs.

IP Address: "Internet Protocol" address. A unique address assigned to a computing device that allows it to send and receive data with other computing devices that have their own unique addresses.

IRC: "Internet Relay Chat." A network over which real-time conversations take place among two or more people in a "channel" devoted to a specific area of interest. See also "chat" or "chat room."

ISP: "Internet Service Provider." The company that provides an Internet connection to individuals or companies. ISPs can help with identifying an individual who posts or sends harassing or threatening words.

Kik (app): A service that facilitates cross-platform (iOS and Android) instant messaging across phones or tablets in an attractive interface. Users can send links, pictures, videos, group messages, etc.

Meme: A virally-transmitted cultural symbol or social idea. Most modern memes are captioned photos or videos that are intended to be funny, often to publicly ridicule human behavior. Others are popular for depicting traits or experiences that many others can totally relate to.

MMORPG: Acronym that stands for: "Massively Multiplayer Online Role-Playing Game." A game in which large numbers of individuals from various locations connect and interact with each other in a virtual world online.

Monitoring: The recording and reporting of online activity, usually through software, which may log a history of all Internet use or just of inappropriate use.

Mutuals: When two individuals friend or follow each other on social media.

Mydol: A chatbot app that is gaining in popularity. It simulates chatting with your favorite K-pop (Korean pop star musician) star. A chatbot is a computer program designed to mimic a conversation with human users. They can sometimes be very natural in their responses, fooling people into believing they are talking to a real person. Some users have mentioned that the conversations can quickly turn to sexual in nature.

Netiquette: "Network etiquette." The unofficial rules of accepted, proper online social conduct.

Network: Two or more computers connected so that they can communicate with each other.

Newbie: Someone who is new to, and inexperienced with, an Internet activity or technology. Also referred to as a newb, n00b, nob, noob, or nub.

Offender: The one who instigates online social cruelty. Also known as the "aggressor."

OnlyFans: A subscription-based online platform that allows creators to sell their video streams and content. It originally gained notoriety during the COVID-19 pandemic and was used by those in the pornography industry, models, escorts, and others to supplement their income.

Periscope: An application (owned by Twitter) that allowed users to broadcast live streaming video. It is now defunct.

Pharming: Pronounced "farming," this is a method by which scammers try to get personal/private information from users by directing them to false, bogus, or "spoof," websites which look legitimate in their web browser.

Phishing: A technique used to gain personal information, usually by means of fraudulent emails.

Photoshopping: The process of altering digital images so that the main subject is placed in a compromising or embarrassing situation. For example, a person might photoshop a picture to append an animal's face to a human's body (or vice versa) or something much worse.

Pinterest (app): An online pinboard and visual discovery engine for finding ideas like recipes, home and style inspiration, and more. Users create, share, and link to boards and "pins" of visual content (largely pictures, memes, and related creations) from across the Web.

Profile: When considered in the context of online social networking, this is a user-customized page that represents that person. Here, a person's background, interests, and friends are listed to reflect who that person is or how that person would like to be seen. Pictures, biographical and contact information, and other interesting facts about the user are often included as well.

Proxy: Software or a website that allows one's Internet connection to be routed or tunneled through a different connection or site. If a user's computer is blocked from accessing certain websites or programs, the user could employ a proxy to redirect the connection to that site or program. For example, if a software filter prohibits a user from directly visiting Facbook, a proxy website could be used to circumvent the filter and provide access.

Rage quitting: A condition in which gamers, through steady provoking, simply cannot take being killed (cheaply or otherwise) anymore and leave a online game game midmatch.

Raiding: On Twitch, creators at the conclusion of their own stream send their audience of streamers to a friend's or colleague's channel to boost their viewership.

Revenge Porn: Sometimes known as nonconsensual porn and defined as the act of distributing intimate photography through different means without the individual's consent

School Climate: The quality, character, social atmosphere, and "feel" of the school, mostly exhibited by patterns of behavior and interactions among and between students and school personnel. Improving school climate reduces both offline and online student interactions.

Screenshot: An image that is captured of what is shown on a phone, tablet, or computer screen.

Secret: An app that gives users the ability to share what they are thinking and feeling with friends from their phone's contact list, while remaining anonymous.

Sexting: The sending or receiving of sexually explicit or sexually suggestive images or video via phone or the Internet.

Sextortion: Threats to expose a sexual image in order to make a person do something or for other reasons, such as revenge or humiliation.

Shoulder Surfing: Peering over the shoulder of someone to see the contents on that person's computer, tablet, or phone screen.

Skype (app): A popular application that enables users to set up profiles, make free phone calls, text chat,

and video chat through their computer or mobile device from any point around the world.

SMS: Acronym that stands for: "Short Message Service." A communications protocol that allows short (160 characters or less) text messages over cell phone.

Snapchat (app): Very popular with youth and young adults, users of this app share text messages, pictures, and videos with friends from their contact list, which generally can be viewed for a period of between 1 to 10 seconds (unless set to "infinity") before disappearing. See also, "snaps."

Snapchat Filters: When users of Snapchat are in particular places, specialized "filters" are available to superimpose onto their "Snap," providing fun, artsy backgrounds, pictures, and word art highlighting that location.

Snapchat Premium (or Premium Snapchat): This expression simply means that the user of the account is willing to share with you snaps that are sexual in nature in return for payment. These users often share their Cash App or Venmo details so you can directly send them money, and they will "subscribe" you to their informal service of sending you their nudes.

Snaps: Pictures or videos sent between users on Snapchat.

Social Networking Sites: Online services that bring together people by organizing them around a common interest and providing an interactive environment of photos, blogs, user profiles, and messaging systems. Examples include Facebook and Instagram.

Spam: Unsolicited electronic mail—usually commercial in nature—sent from someone unknown to the recipient.

Sus: Short for "suspicious." Became popular with the game "Among Us" to call out users who may be the killer.

Tablet: A mobile computing device growing in adoption and popularity. They are smaller than a laptop and bigger than a smartphone, and provide much of the same functionality as both.

Text Bombing: When someone sends large numbers of texts to another, not allowing that person to use their phones because of the annoyance, or because the phone gets overloaded with constant incoming messages.

Texting: Sending short messages via phone.

Threat: Making a statement of taking an action that implies or suggests harm to someone else.

Throwing: To intentionally lose a game on purpose or to lose a game in a notably embarrassing way.

TikTok (app): Previously known as Musical.ly, this app allows users to create and share their own engaging and creative video clips up to 15 seconds long (e.g., lip-syncing to a popular song and dancing around, restating comedic lines from a favorite movie).

Tinder (app): An online dating app that allows people to be matched based on physical attraction. It initially finds potential matches based on filters like gender and location. If two users like each other's pictures, they are able to chat.

Trolling: Deliberately and disingenuously posting information to entice genuinely helpful people to respond (often emotionally). Often done to inflame or provoke others.

Tumblr (app): A social networking site where users can post blogs and follow other people's blogs. The blogs are largely filled with artistic media, content, poetry, creative writing, and multimedia based on user interests (as well as the latest in memes and pop culture). Tumblr makes it easy to share images, GIFs, videos, music, text, links, and more in a very aesthetically pleasing and customizable way.

Tweet: A short (280 character [or less]) message posted on Twitter.

Twitch (app): An app and website that allows anyone to live-stream (or upload and share previously broadcasted videos) themselves doing anything—sharing stories and news, playing a video game, providing commentary on other content they are watching, or whatever else they might be interested in broadcasting— all while interacting with viewers in a text chat on the screen at the same time). Popular Twitchers (live streamers) build and cultivate devoted communi-

ties of fans where hundreds and even thousands log on to watch their broadcasts of whatever it is they want to share with the world.

Twitter (app): Social networking and "microblogging" service that allows users to post what they are doing using up to 280 characters per tweet. It is often used to share images, videos, memes, and links; tweet images can be "tagged" with up to 10 other Twitter users so they can be alerted that they are mentioned or referenced in the post. See also, "tweet."

Twitterstorm: A sudden spike in activity surrounding a certain topic on the Twitter social media site. A Twitterstorm is often started by a single person who sends his or her followers a message often related to breaking news. Using a certain and often original hashtags, the tweet quickly spreads as people are notified of the message and then reuse the hashtag with subsequent retweets and tweets.

Unalive: Refers to dying, typically by suicide. A user on social media might post that they tried to "unalive."

Unfriend (or unfollow): The act of removing a friend from a social circle found on your social media site so they can't see and don't have access to your posts, captions, comments, or anything else you'd like to restrict to a certain audience. Although unfriending has similarities with blocking a friend, it is different in the context of social media. Blocking a person prevents that person's name from appearing in search results as well as prevents that person from contacting the person who has blocked him/her, whereas unfriending would not result in any of these and would just show that the person is no longer in the other person's social circle.

Viber (app): An instant messaging and VoIP app (similar to Skype). Users can also exchange images, video, and audio media messages.

Victim: The person who is on the receiving end of online social cruelty. Also known as the "target."

Vine (app): A video app owned by Twitter (and that is now defunct) that allowed users to capture moments in six seconds and share them with others.

VoIP: Acronym that stands for: "Voice over Internet Protocol." The transmission of voice over an Internet connection. Allows users to make phone calls using the Internet instead of a phone line.

Web: Short for "World Wide Web" and representing the sites and pages linked together via the Internet.

Webcast: A live or prerecorded audio and/or video session that uses the Internet to broadcast.

Webcrastinate: To waste time by browsing around the world wide web instead of getting on with the things one should be doing.

Webdrawls: The act or process of going without the use of the Internet to which one has become addicted.

WhatsApp (app): A cross-platform messaging application that allows users to send texts, pictures, videos, links, user locations, documents, and more. It allows for connections based on one's phone number. It has over 2 billion monthly active users.

Whisper (app): An app that allows users to share their secrets anonymously with other users using text and images. Individuals input their secret (or another self-disclosing message) into the app, select a relevant picture as a background, and then post it for others to like, comment on, and share with others.

Wireless: Communications in which electromagnetic waves carry a signal through space rather than along a wire. Refers primarily to wireless Internet access (Wi-Fi) available in an increasing number of places.

Wireless Device: Electronic devices that can access the Internet without being physically attached by a cable or data line.

YouTube (app): A wildly popular video sharing app and site owned by Google where registered users can upload and share videos with anyone able to access the site. It has over 2.3 billion average monthly users and over 30 billion average daily users, with 300 hours of video uploaded every minute.

Comprehensive Bullying Prevention Fidelity Assessment

COMPONENT: SCHOOL CLIMATE

	In Continuous Improvement	In Progress	Not Yet Initiated
All staff use distinct strategies or methods to build relationships with and among students.			
The school uses distinct strategies or methods to build relationships with and among students.	2	1	0
Teachers intervene immediately when witnessing bullying.	2	1	0
Teachers use the five classroom management principles in their classrooms.	2	1	0
The school has three-to-five schoolwide expectations that are explicitly taught multiple times throughout the year.			
The school has three-to-five schoolwide expectations that are positively stated.	2	1	0
A behavior matrix is created with rules, expectations, and locations (including *online* as one of the locations).	2	1	0
Students are explicitly taught behavior expectations multiple times throughout the year.	2	1	0
The school consistently uses an acknowledgment system to reinforce expected behaviors.			
The school consistently uses immediate, high-frequency recognition as part of its acknowledgment system to reinforce expected behaviors.	2	1	0
Teachers use behavior-specific language when verbally reinforcing students.	2	1	0
The school consistently uses long-term reinforcement as part of its acknowledgment system to reinforce expected behaviors.	2	1	0

(continued)

The school implements an equitable and consistent discipline system that includes how the staff can respond to bullying.			
The school has defined minor, major, and crisis behaviors.	2	1	0
The school has outlined how to respond to minor, major, and crisis behaviors as part of their discipline structure.	2	1	0
Discipline is managed with consideration of multiple factors (e.g., developmental appropriateness, past infractions).	2	1	0
Students are adequately trained and respond appropriately to bullying.			
There are clear procedures outlined for how students can respond to bullying.	2	1	0
Students are explicitly taught the procedure for how to respond to bullying.	2	1	0

COMPONENT: POLICY

	In Continuous Improvement	In Progress	Not Yet Initiated
The school handbook policy is fully aligned with district school board policy.			
The school handbook policy is fully aligned with district school board policy.	2	1	0
The school handbook policy is fully aligned with state law.			
The school handbook policy is fully aligned with state law.	2	1	0
The school bullying prevention policy includes the key features shown to be effective in preventing bullying.			
The school bullying prevention policy includes the definition of bullying.	2	1	0
The school bullying prevention policy includes a statement that bullying is prohibited.	2	1	0
The school bullying prevention policy enumerates federally protected classes as specifically protected by the policy.	2	1	0
The school bullying prevention policy outlines its scope.	2	1	0
The school bullying prevention policy outlines prevention and intervention efforts of the school.	2	1	0
The school bullying prevention policy includes a description of how and where stakeholders can make a report of bullying.	2	1	0
The school bullying prevention policy includes a description of the investigative process when a report of bullying is received.	2	1	0

(continued)

The school bullying prevention policy includes a graduated range of consequences, not solely punitive, for those involved in bullying.	2	1	0
The school bullying prevention policy includes a description of the communication process when incidents of bullying occur.	2	1	0
The school bullying prevention policy includes a description of the record keeping for incidents of bullying.	2	1	0
School staff members are trained on the bullying prevention policy at least once each year.			
Onboarding training on the bullying prevention policy is provided for all new staff members prior to their interaction with students.	2	1	0
Refresher training for returning staff members on the bullying prevention policy is provided at least once each year.	2	1	0

COMPONENT: EVIDENCE-BASED CURRICULA

	In Continuous Improvement	In Progress	Not Yet Initiated
The school uses a structured selection process to choose the curricula.			
When choosing curricula, the *evidence* of curricula is considered.	2	1	0
When choosing curricula, the *usability* of curricula is considered.	2	1	0
When choosing curricula, the *fit* of curricula is considered.	2	1	0
When choosing curricula, the *need* of curricula is considered.	2	1	0
When choosing curricula, the *capacity* of curricula is considered.	2	1	0
When choosing curricula, the *supports* of curricula are considered.	2	1	0
The curriculum is able to be implemented schoolwide.			
The selected curriculum is implemented as a universal support for all students in the school.	2	1	0
Staff members receive ongoing training and coaching for the curriculum.			
Staff members receive ongoing training and coaching for the curriculum.	2	1	0
Adequate time is given to staff members to learn the curriculum.	2	1	0
Staff members who need support in implementing the curriculum are provided coaching.	2	1	0

(continued)

The curriculum serves as one part of a layered continuum of supports to prevent bullying.			
The curriculum at Tier 1 is implemented with fidelity.	2	1	0
Tier 2 supports for bullying are in place and implemented with fidelity.	2	1	0
Tier 3 supports for bullying are in place and implemented with fidelity.	2	1	0

COMPONENT: FAMILY AND COMMUNITY PARTNERSHIPS

	In Continuous Improvement	In Progress	Not Yet Initiated
The school has an inclusive culture that considers equity when making schoolwide decisions.			
The school builds an inclusive culture by ensuring equity when making schoolwide decisions.	2	1	0
The school provides supports for families (e.g., child care, meals) to enable better accessibility to school events.	2	1	0
School events are held at times and locations that enable greater access for families (e.g., weekends, in the community).	2	1	0
The school has multiple methods for two-way communication with families.			
The school provides families with easily accessible ways to provide feedback.	2	1	0
Staff members use strategies to intentionally build positive relationships with families.	2	1	0
The school involves all families by actively working to build their self-efficacy on bullying prevention, by including families in decision making, and by having a policy on engaging families.			
The school actively works to build family self-efficacy around bullying prevention.	2	1	0
The school provides opportunities for families to be part of the decision-making processes.	2	1	0
The school has a policy on actively engaging families.	2	1	0
The school partners with community organizations to strategically support bullying prevention.			
The school partners with community organizations to support bullying prevention.	2	1	0
An Asset Map exists with up-to-date community organizations.	2	1	0
A representative from the community serves on the bullying prevention implementation team.	2	1	0

(continued)

The school provides structured, meaningful opportunities for students to participate in bullying prevention efforts.			
Students support data analysis related to bullying as developmentally appropriate.	2	1	0
Students provide input into bullying prevention strategies.	2	1	0

COMPONENT: DATA-BASED DECISION MAKING

	In Continuous Improvement	In Progress	Not Yet Initiated
The school uses a structured problem-solving process to analyze system-level and individual student bullying concerns.			
The school uses a structured problem-solving process when making data-based decisions.	2	1	0
Precise problem statements are developed and used as part of the structured problem-solving process.	2	1	0
A structured problem-solving process is used to analyze systems issues related to bullying.	2	1	0
A structured problem-solving process is used to analyze individual student issues related to bullying.	2	1	0
The school measures the fidelity of implementation for CBP on an ongoing basis, and data from the assessment are used for problem solving.			
The school measures the fidelity of implementation for CBP.	2	1	0
Fidelity assessments are conducted on an ongoing basis.	2	1	0
Data from fidelity assessments are used for problem solving.	2	1	0
The school measures student outcomes as well as staff and family perceptions related to bullying at least once each year.			
Student-reported frequency of bullying is measured at least once each year.	2	1	0
Staff and family perceptions of bullying are measured at least once each year.	2	1	0
An accessible data warehouse is available for all staff members and is used to support data-based decision making.			
An accessible data warehouse is available for all staff members.	2	1	0
Staff members are trained on how to use the data warehouse.	2	1	0
The data warehouse is accessed and used to support data-based decision making.	2	1	0

Comprehensive Bullying Prevention Drivers Best-Practices Assessment

Driver	Item	In Continuous Improvement	In Progress	Not Yet Initiated
Selection	Selection of team members for the bullying prevention implementation team ensures mutual understanding of roles and responsibilities of team members.	2	1	0
	Selection of team members for the bullying prevention implementation team includes a process to determine their willingness to be open-minded and implement team decisions.	2	1	0
Training	There is someone accountable for the training of staff members on CBP best practices.	2	1	0
	There is someone accountable for the training of staff members on the selected evidence-based curriculum.	2	1	0
	Members of the bullying prevention implementation team provide skill-based training for all stakeholders on bullying prevention best practices.	2	1	0
	There is a training plan developed and used to support professional development.	2	1	0
	The bullying prevention implementation team uses data from trainings for improvement.	2	1	0

(continued)

Adapted with permission from Ward, C., Metz, A., Louison, L., Loper, A., & Cusumano, D. (2018). *Drivers Best Practices Assessment.* Chapel Hill, NC: National Implementation Research Network, University of North Carolina at Chapel Hill. Based on Fixsen, D. L., Blase, K., Naoom, S., Metz, A., Louison, L., & Ward, C. (2015). *Implementation Drivers: Assessing Best Practices.* Chapel Hill, NC: National Implementation Research Network, University of North Carolina at Chapel Hill. Reprinted in *Effective Bullying Prevention: A Comprehensive Schoolwide Approach* by Adam Collins and Jason Harlacher (The Guilford Press, 2023). Permission to photocopy this material is granted to purchasers of this book for personal use or use with students (see copyright page for details). Purchasers can download additional copies of this material (see the box at the end of the table of contents).

Driver	Item	In Continuous Improvement	In Progress	Not Yet Initiated
Coaching	There is someone accountable for the coaching of staff members on CBP best practices.	2	1	0
	There is someone accountable for the coaching of staff members on the selected evidence-based curriculum.	2	1	0
	The coaching provided to staff members uses a layered continuum of supports.	2	1	0
	There is a coaching plan developed and used to support professional development.	2	1	0
	The bullying prevention implementation team uses data from coaching for improvement.	2	1	0
Fidelity	There is someone accountable for the fidelity assessments for CBP.	2	1	0
	There is someone accountable for the fidelity assessments of the evidence-based curriculum.	2	1	0
	Fidelity assessments are conducted on a regular basis by the bullying prevention implementation team.	2	1	0
	The bullying prevention implementation team uses fidelity assessment data to improve implementation of CBP.	2	1	0
	The bullying prevention implementation team uses fidelity assessment data to improve implementation of the evidence-based curriculum.	2	1	0
Data System	There is someone accountable for the data system.	2	1	0
	School staff members have access to relevant data to make decisions.	2	1	0
	Data are useful and usable.	2	1	0
	The bullying prevention implementation team has a structured process for using data for decision making.	2	1	0

(continued)

Comprehensive Bullying Prevention Drivers Best-Practices Assessment *(page 3 of 3)*

Driver	Item	In Continuous Improvement	In Progress	Not Yet Initiated
Administrative Support	Leadership sets aside resources to support the development of staff competency to deliver CBP.	2	1	0
	Leadership develops and/or refines policies or procedures that support CBP.	2	1	0
	Leadership makes changes in school roles, functions, and structures as need to accommodate CBP.	2	1	0
	Leadership engages in regular communication with the staff and stakeholders about CBP.	2	1	0
	Leadership visibly promotes the importance of effectively implementing CBP.	2	1	0
	Leadership problem-solves challenges to implementing CBP effectively.	2	1	0
	Leadership recognizes and appreciates the staff's contributions in implementing CBP.	2	1	0
Stakeholder Engagement	Leadership and staff members engage families and the community in developing a shared understanding of the need for CBP.	2	1	0
	Leadership and staff members create opportunities for families, students, and the community to learn and design solutions together to support CBP.	2	1	0
	School leadership regularly communicates with all stakeholders about CBP.	2	1	0

Stages of Implementation Checklist for Comprehensive Bullying Prevention

EXPLORATION STAGE

	In Continuous Improvement	In Progress	Not Yet Initiated
Develop a bullying prevention implementation team representative of the staff, families, students, and community.	2	1	0
Implement and utilize teaming best practices during implementation team meetings.	2	1	0
Develop communication processes and messages for bullying prevention efforts.	2	1	0
Identify the changes needed, existing assets, and potential root causes of bullying in the school.	2	1	0
Assess what is currently in place to address bullying prevention (e.g., Initiative Inventory).	2	1	0
Outline a plan for readiness, for developing staff capacity, and for needed systems changes.	2	1	0
Identify and learn about other potential practices or programs to address bullying prevention, including CBP.	2	1	0
Assess the fit and feasibility of options to address bullying prevention, considering need, fit, evidence, usability, capacity, and supports (e.g., Hexagon Tool).	2	1	0
Using results from the fit and feasibility assessment (e.g., Hexagon Tool), select the program to implement, choose to reassess need and potential options, or choose not to proceed.	2	1	0
Cultivate relationships with stakeholders who will support bullying prevention efforts.	2	1	0
Cultivate champions of bullying prevention who have the authority and/or cultural capital to promote change.	2	1	0

(continued)

There is someone accountable for the training of staff on CBP best practices.	2	1	0
There is someone accountable for the training of staff on the selected evidence-based curriculum.	2	1	0
There is someone accountable for the coaching of staff on CBP best practices.	2	1	0
There is someone accountable for the coaching of staff on the selected evidence-based curriculum.	2	1	0
There is someone accountable for the fidelity assessments for CBP.	2	1	0
There is someone accountable for the fidelity assessments of the evidence-based curriculum.	2	1	0
There is someone accountable for the data system.	2	1	0
School administration visibly promotes the importance of effectively implementing CBP.	2	1	0
Determine what actions are needed to optimize readiness and develop staff capacity, as well as school system changes needed for CBP and the evidence-based curriculum.	2	1	0

INSTALLATION STAGE

	In Continuous Improvement	In Progress	Not Yet Initiated
Needed perspectives are present on the bullying prevention implementation team (e.g., multiple grade levels, specialists, family members).	2	1	0
The bullying prevention implementation team meets regularly (e.g., once each month) and uses data to support installation activities.	2	1	0
School administration sets aside resources to support the development of staff competency to deliver CBP.	2	1	0
Leadership and staff engage families and the community in developing a shared understanding of the need for CBP.	2	1	0
Leadership makes changes in school roles, functions, and structures as needed to accommodate CBP.	2	1	0
The selected evidence-based bullying prevention curriculum is purchased, as needed.	2	1	0
Bullying prevention implementation team has appropriate knowledge, skills (e.g., bullying prevention best practices), and authority to support systems development and improvement for CBP.	2	1	0

(continued)

The bullying prevention implementation team has an up-to-date training plan that enables all staff to gain the knowledge and skills needed to effectively implement CBP.	2	1	0
The bullying prevention implementation team uses data from trainings for continuous improvement.	2	1	0
The bullying prevention implementation team has an up-to-date coaching plan that enables all staff to receive a layered continuum of supports to effectively implement CBP.	2	1	0
The bullying prevention implementation team uses data from coaching for continuous improvement.	2	1	0
The school has a data warehouse that is accessible by all the staff and informs data-based decision making by the bullying prevention implementation team.	2	1	0
Bullying prevention implementation team trains necessary staff members on how to use the data warehouse.	2	1	0
The bullying prevention implementation team establishes and continually monitors the progress of short- and long-term goals for success.	2	1	0
Initial training is provided to all stakeholders on CBP and the selected evidence-based curriculum.	2	1	0
The bullying prevention implementation team reviews and revises the bullying prevention handbook policy.	2	1	0
Develop and use two-way communication between staff, families, and community organizations to support ongoing, effective communication.	2	1	0

INITIAL IMPLEMENTATION STAGE

	In Continuous Improvement	In Progress	Not Yet Initiated
All the staff use distinct strategies or methods to build relationships with and among students.	2	1	0
The school's three-to-five schoolwide expectations are explicitly taught multiple times throughout the year.	2	1	0
Staff consistently uses an acknowledgment system to reinforce expected behaviors.	2	1	0
The school implements an equitable and consistent discipline system that includes how the staff can respond to bullying.	2	1	0
Students are trained on how to respond appropriately to bullying.	2	1	0

(continued)

	In Continuous Improvement	In Progress	Not Yet Initiated
The school handbook policy is fully aligned with the district bullying prevention policy.	2	1	0
The school handbook policy is fully aligned with state law.	2	1	0
The school bullying prevention policy includes the key features shown to be effective in preventing bullying.	2	1	0
School staff are trained on the bullying prevention policy at least once each year.	2	1	0
School staff implement the selected evidence-based curriculum schoolwide.	2	1	0
Staff receives ongoing training for the curriculum and bullying prevention best practices.	2	1	0
Staff receives ongoing coaching for the curriculum and bullying prevention best practices.	2	1	0
The school implements Tier 2 and Tier 3 supports for bullying.	2	1	0
The school ensures an inclusive culture that considers equity when making schoolwide decisions.	2	1	0
The school implements multiple methods for two-way communication with families.	2	1	0
The school actively builds the self-efficacy of families regarding bullying prevention.	2	1	0
The school includes families in decision making on bullying prevention efforts.	2	1	0
The school has a policy on engaging families.	2	1	0
The school partners with community organizations to strategically support bullying prevention.	2	1	0
The school provides structured, meaningful opportunities for students to participate in bullying prevention efforts.	2	1	0
The school uses a structured problem-solving process to analyze system-level and individual student-level bullying concerns.	2	1	0
The school measures the fidelity of implementation for CBP on an ongoing basis.	2	1	0
The school uses CBP fidelity data for problem solving.	2	1	0
The school measures student outcomes related to bullying at least once each year.	2	1	0

(continued)

The school measures staff and family perceptions of bullying at least once each year.	2	1	0
An accessible data warehouse is available for the staff and is used to support data-based decision making.	2	1	0
Bullying prevention implementation team meets regularly (e.g., once each month) and uses data to analyze and improve implementation.	2	1	0
The school refines its implementation infrastructure (e.g., training, coaching, data systems) based on data and feedback.	2	1	0
School administration recognizes and appreciates staff contributions to implement CBP.	2	1	0

FULL IMPLEMENTATION STAGE

	In Continuous Improvement	In Progress	Not Yet Initiated
Bullying prevention implementation team continues to meet regularly to support CBP.	2	1	0
Bullying prevention implementation team uses data-based decision making to improve implementation of CBP.	2	1	0
The bullying prevention implementation team uses multiple forms of data for decision making to improve CBP.	2	1	0
The school implements the evidence-based bullying prevention curriculum with fidelity schoolwide.	2	1	0
The school implements CBP with fidelity schoolwide.	2	1	0
The bullying prevention implementation team provides CBP onboarding training for new staff.	2	1	0
The bullying prevention implementation team provides refresher training on CBP for all the staff each year.	2	1	0
The school uses two-way communication with all stakeholders to support and improve CBP.	2	1	0
The school surveys students on their experiences with bullying each year.	2	1	0
The school regularly communicates bullying prevention outcomes and efforts to all stakeholders.	2	1	0

References

Akin-Little, K. A., Eckert, T. L., Lovett, B. J., & Little, S. G. (2004). Extrinsic reinforcement in the classroom: Bribery or best practice. *School Psychology Review, 33*(3), 344–362.

Alberto, P. A., & Troutman, A. C. (2013). *Applied behavior analysis for teachers* (9th ed.). Pearson.

Aldridge, J. M., McChesney, K., & Afari, E. (2018). Relationships between school climate, bullying and delinquent behaviors. *Learning Environment Research, 21,* 153–172.

Ali, R. (2010, October 26). Dear colleague letter from Assistant Secretary for Civil Rights [Policy Guidance]. Retrieved from *www2.ed.gov/about/offices/list/ocr/letters/colleague-201010.html.*

Alsaker, F. D. (2004). Bernese programme against victimisation in kindergarten and elementary school. In P. K. Smith, D. Pepler, & K. Rigby (Eds.), *Bullying in schools: How successful can interventions be?* (pp. 289–306). Cambridge University Press.

Anderson, A. R., Christensen, S. L., Sinclair, M. F., & Lehr, C. A. (2004). Check & Connect: The importance of relationships for promoting engagement in school. *Journal of School Psychology, 42*(4), 95–113.

Archer, A., & Hughes, C. (2011). *Explicit instruction: Effective and efficient teaching.* Guilford Press.

Aronson, E. (1978). *The jigsaw classroom.* SAGE.

Aronson, E. (2002). Building empathy, compassion, and achievement in the jigsaw classroom. In J. Aronson (Ed.), *Improving academic achievement: Impact of psychological factors on education* (pp. 209–225). Academic Press.

Aronson, E., & Patnoe, S. (2011). *Cooperation in the classroom: The jigsaw method.* Pinter & Martin.

Astor, R. A., Guerra, N., & Van Acker, R. (2010). How can we improve school safety research? *Educational Researcher, 39,* 69–78.

Averdijk, M., Zirk-Sadowski, J., Ribeaud, D., & Eisner, M. (2016). Long-term effects of two childhood psychosocial interventions on adolescent delinquency, substance use, and antisocial behavior: A cluster randomized controlled trial. *Journal of Experimental Criminology, 12,* 21–47.

Bacallao, M., & Smokowski, P. (2010). Sociometric status and bullying: Peer relationships, aggressive behavior, and victimization. In N. Ramsay & C. R. Morrison (Eds.), *Youth violence and juvenile justice: Causes, intervention, and treatment programs* (pp. 117–138). Nova Science.

Barboza, G. E., Schiamberg, L. B., Oehmke, J., Korzeniewski, S. J., Post, L. A., & Heraux, C. G. (2009).

Individual characteristics and the multiple contexts of adolescent bullying: An ecological perspective. *Journal of Youth and Adolescence, 38*(1), 101–121.

Barrett, S., Eber, L., McIntosh, K., Perales, K., & Romer, N. (2018). *Teaching social-emotional competencies within a PBIS framework.* OSEP Technical Assistance Center on Positive Behavioral Interventions and Supports.

Bauman, S., Rigby, K., & Hoppa, K. (2008). US teachers' and school counsellors' strategies for handling school bullying incidents. *Educational Psychology, 28*(7), 837–856.

Beckner, B. (2013). *From pre-service to practice: What every preschool teacher needs to know.* PBIS Missouri. Retrieved from *https://pbismissouri.org/wp-content/uploads/2017/12/2C_Pre-Service-to-Practice.2013.pdf.*

Bell Carter, B., & Spencer, V. G. (2006). The fear factor: Bullying and students with disabilities. *International Journal of Special Education, 21(1),* 11–23.

Berne, S., Frisén, A., & Oskarsson, J. (2020). High school students' suggestions for supporting younger pupils counteract cyberbullying. *Scandinavian Journal of Psychology, 61*(1), 47–53.

Blake, J. J., Zhou, Q., Kwok, O.-M., & Benz, M. R. (2016). Predictors of bullying behavior, victimization, and bully-victim risk among high school students with disabilities. *Remedial and Special Education, 37*(5), 285–295.

Blase, K. A., Fixsen, D. L., & Van Dyke, M. K. (2018). *Developing usable innovations.* Active Implementation Research Network. Retrieved from *www.activeimplementation.org/resources.*

Bogart, L. M., Elliott, M. N., Klein, D. J., Tortolero, S. R., Mrug, S., Peskin, M. F., et al. (2014). Peer victimization in fifth grade and health in tenth grade. *Pediatrics, 133*(3), 440–447.

Bosworth, K., & Judkins, M. (2014). Tapping into the power of school climate to prevent bullying: One application of schoolwide positive behavior interventions and supports. *Theory into Practice, 53*(4), 300–307.

Bowes, L., Joinson, C., Wolke, D., & Lewis, G. (2015). Peer victimisation during adolescence and its impact on depression in early adulthood: Prospective cohort study in the United Kingdom. *British Medical Journal, 350*, h2469.

Bradshaw, C. (2013). Preventing bullying through positive behavioral interventions and supports (PBIS): A multilayered approach to prevention and integration. *Theory into Practice, 52(4),* 288–295.

Bradshaw, C. P., Sawyer, A. L., & O'Brennan, L. M. (2007). Bullying and peer victimization at school: Perceptual differences between students and school staff. *School Psychology Review, 36*(3), 361–382.

Branson, C. E., & Cornell, D. (2009). A comparison of self and peer reports in the assessment of middle school bullying. *Journal of Applied School Psychology, 25*(5), 5–24.

Brophy, J., & Good, T. (1986). Teacher behavior and student achievement. In M. Wittrock (Ed.), *Handbook of research on teaching* (3rd ed., pp. 328–375). Macmillan.

Cameron, J., & Pierce, W. D. (1994). Reinforcement, reward, and intrinsic motivation: A meta-analysis. *Review of Educational Research, 64*(3), 363–423.

Casella, R. (2000). The benefits of peer mediation in the context of urban conflict and program status. *Urban Education, 35*(3), 324–355.

Centers for Disease Control and Prevention. (2021). Youth Risk Behavior Surveillance System. Retrieved from *www.cdc.gov/healthyyouth/data/yrbs/questionnaires.htm.*

Chaparro, E., Horner, R., Algozzine, B., Daily, J., & Nese, R. N. T. (2022, April). *How school teams use data to make effective decisions: Team-Initiated Problem Solving (TIPS).* Center on PBIS, University of Oregon.

Check & Connect Student Engagement Intervention, Institute on Community Integration. (2020). Retrieved from *https://checkandconnect.umn.edu.*

Christ, T. (2008). Best practices in problem analysis. In A. Thomas & J. Grimes (Eds.), *Best practices in school psychology IV* (pp. 159–176). National Association of School Psychologists.

Chuck, E. (2017, December 4). Bullying drove 13-year-old Rosalie Avila to kill herself, parents say. *NBC News.* Retrieved from *www.nbcnews.com/news/us-news/bullying-drove-13-year-old-rosalie-avila-kill-herself-parents-n826281.*

Cipriano, C., Barnes, T. N., Rivers, S. E., & Brackett, M. (2019). Exploring changes in student engagement through the RULER approach: An examination of students at risk of academic failure. *Journal of Education for Students Placed At Risk, 24* (1) 1–19.

Clemens, N. H., Keller-Margulis, M. A., Scholten, T., & Yoon, M. (2016). Screening assessment within a mult-tiered system of support: Current practices, advances, and next steps. In S. R. Jimerson, M. K. Burns, & A. M. VanDerHeyden (Eds.), *Handbook of response to intervention: The science and practice of multi-tiered systems of support* (2nd ed., pp. 187–213). Springer.

Cohen, J., & Freiberg, J. A. (2013). School climate and bullying prevention. In T. Dary & T. Pickeral (Eds.), *School climate practices for implementation and sustainability.* A School Climate Practice Brief, Number 1. National School Climate Center.

Colorado Department of Education. (2019, July). Colorado bullying prevention and education best practices and model policy. Retrieved from *www.cde.state.co.us/mtss/modelpolicypdf.*

Constantino, S. M. (2015). *Engage every family: Five simple principles.* Corwin.

Cook, C. R., Fiat, A., Larson, M., Daikos, C., Slemrod, T., Holland, E. A., et al. (2018). Positive greetings at the door: Evaluation of a low-cost, high-yield proactive classroom management strategy. *Journal of Positive Behavior Interventions, 20*(3), 1–11.

Cornell, D., & Bandyopadhyay, S. (2009). The assessment of bullying. In S. Jimerson, S. Swearer, & D. Espelage (Eds.), *Handbook of bullying in schools: An international perspective* (pp. 265–276). Routledge/Taylor & Francis Group.

Cougnard, A., Marcelis, M., Myin-Germeys, I., De Graaf, R., Vollebergh, W., Krabbendam, L., et al. (2007). Does normal developmental expression of psychosis combine with environmental risk to cause persistence of psychosis? A psychosis proneness-persistence model. *Psychological Medicine, 37*(4), 513–527.

Crone, D. A., & Horner, R. H. (2015). *Building positive behavior support systems in schools: Functional behavioral assessment* (2nd ed.). Guilford Press.

Cross, D., Lester, L., Barnes, A., Cardoso, P., & Hadwen, K. (2015). If it's about me, why do it without me? Genuine student engagement in school cyberbullying education. *International Journal of Emotional Education, 7*(1), 35–51.

Cusumano, D., & Preston, A. (2018). *Practice profile for coaching.* National Implementation Research Network. Retrieved from *https://nirn.fpg.unc.edu/sites/nirn.fpg.unc.edu/files/resources/Practice%20Profile%20for%20Coaching%20for%20Ai%20Hub%20Module%201.8.pdf.*

Daly, E. J., III, Lentz, F. E., Jr., & Boyer, J. (1996). The instructional hierarchy: A conceptual model for understanding the effective components of reading interventions. *School Psychology Quarterly, 11*(4), 369–386.

Davis, F. E., Lyubansky, M., & Schiff, M. (2015). Restoring racial justice. In R. Scott & S. Kosslyn (Eds.), *Emerging trends in the social and behavioral sciences* (pp. 1–16). Wiley.

de Vries, E., Kaufman, T. M. L., Veenstra, R., Laninga-Wijnen, L., & Huitsing, G. (2021). Bullying and victimization trajectories in the first years of secondary education: Implications for status and affection. *Journal of Youth and Adolescence, 50*(10), 1995–2006.

Decker, D. M., Dona, D. P., & Christenson, S. L. (2007). Behaviorally at-risk African American students: The importance of student-teacher relationships for student outcomes. *Journal of School Psychology, 45,* 83–109.

Deno, S. (2003). Developments in curriculum-based measurement. *Journal of Special Education, 37*(3), 184–192.

Deno, S. (2016). Data-based decision making. In S. Jimerson, M. Burns, & A. VanDerHeyden (Eds.), *Handbook of response to intervention* (pp. 9–28). Springer.

DePry, R. L., & Sugai, G. (2002). The effect of active supervision and pre-correction on minor behavioral incidents in a sixth grade general education classroom. *Journal of Behavioral Education, 11*(4), 255–267.

Didden, R., Scholte, R. H. J., Korzilius, H., de Moor, J. M. H., Vermeulen, A., O'Reilly, M., et al. (2009).

Cyberbullying among students with intellectual and developmental disability in special education settings. *Developmental Neurorehabilitation, 12*(3), 146–151.

Dillman, D. A., & Smyth, J. D. (2014). *Internet, phone, mail, and mixed-mode surveys: The tailored design method* (4th ed.). Wiley.

Dion, E. (2018, Jan 21). 12-year-old's suicide leaves family, police, school officials seeking answers. *Panama City News Herald.* Retrieved from *www.newsherald.com/news/20180121/12-year-olds-suicide-leaves-family-police-school-officials-seeking-answers.*

Dodge, K. A., & Coie, J. D. (1987). Social-information-processing factors in reactive and proactive aggression in children's peer groups. *Journal of Personality and Social Psychology, 53*(6), 1146–1158.

Dodge, K. A., Coie, J. D., & Lynam, D. (2006). Aggression and antisocial behavior in youth. In N. Eisenberg, W. Damon, & R. M. Lerner (Eds.), *Handbook of child psychology: Social, eomotional, and personality development* (pp. 719–788). Wiley.

Donovan, M., Bransford, J. D., & Pellegrino, J. (1999). *How people learn: Bridging research and practice.* National Academies Press.

Ducharme, J. (2017, November 3). An 11-year-old South Carolina girl fatally shot herself because of bullying at school. *Time.* Retrieved from *https://time.com/5009743/toni-rivers-south-carolina-suicide.*

DuFour, R., & Eaker, R. (1998). *Professional learning communities at work: Best practices for enhancing student achievement.* National Educational Service.

DuFour, R., & Marzano, R. (2011). *Leaders of learning: How district, school, and classroom leaders improve student achievement.* Solution Tree.

Dunlap, G., Iovannone, R., Kincaid, D., Wilson, K., Christiansen, K., Strain, P. S., et al. (2010). *Prevent-teach-reinforce: The school-based of individualized positive behavior support.* Brookes.

Durlak, J. A., Weissberg, R. P., Dymnicki, A. B., Taylor, R. D., & Schellinger, K. B. (2011). The impact of enhancing students' social and emotional learning: A meta-analysis of school-based universal interventions. *Child Development, 82*(1), 405–432.

Eliason, B., & Morris, K. (2015). *Drill down tool evaluation brief.* Center on PBIS. Retrieved from *www.pbis.org/resource/drill-down-tool-evaluation-brief.*

Eliot, M., Cornell, D., Gregory, A., & Fan, X. (2010). Supportive school climate and student willingness to seek help for bullying and threats of violence. *Journal of School Psychology, 48,* 533–553.

Elmore, R. F. (2000). Building a new structure for school leadership. *American Educator,* 1–40. Retrieved from *www.aft.org/pdfs/americaneducator/winter9900/NewStructureWint99_00.pdf.*

Elsaesser, C., Russell, B., Ohannessian, C. M., & Patton, D. (2017). Parenting in a digital age: A review of parents' role in preventing adolescent cyberbullying. *Aggression and Violent Behavior, 35,* 62–72.

Espelage, D. L., Aragon, S. R., Birkett, M., & Koenig, B. W. (2008). Homophobic teasing, psychological outcomes, and sexual orientation among high school students: What influence do parents and schools have? *School Psychology Review, 37*(2), 202–216.

Espelage, D. L., Hong, J. S., Rao, M. A., & Low, S. (2013). Associations between peer victimization and academic performance. *Theory Into Practice, 52*(4), 233–240.

Espelage, D. L., Low, S., Polanin, J. R., & Brown, E. C. (2013). The impact of a middle school program to reduce aggression, victimization, and sexual violence. *Journal of Adolescent Health, 53,* 180–186.

Espelage, D. L., Low, S., Polanin, J. R., & Brown, E. C. (2015). Clinical trial of second step middle-school program: Impact on aggression and victimization. *Journal of Applied Developmental Psychology, 37,* 52–63.

Espelage, D. L., Rose, C. A., & Polanin, J. R. (2015). Social-emotional learning program to reduce bullying, fighting, and victimization among middle school students with disabilities. *Remedial and Special Education, 36*(5), 299–311.

Evans, K., & Lester, J. (2012). Zero tolerance: Moving the conversation forward. *Intervention in School and Clinic, 48,* 108–114.

Eyuboglu, M., Eyuboglu, D., Pala, S. C., Oktar, D., Demirtas, Z., Arslantas, D., et al. (2021). Traditional school bullying and cyberbullying: Prevalence, the effect on mental health problems and self-harm behavior. *Psychiatry Research, 297*, 113730.

Facing History and Ourselves. (2019). *How do we know it works? A summary of key evaluation findings.* (2019). Retrieved from *www.facinghistory.org/chunk/how-do-we-know-it-works-summary-key-evaluation-findings.*

Farmer, C. (2019, Oct 21). Reidsville high school seniors go viral after befriending lonely freshman. *Fox 8.* Retrieved from *https://myfox8.com/morning-show/whats-right-with-our-schools/reidsville-high-school-seniors-go-viral-after-befriending-lonely-freshman.*

Farmer, T., Petrin, R., Brooks, D., Hamm, J., Lambert, K., & Gravelle, M. (2012). Bullying involvement and the school adjustment of rural students with and without disabilities. *Journal of Emotional and Behavioral Disorders 20*, 19–37.

Farrington, D. P., & Ttofi, M. M. (2009). School-based programs to reduce bullying and victimization. *Campbell Systematic Reviews, 5*(1), i–148.

Felix, E. D., & You, S. (2011). Peer victimization within the ethnic context of high school. *Journal of Community Psychology, 39*(7), 860–875.

Fixsen, D. L., Blase, K. A., Timbers, G. D., & Wolf, M. M. (2001). In search of program implementation: 792 replications of the Teaching Family Model. In G. A. Bernfeld, D. P. Farrington, & A. W. Leschied (Eds.), *Offender rehabilitation in practice: Implementing and evaluating effective programs* (pp. 149–166). Wiley.

Fixsen, D. L., Naoom, S. F., Blase, K. A., Friedman, R. M., & Wallace, F. (2005). *Implementation research: A synthesis of the literature.* Louis de la Parte Florida Mental Health Institute. Retrieved from *https://nirn.fpg.unc.edu/resources/implementation-research-synthesis-literature.*

Flay, B. R., & Allred, C. G. (2010). The Positive Action Program: Improving academics, behavior, and character by teaching comprehensive skills for successful learning and living. In T. Lovatt, R. Tooney, & N. Clement (Eds.), *International research handbook on values education and student wellbeing* (pp. 471–501). Springer.

Fraenkel, J., Wallen, N., & Hyun, H. (2018). How to design and evaluate research in education (10th ed.). Retrieved from *www.mheducation.com/highered/product/how-design-evaluate-research-education-fraenkel-wallen/M9781259913839.html.*

Freeman, J. (2019, February 22). *Implementing PBIS in high schools: Current trends and future directions.* Paper presented at the meeting of the Association for Positive Behavior Support.

Gaffney, H., Farrington, D. P., Espelage, D. L., & Ttofi, M. M. (2019). Are cyberbullying intervention and prevention programs effective? A systematic and meta-analytical review. *Aggression and Violent Behavior, 45*, 134–153.

Gaffney, H., Farrington, D. P., & Ttofi, M. M. (2019). Examining the effectiveness of school-bullying intervention programs globally: A meta-analysis. *International Journal of Bullying Prevention, 1*(1), 14–31.

Gaffney, H., Ttofi, M. M., & Farrington, D. P. (2019). Evaluating the effectiveness of school-bullying prevention programs: An updated meta-analytical review. *Aggression and Violent Behavior, 45*, 111–133.

Gage, N. A., Katsiyannis, A., Rose, C., & Adams, S. E. (2021). Disproportionate bullying victimization and perpetration by disability status, race, and gender: A national analysis. *Advances in Neurodevelopmental Disorders, 5*, 256–268.

Garofalo, R., Wolf, R. C., Kessel, S., Palfrey, S. J., & DuRant, R. H. (1998). The association between health risk behaviors and sexual orientation among a school-based sample of adolescents. *Pediatrics, 101*(5), 895–902.

George, H. (2009, June). Schoolwide positive behavioral interventions and supports training. In-service provided at Washoe County School District, Reno, NV.

George, H. P., Kincaid, D., & Pollard-SAGE, J. (2009). Primary-tier interventions and supports. In W. Sailor,

G. Dunlap, G. Sugai, & R. H. Horner (Eds.), *Handbook of positive behavior support* (pp. 375–394). Springer.

Gest, S. D., Madill, R. A., Zadzora, K. M., Miller, A. M., & Rodkin, P. C. (2014). Teacher management of elementary classroom school dynamics: Associations with changes in student adjustment. *Journal of Emotional and Behavioral Disorders, 22*(2), 107–118.

Gibb, S. J., Horwood, L. J., & Fergusson, D. M. (2011). Bullying victimization/perpetration in childhood and later adjustment: Findings from a 30-year longitudinal study. *Journal of Aggression, Conflict and Peace Research, 3*(2), 82–88.

Gini, G., & Pozzoli, T. (2009). Association between bullying and psychosomatic problems: A meta-analysis. *Pediatrics, 123*(3), 1059–1065.

Gladden, R. M., Vivolo-Kantor, A. M., Hamburger, M. E., & Lumpkin, C. D. (2014). *Bullying surveillance among youths: Uniform definitions for public health and recommended data elements. Version 1.0.* Centers for Disease Control and Prevention. Retrieved from *https://eric.ed.gov/?id=ED575477.*

GLSEN (Gay, Lesbian & Straight Education Network). (2019). Model district anti-bullying and harassment policy: Model language, commentary and resources (p. 8). Retrieved from *www.glsen.org/sites/default/files/2019–10/GLSEN-Model-District-LGBTQ-Inclusive-Anti-Bullying-Harassment-Policy.pdf.*

Goldberg, J. (2016, July 30). It takes a village to determine the origins of an African proverb. *National Public Radio.* Retrieved from *www.npr.org/sections/goatsandsoda/2016/07/30/487925796/it-takes-a-village-to-determine-the-origins-of-an-african-proverb.*

Good, C., & Lindsay, P. (2013, October 11). *Student voice: Strategies to include students in PBIS.* Paper presented at the National PBIS Leadership Forum. Retrieved from *https://documents.pub/download/chris-good-purnima-lindsay-red-deer-public-schools-alberta-canada-student.*

Good, C. P., McIntosh, K., & Gietz, C. (2011). Integrating bullying prevention into schoolwide positive behavior support. *Teaching Exceptional Children, 44,* 48–56.

Good, R. H., Gruba, J., & Kaminski, R. (2002). Best practices in using dynamic indicators of Basic Early Literacy Skills (DIBELS) in an outcomes-driven model. In A. Thomas & J. Grimes (Eds.), *Best practices in school psychology IV* (4th ed., pp. 679–699). National Association of School Psychologists.

Graham, S., & Bellmore, A. D. (2007). Peer victimization and mental health during early adolescence. *Theory Into Practice, 46*(2), 138–146.

Greenberg, J., Putman, H., & Walsh, K. (2014). *Training our future teachers: Classroom management.* National Council on Teacher Quality. Retrieved from *www.nctq.org/dmsView/Future_Teachers_Classroom_Management_NCTQ_Report on December 2, 2014.*

Gresham, F. M. (2002). Teaching social skills to high-risk children and youth: Preventive and remedial strategies. In M. R. Shinn, H. M. Walker, & G. Stoner (Eds.), *Interventions for academic and behavior problems II: Preventive and remedial approaches* (pp. 403–432). National Association of School Psychologists.

Gruenert, S., & Whitaker, T. (2015). *School culture rewired: How to define, assess, and transform it.* Association for Supervision and Curriculum Development.

Gunter, P. L., Reffel, J., Barnett, C. A., Lee, J. L., & Patrick, J. (2004). Academic response rates in elementary-school classrooms. *Education and Treatment of Children, 27*(2), 105–113.

Guskey, T. R. (1999). *Evaluating professional development.* Corwin Press.

Hall, G. E. (1974). The concerns-based adoption model: A developmental conceptualization of the adoption process within educational institutions. Retrieved from *https://eric.ed.gov/?id=ED111791.*

Hamburger, M. E., Basile, K. C., & Vivolo, A. M. (2011). *Measuring bullying victimization, perpetration, and bystander experiences: A compendium of assessment tools.* Centers for Disease Control and Prevention, National Center for Injury Prevention and Control.

Haring, N. G., Lovitt, T. C., Eaton, M. D., & Hansen, C. L. (1978). *The fourth R: Research in the classroom.* Merrill.

Harlacher, J. E. (2015). *Designing effective classroom management.* Marzano Research.

Harlacher, J. E., Potter, J. B., & Weber, J. M. (2015). A team-based approach to improving core instructional reading practices within response to intervention. *Intervention in School and Clinic, 50*(4), 210–220.

Harlacher, J. E., & Rodriguez, B. J. (2018). *An educator's guide to schoolwide positive behavioral interventions and supports.* Marzano Research.

Harlacher, J. E., Sakelaris, T. L., & Kattelman, N. K. (2013). *Practitioner's guide to curriculum-based evaluation in reading.* Springer.

Hassan, C. (2016, December 1). Teen who was relentlessly bullied kills herself in front of her family. *CNN.* Retrieved from *www.cnn.com/2016/12/01/health/teen-suicide-cyberbullying-trnd.*

Hatzenbuehler, M. L., & Keyes, K. M. (2013). Inclusive anti-bullying policies and reduced risk of suicide attempts in lesbian and gay youth. *Journal of Adolescent Health: Official Publication of the Society for Adolescent Medicine, 53*(10), S21–S26.

Hawken, L., Crone, D., & Bundock, K., & Horner, R. H. (2021). *Responding to problem behavior in schools* (3rd ed.). Guilford Press.

Hawkins, D. L., Pepler, D. J., & Craig, W. M. (2001). Naturalistic observations of peer interventions in bullying. *Social Development, 10*(4), 512–527.

Haydon, T., Conroy, M. A., Scott, T. M., Sindelar, P. T., Barber, B. R., & Orlando, A. (2010). A comparison of three types of opportunities to respond on student academic and social behaviors. *Journal of Emotional and Behavioral Disorders, 18*(1), 27–40.

Haydon, T., Marsicano, R., & Scott, T. M. (2013). A comparison of choral and individual responding: A review of the literature. *Preventing School Failure, 57*(4), 181–188.

Heifetz, R. A., & Laurie, D. L. (1997). The work of leadership. *Harvard Business Review, 75*(1), 124–134.

Heifetz, R. A., Linsky, M., & Grashow, A. (2009). *The practice of adaptive leadership: Tools and tactics for changing your organization and the world.* Harvard Business Press.

Heitzeg, N. (2009). Education or incarceration: Zero tolerance policies and the school to prison pipeline. *Forum on Public Policy: A Journal of the Oxford Round Table, 2009,* 2.

Henderson, A. T., Mapp, K. L., Johnson, V. R., & Davies, D. (2007). *Beyond the bake sale: The essential guide to family/school partnerships.* New Press.

Hess, M., Wirtz, S., Allroggen, M., & Scheithauer, H. (2017). Intervention and therapy for perpetrators and victims of bullying: A systematic review. *Praxis Der Kinderpsychologie Und Kinderpsychiatrie, 66*(10), 740–755.

Hinduja, S., & Patchin, J. W. (2018). Connecting adolescent suicide to the severity of bullying and cyberbullying. *Journal of School Violence, 18*(3), 1–14.

Hinduja, S., & Patchin, J. (2023, February 2). *Cyberbullying fact sheet: Identification, prevention, and response.* Cyberbullying Research Center. Retrieved from *http://cyberbullying.org/cyberbullying-fact-sheet-identification-prevention-and-response.*

Holt, M. K., Vivolo-Kantor, A. M., Polanin, J. R., Holland, K. M., DeGue, S., Matjasko, J. L., et al. (2015). Bullying and suicidal ideation and behaviors: A meta-analysis. *Pediatrics, 135*(2), e496–e509.

Hoover-Dempsey, K. V., & Sandler, H. M. (1997). Why do parents become involved in their children's education? *Review of Education Research, 67*(1), 3–42.

Hoover-Dempsey, K. V., Walker, J. M. T., Sandler, H. M., Whetsel, D., Green, C. L., Wilkins, A. S. et al. (2005). Why do parents become involved? Research findings and implications. *Elementary School Journal, 106*(2), 105–130.

Horner, R. H., Sugai, G., Todd, A. W., & Lewis-Palmer, T. (2005). Schoolwide positive behavior support. In L. M. Bambara & L. Kern (Eds.), *Individualized supports for students with problem behaviors: Designing positive behavior plans* (pp. 359–390). Guilford Press.

Hosp, J. L. (2008). Best practices in aligning academic assessment with instruction. In A. Thomas & J. Grimes (Eds.), *Best practices in school psychology V* (pp. 363–376). NASP Publications.

Hosp, J. L., Huddle, S., Ford, J. W., & Hensely, K. (2016). Learning disabilities/special education. In S. R.

Jimerson, M. K. Burns, & A. M. VanDerHeyden (Eds.), *Handbook of response to intervention: The science and practice of multi-tiered systems of support* (2nd ed., pp. 43–58). Springer.

Huang, F. L., & Cornell, D. G. (2015). The impact of definition and question order on the prevalence of bullying victimization using student self-reports. *Psychological Assessment, 27*(4), 1484–1493.

Hunter, S. C., Durkin, K., Boyle, J. M. E., Booth, J. N., & Rasmussen, S. (2014). Adolescent bullying and sleep difficulties. *Europe's Journal of Psychology, 10*(4), 740–755.

Iannotti, R. J. (2013). Health behavior in school-aged children (HBSC), 2009–2010. Inter-University Consortium for Political and Social Research.

IRIS Center. (2021). *How do you know whether an EBP is effective with your children or students?* Retrieved from *https://iris.peabody.vanderbilt.edu/module/ebp_03/cresource/q4/p08.*

Jennings, P. A., & Greenberg, M. T. (2009). The prosocial classroom: Teacher social and emotional competence in relation to student and classroom outcomes. *Review of Educational Research, 79*(1), 491–525.

Jimerson, S., Burns, M. K., & VanDerHeyden, A. (Eds.). (2016). *Handbook of response to intervention: The science and practice of multi-tiered systems of support.* Springer.

Jones, S. M., & Kahn, J. (2017). *The evidence base for how we learn: Supporting students' social, emotional, and academic development.* The Aspen Institute, National Commission on Social, Emotional, and Academic Development.

Joyce, B. R., & Showers, B. (2002). *Student achievement through staff development* (3rd ed.). Association for Supervision and Curriculum Development.

Juvonen, J., & Graham, S. (2014). Bullying in schools: The power of bullies and the plight of victims. *Annual Review of Psychology, 65*(1), 159–185.

Juvonen, J., Nishina, A., & Graham, S. (2001). Self-views versus peer perceptions of victim status among early adolescents. In J. Juvonen & S. Graham (Eds.), *Peer harassment in school: The plight of the vulnerable and victimized* (pp. 105–124). Guilford Press.

Juvonen, J., Nishina, A., & Graham, S. (2006). Ethnic diversity and perceptions of safety in urban middle schools. *Psychological Science, 17*(5), 393–400.

Kidger, J., Heron, J., Leon, D. A., Tilling, K., Lewis, G., & Gunnell, D. (2015). Self-reported school experience as a predictor of self-harm during adolescence: A prospective cohort study in the South West of England (ALSPAC). *Journal of Affective Disorders, 173,* 163–169.

Klein, J., & Cornell, D. (2010). Is the link between large high schools and student victimization an illusion? *Journal of Educational Psychology, 102,* 933–946.

Klein, J., Cornell, D., & Konold, T. (2012). Relationships between bullying, school climate, and student risk behaviors. *School Psychology Quarterly, 27*(3), 154–169.

Klomek, A. B., Sourander, A., & Elonheimo, H. (2015). Bullying by peers in childhood and effects on psychopathology, suicidality, and criminality in adulthood. *The Lancet, Psychiatry, 2*(10), 930–941.

Kosciw, J., Clark, C., Truong, N., & Zongrone, A. (2020). *The 2019 national school climate survey: The experiences of lesbian, gay, bisexual, transgender, and queer youth in our nation's schools.* GLSEN.

Koth, C. W., Bradshaw, C. P., & Leaf, P. J. (2008). A multilevel study of predictors of student perceptions of school climate: The effect of classroom-level factors. *Journal of Educational Psychology, 100*(1), 96–104.

Kratochwill, T. R., Elliott, S. N., & Callan-Stoiber, K. (2002). Best practices in school-based problem-solving consultation. In A. Thomas & J. Grimes (Eds.), *Best practices in school psychology IV* (pp. 583–608). Bethesda, MD: National Association of School Psychologists.

Kretzmann, J. P., & McKnight, J. L. (1993). *Building communities from the inside out: A path toward finding and mobilizing a community's assets.* ACTA Publications.

Kriete. R., & Davis, C (2014). *The morning meeting book* (3rd ed.). Northeast Foundation for Children.

Kull, R. M., Greytak, E. A., Kosciw, J. G., & Villenas, C. (2016). Effectiveness of school district antibullying policies in improving LGBT youths' school climate. *Psychology of Sexual Orientation and Gender Diversity, 3*(4), 407–415.

Ladd, G. W., Ettekal, I., & Kochenderfer-Ladd, B. (2017). Peer victimization trajectories from kindergarten through high school: Differential pathways for children's school engagement and achievement? *Journal of Educational Psychology, 109*(6), 826–841.

Langland, S., Lewis-Palmer, T., & Sugai, G. (1998). Teaching respect in the classroom: An instructional approach. *Journal of Behavioral Education, 8,* 245–262.

Lee, M., & Friedrich, T. (2007). The "smaller" the school, the better? The Smaller Learning Communities (SLC) in U.S. high schools. *Improving Schools, 10*(3), 261–282.

Leff, S. S., Evian Waasdorp, T., Paskewich, B., Lakin Gullan, R., Jawad, A. F., Paquette MacEvoy, J., et al. (2010). The preventing relational aggression in schools everyday program: A preliminary evaluation of acceptability and impact. *School Psychology Review, 39*(4), 569–587.

Leff, S., & Waasdorp, T. (2013). Effect of aggression and bullying on children and adolescents: Implications for prevention and intervention. *Current Psychiatry Reports, 15,* 343.

Lemstra, M. E., Nielsen, G., Rogers, M. R., Thompson, A. T., & Moraros, J. S. (2012). Risk indicators and outcomes associated with bullying in youth aged 9–15 years. *Canadian Journal of Public Health, 103*(1), 9–13.

Lencioni, P. (2002). *The five dysfunctions of a team: A leadership fable.* Jossey-Bass.

Lereya, S. T., Samara, M., & Wolke, D. (2013). Parenting behavior and the risk of becoming a victim and a bully/victim: A meta-analysis study. *Child Abuse and Neglect, 37*(12), 1091–1108.

Lewis, K. M., Schure, M., Bavarian, N., DuBois, D., Day, J., Ji, P., et al. (2013). Problem behavior and urban, low income youth: A randomized controlled trial of Positive Action in Chicago. *American Journal of Preventative Medicine, 44*(6), 622–630.

Lewis, T. J., Hudson, S., Richter, M., & Johnson, N. (2004). Scientifically supported practices in emotional and behavioral disorders: A proposed approach and brief review of current practices. *Behavioral Disorders, 29*(3), 247–259.

Li, K., Washburn, I., DuBois, D., Vuchinich, S., Ji, P., Brechling, V., et al. (2011). Effects of the Positive Action programme on problem behaviours in elementary school students: A matched-pair randomised control trial in Chicago. *Psychology and Health, 26*(2), 187–204.

Limber, S. P., Olweus, D., Wang, W., Masiello, M., & Breivik, K. (2018). Evaluation of the Olweus bullying prevention program: A large scale study of U. S. students in grades 3–11. *Journal of School Psychology, 69,* 56–72.

Losen, D. J., Hodson, C. L., Keith, M. A. II, Morrison, K., & Belway, S. (2015). Are we closing the school discipline gap? Retrieved from *https://escholarship.org/uc/item/2t36g571.*

Lynass, L., Tsai, S., Richman, T. D., & Cheney, D. (2012). Social expectations and behavioral indicators in school-wide positive behavior supports: A national study of behavior matrices. *Journal of Positive Behavior Interventions, 14*(3), 153–161.

Martinez, S., Kern, L., Hershfeldt, P., George, H. P., White, A., Flannery, B., et al. (2019). *High school PBIS implementation: Student voice.* OSEP TA Center on PBIS, University of Oregon. Retrieved from *www.pbis.org.*

McDougall, P., & Vaillancourt, T. (2015). Long-term adult outcomes of peer victimization in childhood and adolescence: Pathways to adjustment and maladjustment. *American Psychologist, 70*(4), 300–310.

McIntosh, K., & Goodman, S. (2016). *Integrated multi-tiered systems of support: Blending RTI and PBIS.* Guilford Press.

McKevitt, B. C., & Braaksma, A. (2008). Best practices in developing a positive behavior support system at the school level. In A. Thomas & J. Grimes (Eds.), *Best practices in school psychology* V (pp. 735–747). National Association of School Psychologists.

McNeely, C. A., Nonnemaker, J. M., & Blum, R. W. (2002). Promoting student connectedness to school: Evidence from the national longitudinal study of adolescent health. *Journal of School Health, 72,* 138–146.

Meints, C. A. (2007). *Target bullying intervention: Continuation, expansion, and sustainability*. (Educational Specialist Research Project). School Psychology Program, Department of Educational Psychology, University of Nebraska–Lincoln.

Metz, A., & Louison, L. (2019). *The Hexagon tool: Exploring context*. National Implementation Research Network, Frank Porter Graham Child Development Institute, University of North Carolina at Chapel Hill.

Murray, A. L., Booth, T., Eisner, M., Ribeaud, D., McKenzie, K., & Murray, G. (2019). An analysis of response shifts in teacher reports associated with the use of a universal school-based intervention to reduce externalising behaviour. *Prevention Science, 20*, 1265–1273.

Naito, T., & Gielen, U. (2006). Bullying and Ijime in Japanese schools. In F. L. Denmark, H. H. Krauss, R. W. Wesner, E. Midlarsky, & U. Gielen (Eds.), *Violence in schools: Cross-national and cross-cultural perspectives* (pp. 169–190). Springer.

Nakamoto, J., & Schwartz, D. (2010). Is peer victimization associated with academic achievement? A meta-analytic review. *Social Development, 19*(2), 221–242.

National Implementation Research Network. (2020). *Implementation stages planning tool*. National Implementation Research Network, FPG Child Development Institute, University of North Carolina at Chapel Hill.

National School Climate Center (NSCC). (2007). *The school climate challenge: Narrowing the gap between school climate research and school climate policy, practice guidelines and teacher education policy*. Retrieved from *www.schoolclimate.org/themes/schoolclimate/assets/pdf/policy/school-climate-challenge-web.pdf*.

National School Climate Center (NSCC). (n.d.). What is school climate? Retrieved from *www.schoolclimate.org/about/our-approach/what-is-school-climate*.

National Threat Assessment Center. (2021). *Averting targeted school violence: A U.S. Secret Service analysis of plots against schools*. U.S. Secret Service, Department of Homeland Security.

Neary, A., & Joseph, S. (1994). Peer victimization and its relationship to self-concept and depression among schoolgirls. *Personality and Individual Differences, 16*(1), 183–186.

Nese, R. N. T., Horner, R. H., Dickey, C. R., Stiller, B., & Tomlanovich, A. (2014). Decreasing bullying in middle school: Expect respect. *School Psychology Quarterly, 29*(3), 272–286.

Newmann, F. M., Smith, B., Allensworth, E., & Bryk, A. S. (2001). Instructional program coherence: What it is and why it should guide school improvement. *Educational Evaluation and Policy Analysis, 23*(4), 297–321.

Newton, J. S., Horner, R. H., Algozzine, B., Todd, A. W., & Algozzine, K. (2012). A randomized wait-list controlled analysis of the implementation integrity of team-initiated problem solving processes. *Journal of School Psychology, 50*(4), 421–441.

Newton, J. S., Todd, A. W., Algozzine, K. M., Horner, R. H., & Algozzine, B. (2009). *Team-initiated problem solving training manual*. University of Oregon, Educational and Community Supports.

O'Higgins Norman, J., & Hinduja, S. (2019). Inaugural editorial. *International Journal of Bullying Prevention, 1*(1), 1–2.

O'Neil, R. E., Albin, R. W., Storey, K., Horner, R. H., & Sprague, J. (2014). *Functional assessment and program development for problem behavior: A practical handbook* (3rd ed.). Cengage Learning.

Oliver, R., Wehby, J., & Reschly, D. J. (2011). Teacher classroom management practices: Effects on disruptive or aggressive student behavior. *Campbell Systematic Reviews, 2011*(4).

Olweus, D. (1978). *Aggression in the schools: Bullies and whipping boys*. Hemisphere.

Olweus, D. (1993). *Bullying at school: What we know and what we can do*. Blackwell.

Olweus, D. (1994). Bullying at school: Basic facts and effects of a school-based intervention program. *Journal of Child Psychology and Psychiatry, 35*(7), 1171–1190.

Olweus, D. (2006). *Revised Olweus bully/victim questionnaire*. APA PsycTests. Retrieved from *https://doi.org/10.1037/t09634-000*.

Olweus, D., Limber, S. P., Crocker Flerx, V., Mullin, N., Riese, J., & Snyder, M. (2007). *Olweus bullying program: Schoolwide guide.* Hazelden.

Ortega, L., Lyubansky, M., Nettles, S., & Espelage, D. (2016). Outcomes of a restorative circles program in a high school setting. *Psychology of Violence, 6*(3), 459–468.

Patchin, J. W., & Hinduja, S. (2006). Bullies move beyond the schoolyard: A preliminary look at cyberbullying. *Youth Violence and Juvenile Justice, 4*(2), 148–169.

Patchin, J. W., & Hinduja, S. (2013). *Words wound: Delete cyberbullying and make kindness go viral.* Free Spirit.

Patel, M. M., Liddell, J. L., & Ferreira, R. J. (2018). An evaluation of the Positive Action program for youth violence: From schools to summer camps. *Child and Adolescent Social Work Journal, 35,* 519–530.

PBIS Apps. (2011). SWIS suite. Retrieved from *www.pbisapps.org/Applications/Pages/SWIS-Suite.aspx.*

PBIS Apps. (2020). SWIS facilitator's guide. Retrieved from *www.pbisapps.org/Resources/SWIS%20 Publications/SWIS%20Facilitators%20Guide.pdf*

Peeters, M., Cillessen, A. H. N., & Scholte, R. H. J. (2010). Clueless or powerful? Identifying subtypes of bullies in adolescence. *Journal of Youth and Adolescence, 39*(9), 1041–1052.

Pepler, D., Craig, W., & O'Connell, P. (2010). Peer processes in bullying: Informing prevention and intervention strategies. In S. Jimerson, S. Swearer, & D. Espelage (Eds.), *Handbook of bullying in schools: An international perspective* (pp. 469–479). Routledge/Taylor & Francis Group.

Perry, D. G., Kusel, S. J., & Perry, L. C. (1988). Victims of peer aggression. *Developmental Psychology, 24,* 807–814.

Petrosino, A., Guckenburg, S., DeVoe, J., & Hanson, T. (2010). *What characteristics of bullying, bullying victims, and schools are associated with increased reporting of bullying to school officials?* (Issues & Answers Report, REL 2010 No. 092). Washington, DC: U.S. Department of Education, Institute of Education Sciences, National Center for Education Evaluation and Regional Assistance, Regional Educational Laboratory Northeast and Islands. Retrieved from *http://ies.ed.gov/ncee/edlabs.*

Planalp, B., & Scott, J. (2020). *Family of 8-year-old CPS student who died by suicide win key court battle.* Fox Now. Retrieved from *www.fox19.com/2020/12/29/family-yo-cps-student-who-died-by-suicide-wins-key-court-battle.*

Polanin, J. R., Espelage, D. L., & Pigott, T. D. (2012). A meta-analysis of school-based bullying prevention programs' effects on bystander intervention behavior. *School Psychology Review, 41*(1), 47–65.

Porowski, A., O'Conner, R., & Passa, A. (2014). *Disproportionality in school discipline: An assessment of trends in Maryland, 2009–12* (REL 2014–017). U.S. Department of Education, Institute of Education Sciences, National Center for Education Evaluation and Regional Assistance, Regional Educational Laboratory Mid-Atlantic. Retrieved from *https://ies.ed.gov/ncee/edlabs.*

Positive Action. (n.d.). Introduction. *https://www.positiveaction.net/introduction.*

Radliff, K. M., Wheaton, J. E., Robinson, K., & Morris, J. (2012). Illuminating the relationship between bullying and substance use among middle and high school youth. *Addictive Behaviors, 37*(4), 569–572.

Redding, S., Murphy, M., & Sheley, P. (2011). *Handbook on family and community engagement.* Information Age.

Reyes, M. R., Brackett, M. A., Rivers, S. E., White, M., & Salovey, P. (2012). Classroom emotional climate, student engagement, and academic achievement. *Journal of Educational Psychology, 104*(3), 700–712.

Richard, J. F., Schneider, B. H., & Mallet, P. (2012). Revisiting the whole-school approach to bullying: Really looking at the whole school. *School Psychology International, 33*(3), 263–284.

Rivara, F., & Le Menestrel, S. (2016). *Preventing bullying through science, policy, and practice.* National Academies Press.

Rogers, E. M. (1995). *Diffusion of innovations* (4th ed.). Free Press.

Rose, C. A., & Gage, N. A. (2017). Exploring the involvement of bullying among students with disabilities over time. *Exceptional Children, 83*(3), 298–314.

Ross, S. W., & Horner, R. H. (2009). Bully prevention in positive behavior support. *Journal of Applied Behavior Analysis, 42,* 747–759.

Ross, S. W., & Horner, R. H. (2013). Bully prevention in positive behavior support: Preliminary evaluation of third-, fourth-, and fifth-grade attitudes toward bullying. *Journal of Emotional and Behavioral Disorders, 22*(4), 225–236.

Ross, S., Horner, R. H., & Stiller, B. (2012). *Bully prevention in positive behavior support.* Educational and Community Supports. Retrieved from *www.pbis.org/common/cms/files/pbisresources/bullyprevention_ES.pdf.*

Rothman, M. (2018, March 20). *"Stranger Things" cast rallies behind fan after no one showed to his birthday party.* Good Morning America. Retrieved from *www.goodmorningamerica.com/culture/story/stranger-things-cast-rallies-fan-showed-birthday-party-53878864.*

Rupp S., Elliott S., & Gresham F. (2018). Assessing elementary students' bullying and related social behaviors: Cross-informant consistency across school and home environments. *Children and Youth Services Review, 93,* 458–466.

Russell, S. T., Everett, B. G., Rosario, M., & Birkett, M. (2014). Indicators of victimization and sexual orientation among adolescents: Analyses from youth risk behavior surveys. *American Journal of Public Health, 104*(2), 255–261.

Saewyc, E. M., Konishi, C., Rose, H. A., & Homma, Y. (2014). School-based strategies to reduce suicidal ideation, suicide attempts, and discrimination among sexual minority and heterosexual adolescents in Western Canada. *International Journal of Child, Youth and Family Studies: IJCYFS, 5*(1), 89–112.

Salmivalli, C., Lagerspetz, K., Björkqvist, K., Österman, K., & Kaukiainen, A. (1996). Bullying as a group process: Participant roles and their relations to social status within the group. *Aggressive Behavior, 22*(1), 1–15.

Schmoker, M. J. (2006). *Results now: How we can achieve unprecedented improvement in teaching and learning.* Association for Supervision & Curriculum Development.

Shinn, M. R. (2008). Best practices in curriculum-based measurement and its use in a problem-solving model. In A. Thomas & J. Grimes (Eds.), *Best practices in school psychology V* (pp. 243–262). National Association of School Psychologists.

Shriberg, D., Brooks, K., Jenkins, K., Immen, J., Sutter, C., & Cronin, K. (2017). Using student voice to respond to middle school bullying: A student leadership approach. *School Psychology Forum, 11*(1). 20–33.

Simonsen, B., Fairbanks, S., Briesch, A., Myers, D., & Sugai, G. (2008). Evidence-based practices in classroom management: Considerations for research to practice. *Education and Treatment of Children, 31,* 351–380.

Simonsen, B., & Myers, D. (2015). *Classwide positive behavior interventions and supports: A guide to proactive classroom management.* Guilford Press.

Simonsen, B., Robbie, K., Meyer, K., Freeman, J., Everett, S., & Feinberg, A. (2021, November). *Multi-tiered system of supports (MTSS) in the classroom.* Center on PBIS, University of Oregon.

Simpson, D. D. (2002). A conceptual framework for transferring research to practice. *Journal of Substance Abuse Treatment, 22*(4), 171–182.

Skiba, R. J. (2014). The failure of zero tolerance. *Reclaiming Children and Youth, 22*(4), 27–33.

Smith, B. J., Fox, L., Binder, D. P., Bovey, T., Jones, A., McCullough, K., et al. (2018). *Statewide implementation guide.* Early Childhood Technical Assistance Center. Retrieved from *https://ectacenter.org/sig.*

Son, E., Peterson, N. A., Pottick, K. J., Zippay, A., Parish, S. L., & Lohrmann, S. (2014). Peer victimization among young children with disabilities: Early risk and protective factors. *Exceptional Children, 80*(3), 368–384.

Stiller, B., Nese, R. N. T., Tomlanovich, A. K., Horner, R. H., & Ross, S. W., (2013). *Bullying and harassment prevention in positive behavior support: Expect respect.* Educational and Community

Supports. Retrieved from *www.pbis.org/resource/bullying-prevention-in-pbis-expect-respect-middle-high-school-level.*

Stinchcomb, J. B., Bazemore, G., & Riestenberg, N. (2006). Beyond zero tolerance: Restoring justice in secondary schools. *Youth Violence and Juvenile Justice, 4*(2), 123–147.

Stoiber, K. C., & Gettinger, M. (2016). Multi-tiered systems of support and evidence-based practices. In S. R. Jimerson, M. K. Burns, & A. M. VanDerHeyden (Eds.), *Handbook of response to intervention: The science and practice of multi-tiered systems of support* (pp. 121–142). Springer.

Sugai, G. (2004). *Committee/group self-assessment and action planning (working smarter matrix).* Center on Positive Behavioral Interventions and Supports, University of Oregon.

Sugai, G. (2020, April 22). *MTSS: Proactively shaping for "new normal."* Invited keynote at the Virtual MTSS Fest 2020. University of Washington, Office of Superintendent for Public Instruction.

Sugai, G., & Horner, R. H. (2006). A promising approach for expanding and sustaining school-wide positive behavior support. *School Psychology Review, 35*(2), 246–259.

Sugai, G., & Horner, R. H. (2009). Defining and describing schoolwide positive behavior support. In W. Sailor, G. Dunlap, G. Sugai, & R. Horner (Eds.), *Handbook of positive behavior support* (pp. 307–326). Springer.

Sullivan, T. N., Farrell, A. D., Sutherland, K. S., Behrhorst, K. L., Garthe, R. C., & Greene, A. (2021). Evaluation of the Olweus Bullying Prevention Program in US urban middle schools using a multiple baseline experimental design. *Prevention Science, 22*(8), 1134–1146.

Sutherland, K. S., & Wehby, J. H. (2001). Exploring the relationship between increased opportunities to respond to academic requests and the academic and behavioral outcomes of students with EBD: A review. *Remedial and Special Education, 22*(2), 113–121.

Sutherland, K. S., Wehby, J. H., & Copeland, S. R. (2000). Effect of varying rates of behavior-specific praise on the on-task behavior of students with EBD. *Journal of Emotional and Behavioral Disorders, 8*(1), 2–8.

Swearer Bully Survey. (2021). Retrieved from *https://cehs.unl.edu/bullyingprevention/swearer-bully-survey.*

Swearer, S. M., Espelage, D. L., & Napolitano, S. A. (2009). *Bullying prevention and intervention: Realistic strategies for schools.* Guilford Press.

Swearer, S. M., Wang, C., Collins, A., Strawhun, J., & Fluke, S. (2014). Bullying: A school mental health perspective. In M. Weist, N. A. Lever, C. P. Bradshaw, & J. S. Owens (Eds.), *Handbook of school mental health* (2nd ed., pp. 341–354). Springer.

Taylor-Greene, S., Brown, D., Nelson, L., Longton, J., Gassman, T., Cohen, J., et al. (1997). School-wide behavioral support: Starting the year off right. *Journal of Behavior Education, 7*(1), 99–112.

Thapa, A., Cohen, J., Guffey, S., & Higgins-D'Alessandro, A. (2013). A review of school climate research. *Review of Educational Research, 83*(3), 357–385.

Tharp-Taylor, S., Haviland, A., & D'Amico, E. J. (2009). Victimization from mental and physical bullying and substance use in early adolescence. *Addictive Behaviors, 34*(6–7), 561–567.

Thomas, R. M. (2006). *Violence in America's schools: Understanding, prevention, and responses.* Praeger.

Thunfors, P., & Cornell, D. (2008). The popularity of middle school bullies. *Journal of School Violence, 7*(1), 65–82.

Totenberg, N. (2021, June 23). Supreme Court rules cheerleader's F-bombs are protected by the first amendment. *National Public Radio.* Retrieved from *www.npr.org/2021/06/23/1001382019/supreme-court-rules-cheerleaders-f-bombs-are-protected-by-the-first-amendment.*

Trivette, C. M., Dunst, C. J., Hamby, D. W., & O'Herin, C. E. (2009). Characteristics and consequences of adult learning methods and strategies. *Practical Evaluation Reports, 2*(1).

Ttofi, M., & Farrington, D. (2009). What works in preventing bullying: Effective elements of anti-bullying programmes. *Journal of Aggression, Conflict and Peace Research, 1*(1), 13–24.

Ttofi, M. M., & Farrington, D. P. (2011). Effectiveness of school-based programs to reduce bullying: A systematic and meta-analytic review. *Journal of Experimental Criminology, 7*(1), 27–56.

University of Tennessee Knoxville. (2019, December 11). *Shirt designed by fourth grader raises nearly $1M for STOMP out bullying.* University of Tennessee Knoxville News. Retrieved from *https://news.utk. edu/2019/12/11/ut-shirt-designed-by-fourth-grader-raises-nearly-1-million-for-stomp-out-bullying.*

U.S. Department of Education. (2019). *Student Reports of Bullying: Results from the 2017 school crime supplement to the National Crime Victimization Survey.* National Center for Education Statistics. Retrieved from *https://nces.ed.gov/pubsearch/pubsinfo.asp?pubid=2019054.*

Vaillancourt, T., Brittain, H. L., McDougall, P., & Duku, E. (2013). Longitudinal links between childhood peer victimization, internalizing and externalizing problems, and academic functioning: Developmental cascades. *Journal of Abnormal Child Psychology, 41*(8), 1203–1215.

Van Geel, M., Vedder, P., & Tanilon, J. (2014). Relationship between peer victimization, cyberbullying, and suicide in children and adolescents: A meta-analysis. *JAMA Pediatrics, 168*(5), 435–442.

Van Ryzin, M. J., & Roseth, C. J. (2018). Cooperative learning in middle school: A means to improve peer relations and reduce victimization, bullying, and related outcomes. *Journal of Educational Psychology, 110*(8), 1192–1201.

Wang, C., Berry, B., & Swearer, S. M. (2013). The critical role of school climate in effective bullying prevention. *Theory into Practice, 52*(4), 296–302,

Wang, M., & Degol, J. L. (2016). School climate: A review of the construct, measurement, and impact on student outcomes. *Educational Psychology Review, 28*(2), 315–352.

Watkins, C. L., & Slocum, T. A. (2004). The components of direct instruction. *Journal of Direct Instruction, 3,* 75–110.

Wolke, D., Lereya, S. T., Fisher, H. L., Lewis, G., & Zammit, S. (2014). Bullying in elementary school and psychotic experiences at 18 years: A longitudinal, population-based cohort study. *Psychological Medicine, 44*(10), 2199–2211.

Wolke, D., Woods, S., Bloomfield, L., & Karstadt, L. (2001). Bullying involvement in primary school and common health problems. *Archives of Disease in Childhood, 85*(3), 197–201.

Woodbury, M. G., & Kuhnke, J. L. (2014). Evidence-based practice vs. evidence-informed practice: What's the difference? *Wound Care Canada, 12*(1), 26–29.

Ybarra, M. L., Espelage, D. L., & Mitchell, K. J. (2014). Differentiating youth who are bullied from other victims of peer-aggression: The importance of differential power and repetition. *Journal of Adolescent Health: Official Publication of the Society for Adolescent Medicine, 55*(2), 293–300.

Yeager, D. S., Fong, C. J., Yeon Lee, H., & Espelage, D. L. (2015). Declines in efficacy of anti-bullying programs among older adolescents: Theory and a three-level meta-analysis. *Journal of Applied Developmental Psychology, 37,* 36–51.

Yoder, N., & Gurke, D. (2017). *Social and emotional learning coaching toolkit: Keeping SEL at the Center.* American Institutes for Research.

Zolkoski, S. M. (2019). The importance of teacher-student relationships for students with emotional and behavioral disorders. *Prevention School Failure: Alternative Education for Children and Youth, 63*(3), 236–241.

Index

Note. *f* or *t* following a page number indicates a figure or a table.